Spectacular Narratives

SPECTACULAR NARRATIVES

Hollywood in the Age of the Blockbuster

Geoff King

I.B.Tauris *Publishers*
LONDON • NEW YORK

Published in 2000 by I.B.Tauris & Co Ltd
Victoria House, Bloomsbury Square, London WC1B 4DZ
175 Fifth Avenue, New York NY 10010
Website: http://www.ibtauris.com

In the United States and Canada distributed by St. Martin's Press
175 Fifth Avenue, New York NY 10010

ISBN 1 86064 572 0 Hardback
1 86064 573 9 Paperback

A full CIP record for this book is available from the British Library
A full CIP record for this book is available from the Library of Congress

Library of Congress catalog card: available

Typeset by The Midlands Book Typesetting Company, Loughborough, Leicestershire
Printed and bound in Great Britain by MPG Books Ltd, Bodmin, Cornwall

Contents

General Editor's Introduction

A recent Sky television poll to find the hundred best films of the millennium placed *Star Wars*, *Titanic* and *Gone With The Wind* in first, second and third places respectively – clear evidence of a continuing audience taste for Hollywood spectacle. A common criticism of the recent cycle of spectacles is that they are all special effects and no plot. In his thoughtful and thought-provoking analysis, Geoff King argues that narrative and ideology remain vital ingredients of the spectacle film. His argument is carefully contextualized in the production and marketing strategies of Hollywood, in the nature of the viewing experience and in the role of films within a wider merchandizing world of toys, games and theme parks.

King sees the myth of the frontier as integral to many latter-day spectacles. It is certainly the case that classic westerns have been reworked as space adventures (*High Noon* as *Outland*, *The Magnificent Seven* as *Battle Beyond the Stars*) and that western and science fiction were fused in Michael Crichton's *Westworld* with its robot gunfighters. But King ranges much more widely across the genres in pursuit of his thesis. He sees the pure classic frontier mythology and the myth of technological modernity pitted against each other in *Twister* and *Independence Day*. He focuses on the conflict of nature and culture in *Titanic* and *Jurassic Park*. He examines attitudes to 'the final frontier' – space – in *2001*, *Star Wars*, *The Right Stuff* and *Apollo 13*. He assesses action pictures such as *The Rock*, *Armageddon* and *The Long Kiss Goodbye* in the context of gender politics. He considers disaster movies like *Deep Impact* and *Volcano* in the light of pre-millennial anxieties. He explores the dilemma of authenticity versus art in war movies like *Saving Private Ryan* and *Apocalypse Now*. Thanks to King, we can now see that there is much more to the Hollywood spectacle than just special effects and we can begin to view these films in the light of fundamental cultural and ideological debates.

Jeffrey Richards

Acknowledgements

Thanks to Thomas Austin, Geoff Hemstedt, Leon Hunt, Tanya Krzywinska and Alan Miller for reading all or part of the manuscript at various stages and for offering numerous useful suggestions and encouragement. Special thanks to Alan Miller and Julian Wheeler for essential help in obtaining video copies of some of the films analysed, and to Alison for (mostly) tolerating the screening of large numbers of not her favourite films. This book was completed with the assistance of BRIEF award funding from Brunel University.

Introduction: Spectacle, Narrative and 'Frontier' Mythology

> One of the greatest obstacles to any fruitful theory of genre has been the tendency to treat the genres as discrete. An ideological approach might suggest why they can't be, however hard they may appear to try: at best, they represent different strategies for dealing with the same ideological tensions.
>
> Robin Wood[1]

> Reports of the death of narrative in Hollywood filmmaking … are surely much exaggerated.
>
> Murray Smith[2]

From epic landscape to sumptuous interior; from visions of space, aliens and future cityscapes to explosive action and adventure: expansive vistas spread out across the width of the big screen, their presence magnified by the aural impact of multichannel sound. Everything is larger than life; not real but hyperreal, leading us into the imaginary worlds of the cinema but also leaving us to sit back and wonder at its creations. That is the intention, at least.

The spectacular qualities of the audio-visual experience have become increasingly important to Hollywood in recent decades. An emphasis on spectacle formed a central part of a post-war strategy aimed at tempting lost audiences back to the cinema in the face of demographic changes and the development of television and other domestic leisure activities. More recently, in an age in which the big Hollywood studios have become absorbed into giant conglomerates, the prevalence of spectacle and special effects has been boosted by a growing demand for products that can be further exploited in multimedia forms such as computer games and theme-park rides – secondary outlets that sometimes generate more profits than the films on which they are based. Spectacular display might also be driven by the increased importance of the overseas market in Hollywood's economic calculations, as it tends to translate more easily than other dimensions across cultural and language boundaries. These and other developments have led some to announce the imminent demise of narrative as a central or defining component of Hollywood cinema, or at least its dominant spectacular form. But the case has been considerably overstated.[3]

Narrative is far from being eclipsed, even in the most spectacular and effects-oriented of today's blockbuster attractions. These films still tell reasonably coherent stories, even if they may sometimes be looser and less well integrated than some classical models.[4] This is one dimension of narrative that needs to be considered: the forward-moving development of plot. More central to my argument, contemporary spectaculars also continue to manifest the kinds of underlying thematic oppositions and reconciliations associated with a broadly 'structuralist' analysis of narrative. This dimension has been largely ignored by those who identify, celebrate or more often bemoan a weakening of plot or character development in many spectacular features. Plenty of significant underlying thematic structures can be found amid the extravagances of contemporary Hollywood.

To assert the importance of narrative need not be to disregard the role of spectacle. Narrative and spectacle can work together in a variety of changing relationships and there is no single, all-embracing answer to the question of how the two are related. The aim of this book is to chart some of the contours of this relationship in contemporary Hollywood. A number of thematic narrative structures will be identified, although one particular discourse will be emphasized: the continued saliency of something akin to the myth or ideology of the American 'frontier'. One of the oldest and most familiar American narrative frameworks, the myth of the frontier offers a series of thematic oppositions and reconciliations that continue to be drawn upon, implicitly or explicitly, by a range of films, whatever the status of their 'surface' plots. The traditional generic western may be in a state of near-terminal decline, but many aspects of the mythic or ideological narrative that animated it remain alive and well in Hollywood.

A version identified in many of the films examined in this book establishes a series of oppositions between a construction of the 'frontier', or its contemporary analogues, and an articulation of technological or bureaucratic modernity. This narrative framework comes in different varieties, some more explicitly related to frontier mythology than others. Hollywood spectacle also comes in more than one guise and *Spectacular Narratives* pays equal attention to the analysis of some of the spectacular strategies used in the latter part of the twentieth century. A number of different, although sometimes overlapping, versions will be considered, ranging from the slow contemplative visions of *2001: A Space Odyssey* (1968) and the large-scale special effects of *Titanic* (1997) to the explosive rhetorics of the contemporary action cinema.

One of the reasons for the hasty dismissal of the importance of narrative in contemporary Hollywood may be the overstatement by influential theorists such as David Bordwell[5] of the degree of its coherence in, and dominance of, the 'classical' Hollywood of the studio era. Narrative coherence is an important factor in classical Hollywood, but only as one of a number of competing dynamics. Other attractions, such as distracting star performances or other spectacles, might be thrown in at any time.[6] The industry's promotional discourses actively seek to play up such multiple appeals and distractions, to encourage 'diverse positions of viewing' and maximize potential audiences.[7] This is an important characteristic of the contemporary Hollywood blockbuster, but it is far from new to the industry. The connotations of the term 'classical' are part of the problem, including an emphasis on 'decorum, proportion, formal harmony',[8] characteristics that were not always given priority.

Numerous commentators on contemporary, 'new' or 'post-classical' Hollywood seem to rely at least in part on such implicit assumptions about the cinema that went before.[9] The point is not to deny that there have been changes in the precise relations between narrative and spectacle from one period to another, but to question any suggestion that there was a point of departure at which 'classical' narrative existed in anything like a 'pure' state, uncontaminated by various kinds of evasions and distractions. From the very start, throughout the 'classical' era, and today, narrative and spectacle have existed in a series of shifting relationships in which neither has ever been entirely absent. The relative absence of coherent plot or character development in specific instances, even, does not entail an evacuation of underlying narrative themes and oppositions of a structural kind.

Spectacle may disrupt narrative. Spectacular elements that seem to exist purely for their own sake, rather than being integrated into the film as a whole, may take on the character of 'cinematic excess', as Kristin Thompson puts it.[10] But this view is premised on an assumption, drawn in this instance from the work of Stephen Heath, that the mission of cinema is to produce homogeneity. If some of the products of the studio era do seem unified, balanced, coherent and 'well-made', it is doubtful that this was ever an overriding imperative. Profitability has usually been more important than unity or homogeneity. The desire to appeal to a mass market is likely to produce a degree of built-in *in*coherence and conflicting demands. Spectacle is often just as much a core aspect of Hollywood cinema as coherent narrative and should not necessarily be seen as a disruptive intrusion from some place outside. The coherence, or drive towards coherence, often ascribed to classical Hollywood films can be a product of a particular kind of critical reading rather than a quality of the text itself.

My aim is to chart a course somewhere between two opposite but connected tendencies. As Yvonne Tasker argues, 'academic film criticism has often placed an inordinate emphasis on the operations of narrative, hence the significance given to the moment of narrative resolution as a way to decode the politics of a given text.'[11] This over-emphasis on narrative may have encouraged a response that too readily dismisses the importance of the narrative dimension of Hollywood spectacle. Shifts from one kind of reading to the other might more usefully be replaced by a recognition of the multiple logics at work in Hollywood cinema.[12] My approach follows that of Tasker to a significant extent. The audience, she suggests, is subject to contradictory desires: 'We want to find out, to follow the narrative through to its conclusion and the revelation of knowledge that accompanies this. At the same time we wish to stop and stare, to linger over details.'[13] Each of these dimensions offers its own particular pleasures. The business of 'finding out', following the plot, involves an engagement in what is often a carefully structured process of 'knowing' and 'not knowing', of enigma and revelation. A balance is struck between stability and instability, comfortable expectation and surprise or suspense, the precise characteristic of which depends on the kind of film involved.

Spectacle, the production of images at which we might wish to stop and stare, has long played an important part in the creation of popular entertainment, from contemporary and early cinema to pre-cinematic forms such as the diorama and the magic lantern show, theatre, and whole traditions of religious and secular ritual. Spectacle offers a range of pleasures associated with the enjoyment of 'larger than life' representations, more luminous or intense than daily reality, qualities that will be explored in more detail in the rest of this book. The extent to which these desires are contradictory, or can work together, is one of the central issues to be considered. Pleasure is also provided by the level of narrative to which Tasker does not draw attention in her formulation, the working out of underlying narrative dynamics, a subject to which I will return shortly.

In some cases spectacle reinforces, rather than interferes with, the work of narrative. Moments of spectacle sometimes help to move the plot significantly forward. They can also contribute to the play of underlying narrative structures. This is one way of reading the 'frontier' rhetorics of contemporary Hollywood. In terms of narrative themes, an experience of something like the frontier might be offered as a spectacular intrusion into (or escape from) everyday life. Contemporary frontier narratives establish oppositions between the moment of the frontier – sharp, clear-cut, 'authentic' – and a dull, decadent or corrupting version of 'civilization'. The frontier of the original myth is a point at which proximity to the untamed wilderness (or its contemporary equivalents) is supposed to keep civilization fresh and sharply attuned.

A structural equivalent of the frontier experience is created in many films by disruptive intrusions into normality, intrusions that cut through the routines of quotidian life to a supposedly more authentic and immediate level of existence. Many contemporary Hollywood productions promise a kind of surrogate 'frontier' experience for the viewer at the level of audio-visual spectacle. The films themselves are presented as spectacular intrusions into the daily life of the viewer. Hollywood spectacle is offered as an alternative to the domestic routine. It claims – however dubiously or paradoxically – to impinge directly on the spectator, to offer an authentic experience, filled with a vivid sense of large scale *presence*, contrasted to both everyday life and domestic media such as television. The spectacular experience offered to the viewer is in a sense presented as a vicarious equivalent of the frontier experience celebrated thematically at the level of narrative.

Spectacle and narrative will be considered in this book in a variety of contexts, ranging from the industrial and institutional strategies of Hollywood to broader social, cultural, political and historical issues. The increased centrality of spectacle can be understood primarily in the context of changing industrial strategies dating back to the 1950s. If an emphasis on the provision of lavish spectacle is seen as part of an attempt to regain audiences, it can also be understood in terms of the political economy of contemporary Hollywood. Expensive productions maintain or raise 'barriers to entry' that help to ensure continued oligopoly control by the major studios. The mobilization of aspects of frontier narrative also needs to be viewed in context.

Spectacular Narratives adopts a broadly structuralist view of both narrative in general and the particular narrative associated with evocations of the American frontier experience,[14] although this is qualified and complicated by consideration of the industrial context of Hollywood cinema and its address to audiences. Narratives are seen here as story-telling mechanisms that serve, in loose and very general terms, to help to make sense of their world. This often involves a process in which difficult issues facing a particular group or culture are taken up, however superficially, and resolved in some imaginary way. Mythic narratives often entail a move towards the imaginary resolution of contradictions that cannot be resolved in reality. Seen this way, the original myth of the frontier appears as a way of reconciling, at least momentarily, the competing demands of 'civilization' and a version of 'untamed wilderness' or open space deemed to have given America its unique character. Hence the focus on characters – classic protagonists of the western – who straddle the border or 'frontier' between the two, offering the best of both worlds, or at least avoiding the worst extremes of either.

The extent to which this pattern is replicated in many contemporary non-westerns will be demonstrated by tracing a series of discursive articulations around the rival demands of family/domesticity and spectacular heroics. The imaginary reconciliation offered by such articulations is a rhetorical construct, a largely unexamined assertion, far more than any coherent or rational argument. In Hollywood cinema it is usually dependent on identification with characters, emotional manipulation and narrative sleights of hand, rather than a more substantial engagement with the issues. The original frontier was defined in terms of the availability of allegedly 'free', open or 'empty' landscapes into which it was possible to keep moving. The closure of the domestic historical frontier, officially announced in 1890, led to the creation of new frontiers, both imaginary and real. One possibility was to move on elsewhere, ultimately to open a potentially infinite new frontier in space. Another was to imagine an opening of 'frontier' zones closer to home, moments that recreated something of the frontier dynamic. Both kinds of 'new frontier', loosely conceived, can be identified in the narratives of contemporary Hollywood. The western in its original form may have become a rarity, a protected species almost, but the underlying issues to which the myth responded have not gone away and continue to be addressed in many films.[15]

None of this should be taken to suggest that Hollywood films can be read unproblematically as simple reflectors of American culture, even when they attract large audiences. Hollywood cinema remains the product of highly specific industrial and institutional mediations. The popularity of any film can be shaped by arbitrary factors such as promotional expenditure and the presence or absence of competition at the moment of release. Much of the work of distribution today is centred around the organization of this process. The major studios are now defined chiefly by their functions as distributors and financiers of films, rather than by their activities in production. They tend to produce only a relatively small number of films themselves. But these films are often given a disproportionately large share of the promotions budget, an expenditure deemed worthwhile given that the studios make profits on these movies at more levels than those they only finance and/or distribute.[16] The market is further skewed by the tight control maintained by the majors over the commercially crucial summer, Christmas and Easter exhibition seasons, and efforts to stagger the release of blockbusters to some extent within these periods. Such manipulations mean we cannot read directly from the hit status of texts to argue that they plug immediately into contemporary cultural concerns.

It would be equally implausible to suggest that there was no connection between films that attract large audiences and wider cultural or ideological currents. Some kind of mediated relationship can be asserted, especially in cases such as popular genres or otherwise repeatedly successful frameworks. Successful genres, or shorter-term cycles of films, are industrially and critically fabricated structures which, for all their mediations, demonstrate a sustained popularity sufficient to enable us to speculate with some conviction about their connections to the level of mythology or ideology. It seems significant, for instance, that the conflicting imperatives of 'frontier' and civilization repeatedly offered a degree of mythological resolution in the western and the films examined in this book are also structured into seemingly very different settings such as the musical and numerous form of Hollywood comedy.[17]

A threshold of ubiquity is reached at which stronger arguments can be made about the relations of such highly mediated, industrial products to the broader cultural landscape in which they are situated, even if 'scientific' standards of provable connection remain absent, as they usually are in any debates about the 'meaning' of cultural products. It is much easier to identify elements of myth or ideology in Hollywood films than to account for exactly what this means: how these meanings come to be created or what individual or collective members of the audience 'do' with them.

Particular meanings, or leanings, can be identified at a textual level. Commercial imperatives go some way to explaining their presence, as does the broader social or historical context. Viewers can be interviewed about their own perceptions of the cinema-going experience. Between viewer and text come numerous other mediations and meaning-creating factors. The broad social–cultural context imposes certain horizons of interpretation – limitations on the kinds of interpretations likely to be made.[18] So do more particular contextual factors such as class, gender or racial background, or narrower group or personal histories. Viewers are far from entirely free to make their own individual readings of textual material. In some respects, and at some levels, similar social horizons of interpretation are likely to be shared by large groups. In others more radical divergences might be found. Promotional and other extra-textual discourses directly associated with the film industry – including trailers, adverts and reviews – also help to establish discursive frameworks within which viewers are encouraged to place individual films.

Much can be deduced, particularly through the combination of different levels of analysis, even if absolute certainty remains impossible. But the way popular entertainment forms 'tap into', or play on, broader cultural concerns is no magical process. It makes good commercial sense to pick up, mix and ring the changes on well-established discourses such as the myth of the frontier and/or to blend these with issues that have a more immediate currency, such as the impact of new technologies. What is involved here is not an act of direct mythical response to cultural contradictions but the way in which the entertainment industry confects a product that, however loosely or superficially, seeks to gain a degree of purchase in this dimension and to appeal to one audience group or another.

Any assertion of the cultural or mythic role of Hollywood cinema also has to be qualified by consideration of historical trends in the relationship between the industry and audiences. The notion that even classical Hollywood appealed to a mass and undifferentiated audience, and thus could be seen less problematically as embodying an 'expression' of cultural dynamics, has been shown to be little more than industry propaganda designed to inflate its status as a supposedly democratic institution.[19] From at least the 1930s onwards, the industry identified a number of specific audience groups, distinguished on grounds such as age, gender and relative 'sophistication'. The industry sought to combine ingredients that would appeal to more than one of these 'taste publics'.[20] If classical Hollywood offered an element of mythic reconciliation, this may partly have been a reconciliation of the qualities sought by different sections of the audience, a practice driven by specifically industrial imperatives which continues today.

Appealing to a range of potential audience groups can also generate incoherence, however, a tendency emphasized by a number of recent commentators. *Spectacular Narratives* argues for a position somewhere between the extremes of reconciliation and incoherence. Many contemporary Hollywood features offer a component of mythic/ideological reconciliation but this is often a blurry rather than hard-edged process, which leaves room for more than one point of entry. 'Having it both ways' is a pleasure offered by many of the films discussed in this book, a pleasure that might itself begin to square the circle between the *textual* reconciliation of thematic oppositions and the *commercial* mixture of elements designed to appeal to differing audience groups. The interface between the two – the point at which the social or cultural 'meanings' of films overlap with, or appear to contradict, industrial imperatives – is fruitful territory for analysis but far from clear-cut. One of the strongest and most obvious grounds for reading popular entertainment forms in terms of the cultural implications of their 'meanings' is the fact that industry strategists are likely to pay some attention at least to what are perceived to be the interests and concerns of potential audiences. Such interests are not clear-cut or expressed fully or directly, but they can hardly be ignored if commercial success is to be achieved.

Many elements of the audience on which Hollywood had depended were lost in the post-war consumer boom, the move to the suburbs and the expansion of other leisure activities, including television. What was left, or reconstructed, was an increasingly segmented audience: the 'youth' and 'family' audiences, for example, and those seeking more 'adult' or challenging fare.

The targeting of different films to different audiences was heightened and institutionalized by the advent of the ratings system in 1968. The blockbuster format of the last quarter century has evolved as part of an effort to create a much wider audience for certain films, an industrial strategy that might in the process give these attractions a larger measure of cultural centrality. The peak of success, achieved by examples such as *Star Wars* (1977) and *E.T. The Extraterrestrial* (1982), is to gain the resonance of a broader cultural event. Blockbusters seek to mobilize an audience beyond those who attend regularly, although this strategy is still rooted in appeals to particular groups perceived as 'core' cinemagoers, the precise nature of which might change with the demographic tide.[21] Cultural resonances that might tap into the concerns of potential moviegoers are taken explicitly into account by market researchers employed in the preparation of such films.[22] Advertising and promotional strategies are often based around attempts to sell blockbusters as special events that *everybody* is going to see. To miss them, therefore, is to miss out, to be excluded.

A similar dynamic is implied in a great deal of advertising, which often promises not just the product but membership of a community of fellow consumers. Some reconciliation of differences is built into the blockbuster strategy at an industrial level, a fact that might help to explain or ground some of the mythic 'work' in which these films appear to engage. We should also bear in mind that Hollywood films continue to have a cultural reach far greater than that measured by cinema admissions, the majority of viewing experiences having occurred on television and video since the mid-to-late 1980s.

Mythic narratives shade over into ideologies – in the critical, Marxist, sense of the term – where they can be seen to serve particular interests, especially those of dominant groups or classes. To give the impression of resolving real material contradictions could benefit those in existing positions of power, those whose positions might be threatened if the implications of such contradictions were brought to the surface. A mythology could, in principle, exist without serving an ideological purpose: it could offer reconciliations of troubling contradictions in the cultural life of a group or society in a situation in which no particular group benefited materially as a result. But mythic oppositions are often drawn up in such a way as to short-circuit the real issues to more pointed effect. The opposition between 'the frontier' and 'civilization' or the technocratic state is a false one that can be given imaginary reconcilation – and thus the emotional satisfaction derived from creating the impression of taking on problems and resolving them – without addressing the underlying contradictions (of class, race, gender, and so on) that characterize contemporary American society.

The two poles of the opposition are illusory. They underpin ideological conceptions of transcendent individualism at one extreme and the demonization of any notion of large-scale state or enterprise at the other. The former is celebrated as the essence of what it is to be truly 'American', while the impression is given that the latter is merely secondary, intrusive and inessential. Any critique of the state or American-based multinational capital that might have more radical dimensions is safely channelled into an individualistic ideology that underpins, rather than offers an alternative to, much of the economic and social formation. The whole idea of human existence as something essentially self-present and immediate denies the culturally constructed nature of the realities we inhabit, and so denies that these are contingent and changeable rather than immutable. These discourses are circulated with a persistence and frequency that can hardly be ignored or without consequence, even if any clear-cut ideological 'effects' remain impossible to quantify or to separate from other influences.

A distinction can be made, then, between the mythological dimension of Hollywood narrative – providing pleasure and reassurance through the apparent reconciliation of contradictions – and the ideological dimension, in which certain interests benefit as a result. In this way the reassertion of mythic narratives, such as those revolving around images of the frontier, can be understood without need to resort to any kind of conspiracy theory assuming the conscious or organized activity of those with material interests in the viability of the myth. The motivations of the Hollywood film industry are structured around the creation of pleasurable, and hence profitable, movies, rather than being directly political or ideological in character. This alone is sufficient to lead it largely towards the representation of dominant myths and ideologies.

A further distinction can be made between the mythic/ideological and the industrial dimension. Elements of both reconciliation and contradiction can result from industrial strategies aimed at attracting particular audience segments. As a popular form seeking to appeal to a wide range of viewers, Hollywood cinema is subject to multiple determinations. In some cases these coincide, perhaps reinforcing reconciliatory dynamics, but the result is often a good deal more amorphous.

If the structuralist approach pioneered by Lévi-Strauss needs to be supplemented by a more critical perspective, cognizant of the ideological potential of mythology and the commercial imperatives of Hollywood, it also needs to be historicized. Myths and ideologies are not timeless entities. The mythology of the frontier has played a dominant role in American culture for many years, but it does not necessarily have the same precise resonances in all times and places. One of the aims of this study will be to situate aspects of this mythic narrative, historically and politically, as it functions in contemporary Hollywood. Frontier mythology appears to have been mobilized with particular force in recent decades.

Central elements of American myth came under question during a complex of events in the 1960s and early 1970s – including uprisings of racial unrest, the Vietnam war, Watergate and the loss of global economic hegemony – that combined, more or less, to form an amorphous threat to dominant or preferred ideologies for many if not all Americans. This did not translate immediately into the more questioning stance of some of the 'Hollywood Renaissance' films of the period. The fact that elements of traditional American ideology could be questioned was partly to do with the specific strategies of studios that were in financial difficulties and willing, temporarily at least, to widen the bounds of the permissible in the search for audiences.

At times when the industry is more stable Hollywood has managed largely to ignore substantial 'real world' threats to its favourite mythologies, as Robert Ray suggests in his examination of the mobilization of frontier mythology during the Second World War. The war might have undermined one of the central presuppositions of the myth: that America held an 'exceptional' and essentially 'free' frontier status because it remained free of entanglements with others. The implications of this were contained, however, by narratives that continued to insist that involvement in the problems of others (typically, the intervention of the 'reluctant hero') need only be temporary and not permanently restrictive.[23]

By the late 1960s this act of containment was proving more difficult. If any Americans believed they could return to a position of supposed 'isolation' after the Second World War (notwithstanding the fact that the United States was already heavily implicated in operations in plenty of other parts of the world as far back at least as the turn of the century), the

Korean war and especially the conflict in Vietnam made it painfully clear that this was not possible. The combination of the scale of the upheavals of the 1960s and the contemporary economic troubles of Hollywood was sufficient to open at least parts of the mythology to question on screen, even if oppositional forces such as those of the 'counterculture' maintained a sizeable investment themselves in the rhetoric and imagery of the frontier. The mythology of the frontier has since been reasserted more unequivocally as a way of bypassing any complications manifested in the late 1960s or early 1970s; mapping a difficult and complex terrain back into a series of simple, reassuring – and flattering – binary oppositions.

One danger in making such a claim is that it may be accused of treating a subject so ubiquitous as to disappear into nothingness. But this is exactly what the most potent ideologies do. It is the ultimate achievement of ideology to become so ubiquitous as to become almost ungraspable, to become part of the conceptual air we breathe; and, as a result, hard to recognize for what it really is. This is a powerful defence against being subjected to analysis. The analyst risks being accused of merely stating the obvious or the banal. Ideologies that have reached this ideal state of ubiquity are thus liable to slip beneath the critical radar. This should not be allowed. The prevalence of aspects of frontier mythology and ideology in Hollywood cinema is significant and should not be left unexamined on the dangerous assumption that it seems merely 'obvious'. Critical approaches that describe contemporary Hollywood spectaculars in terms of the absence of any significant narrative dimension risk complicity in the establishment of the 'invisibility' of such ideological structures, however banal they might at first appear.

The problem is particularly acute in the case of the conceptions of the narrative myth/ideology of the 'frontier' used in much of this book. The frontier in American culture has concrete historical and social points of reference, even if these have always been contested. But 'the frontier' as a part of discourse is very slippery, hence the need often to put the term within quotation marks. It is a notion hallowed in much of mainstream (and a good deal of alternative) American culture, but can have many different uses and resonances. Discourses that play on the resonances of the frontier are not consistent or free from contradictions, and we should not expect them to be. Popular cultures and mythologies rarely are. It may seem at times as if I am using the concept somewhat loosely, but I would argue that this is largely unavoidable given the nature of the phenomenon itself. The frontier is a concept *mobilized* loosely in its mythic or ideological dimensions. Frontier discourses are sufficiently well entrenched in American culture to provide a repository that can be drawn upon in many different ways that do not necessarily add up to any coherent whole. The absence of a single unambiguous meaning or use of 'the frontier' should not be an excuse for a lack of analytical rigour, of course. But it is necessary to underline the protean nature of the phenomenon. Slipperiness is a quality to which the most effective ideologies might aspire: the fact that we cannot always nail them down precisely does not mean we should not try to scoop them up where we can.

The 'frontier' or the 'frontier experience' can mean many things, and is not always defined in its own terms. It is often defined negatively, in terms of what it is not, which is an additional hazard to analysis. That which is defined negatively does not have fully to be articulated. It is here, again, that much of its ideological power lies: it does not have to be given explicit voice – a voice that could be challenged – for the resonances to be present.[24] Quite what those resonances are will always remain open to argument, precisely because they can be so intangible. I suggest that in contemporary Hollywood cinema they can often be read in terms of something very like frontier mythology, but I accept that this may sometimes be contested. Thematic oppositions between constructions of individual freedom, 'nature' and 'authenticity' – on one side – and oppressive institutions, 'decadence' and over-reliance on technology on the other, are established strongly enough as a central part of the dynamics of many films, whether or not it is always necessary or useful to view them in the light of frontier mythology. The argument that Hollywood spectacle continues to invest significantly in this narrative dimension is not dependent on an acceptance of the emphasis I have placed, as a unifying theme of this book, on the relationship between these themes and aspects of frontier discourse. No texts, cinematic or otherwise, can be reduced to single meanings, especially if they seek to appeal to mass audiences. But neither are they open to an infinite play. Polysemy is almost always structured in one way or another, which leaves plenty of room for dispute. My argument is that certain discourses relating to the mythology of the frontier are called upon or available to structure the interpretation of elements of a wide range of contemporary Hollywood movies, at the levels of both narrative and spectacle. There is always a risk of 'reading too much into' the texts in order to construct a coherent argument, but an element of 'reading into' is involved in all acts of narrative comprehension, not just those that make it into print.[25]

I am not claiming that the meanings I ascribe to frontier discourse in these films are in any way exclusive to the myth or ideology of the American frontier. Oppositions such as that between 'frontier' authenticity and alienating technology or bureaucracy are also found in many other cultural frameworks and need not always be figured in frontier terms, even in America. Most popular narratives are structured around the 'disruption' of equilibrium – which is widely seen as a fundamental characteristic of narrative – so why read this disruption in terms of the frontier? It might not always be appropriate to do so.

My point is that in dominant American cultures such phenomena are often expressed in or refracted through the discourses of the frontier, or lend themselves to such readings, even if that does not exhaust all possible resonances. This is partly because these discourses have so much sheer presence in America – they are constantly available and at hand – and also because they are so greatly valorized in most cases. Frontier tropes are a favoured medium for any argument that wishes to claim the moral high ground, through appeals to either the 'essence of America' in ideal/historical terms or to a future at the 'cutting edge'. I am not suggesting that the reassertion of frontier mythology is the *only* narrative activity in the films to be examined, or that it is free from its own contradictions. It is present in varying degrees, sometimes very much in the foreground, sometimes as just one of a number of potential resonances. Its particular function, among other narrative frameworks, might be to lend its prestige to the assertion of similar or other oppositions and/or reconciliations.

This book examines the relationship between narrative and spectacle in recent Hollywood cinema at a number of levels. Analysis of film texts is situated within various contexts. Readings of individual films or genres are supported by consideration of their status as social phenomena and as particular kinds of commercial products crafted to offer a variety of appeals to their audiences. *Spectacular Narratives* makes no claim to be a study of the whole of contemporary Hollywood cinema. Many types of film are not included, particularly the more modestly budgeted or less spectacular products that continue to play a significant part in the broader industrial strategy. Neither are all aspects of the films given the same degree of attention. The roles of performance and stardom, for example, are only considered in passing. The overall focus of the book is established further in Chapter 1 '"Frontier" Narrative and Spectacle in *Twister* and *Independence Day*'.

The impact of new generations of special effects technologies has done much to drive recent debates about the relationship between spectacle and narrative in contemporary Hollywood and it is to this aspect of the question that I turn in Chapter 2, 'Digital Dinosaurs: From T-Rex to Titanic'. Close textual analysis of *Jurassic Park* (1993) and *Titanic* (1997) is used to give a more detailed account of the moment-by-moment operations of their spectacular and narrative dynamics. In Chapter 3, 'The Final Frontier: Space Fictions', science fiction is viewed as the *locus classicus* of the contemporary transposed frontier, a genre thriving in the period that saw the decline of the traditional western and the increased centrality of Hollywood spectacle.

How exactly the noisier elements of spectacle are constructed is the subject of Chapter 4, 'Maximum Impact: Action Films', which brings elements of Soviet Montage theory and study of Hollywood audiences to bear on an examination of *The Long Kiss Goodnight* (1996) and *The Rock* (1996). Chapter 5, 'Seriously Spectacular: "Authenticity" and "Art" in the War Epic' – which includes readings of *Saving Private Ryan* (1998), *Apocalypse Now* (1979) and *Platoon* (1986) – considers a brand of spectacular narrative that makes claim to a greater cultural 'respectability'. From fire and flood to the threat of comets hurtling towards the earth, the representation of disaster offers another ideal arena for the combination of narrative and spectacular dynamics. The disasters presented in films such as *Volcano* (1997), *Armageddon* (1998) and *Deep Impact* (1998) are examined in Chapter 6, 'Apocalypse, Maybe: Pre-millennial Disaster Movies', which includes consideration of the extent to which the structure of some of these films can be understood in terms of how they are designed to appeal on the basis of gender. The blockbuster features of contemporary Hollywood are commonly referred to as 'thrill rides', in both criticism and their own publicity. What happens, then, when the film becomes a vehicle for actual theme-park rides, computer games or other profitable spin-off products? This is the subject of chapter 7, 'Conclusion Into the Spectacle?', which argues that a blend of narrative and spectacle continues to characterize both the films and their more immersive or interactive progeny.

1

'Frontier' Narrative and Spectacle in *Twister* and *Independence Day*

> The American must cross the border into 'Indian country' and experience a 'regression' to a more primitive and natural condition of life so that the false values of the 'metropolis' can be purged and a new, purified social contract enacted.
>
> Richard Slotkin[1]

The hero of *Twister* (1996) sniffs the air, picks up a handful of dirt and lets it fall slowly through his fingers before looking up into the sky, instinctively reading the natural signs that tell him when and where a tornado is brewing. His arch-rival has little time for such niceties, relying not on his own senses but on vanloads of expensive computerized technology paid for by corporate funds. The hero Bill Harding (Bill Paxton), in his jeans, is marked clearly as heir to the frontier tradition. His opponent Jonas Miller (Cary Elwes), in military-looking cap and fatigues, is a representative of corporate-sector technological might and accorded a far less sympathetic hearing. *Twister*'s engagement with these terms appears to be simplistic and entirely in favour of frontier nostalgia. The dramatic clash between the central characters is loaded, to an almost comic-book extent: Harding is the good guy, Miller the bad, and their personal fates are predetermined accordingly. A more subtle process of negotiation is also involved, however. A distinction can be made between value judgements about the quality of 'surface' narrative found in this kind of film – usually declared wanting in terms of complexity and subtlety – and the identification of 'underlying' narrative patterns that merit more sustained analysis. A similar structure of oppositions is implicit, if less obviously so, in *Independence Day*, the other big effects-led blockbuster of the summer of 1996, in which alien attack provides the catalyst for the juxtaposition of 'frontier' individual and technological realms. The fact that such themes continue to influence the way we are invited to read popular films underlines their centrality to some of the strains within American myth/ideology in the late twentieth century, however inflated the spectacular dimension might become.

This chapter will begin by considering the thematic oppositions that underpin the texts, emphasizing the points of relation to frontier mythology and situating the films in their ideological and political contexts. *Twister* and *Independence Day* will also be examined within the industrial and aesthetic landscape of contemporary Hollywood. This will require analysis of the social and cultural position of Hollywood cinema and its formal strategies, particularly the relationship between narrative and spectacle. Consideration will also be given to the place Hollywood now occupies within the historical context of frontier mythology.

Narrative oppositions and resolutions: frontier zone vs. technological modernity

Elemental force in *Twister* and *Independence Day* is presented as both lethal danger and potential source of redemption, precisely the role played by the wilderness and its occupants in the classic American frontier tradition. To those lacking the requisite knowledge and attitude, the wild, manifested by prodigious tornado or alien, is an unpredictable and unfathomable enemy. But to certain privileged individuals it offers the possibility of a special kind of supposedly authentic experience.[2] This is offered as valuable both in itself and as providing a more widely applicable cure for a range of social ills. The 'frontier' realm opened up by these forces can also become a domain in which such individuals can make a difference, where immediate human agency is presented as free from social constraint.

Chasing the tornados of *Twister* offers an opportunity for excitement, adventure and an engagement with undomesticated natural extremity. The space within and immediately around the tornado becomes a mobile frontier zone in which such possibilities are unleashed amid otherwise mundane existence. The heart of the tornado is a place of carnivalized disruption, where normal rules do not apply. The frontier is often seen as a place where the usual weight of social norms is lessened or removed. Within the force-fields of the tornado the metaphor is literalized. The laws of gravity are rescinded, at least temporarily. Heavy vehicles and entire buildings are freed from their bounds. The result is chaotic and hazardous, but also liberating and exhilarating. Harding and his partner Jo (Helen Hunt) are portrayed as having what it takes to inhabit this privileged space, to get close enough to penetrate to the heart of the tornado and to survive the experience. Miller remains alienated from such possibility. His dependence on technology leads him astray. He usually misses the target and his one direct encounter leads to his death.

Engagement with the alien invaders of *Independence Day* offers similar possibility of escape from the mess, tedium and corruption of daily life in late twentieth-century America: it is in such terms, avoiding any more substantial causal factors, that the fruits of contemporary capitalism tend to be rendered. Abandoning the metropolis for a showdown launched from the New Mexico desert, the central characters move from an alienated state to a form of elemental combat that enables them to prove themselves in a break from dull or oppressive routine. This version of the renewed frontier experience produces the appearance of enemies that are unambiguously defined and against which a clear definition of virtuous self can be articulated. The contrast between desert and cityscape is starkly drawn in *Independence Day*, the original westward frontier movement echoed in the image of a caravan of motor-homes moving across the empty expanses of Nevada.

The personification of wilderness or exterior force seems to relish assaults on what might be seen as sources of 'decadence', in a pattern of retributive violence that echoes puritan strictures on the dangers of moral 'backsliding'. The aliens of *Independence Day* destroy the heart of the

Redemptive force from above, I: an alien ship destroys the White House, a source of 'decadence' and corruption in Independence Day, *© Twentieth Century Fox Film Corporation, 1996. Ronald Grant archive*

metropolis, bringing fiery vengeance like some latter-day Old Testament god. In *Twister* the tornado brings real terror to a drive-in performance of *The Shining* (1980), an intertextual joke that also implies a distinction between the status of the two films. *The Shining* is located, within the fictional world, as a source of decadent or artificial thrills, rudely interrupted by a force of nature. *Twister*, in the process, allies itself with the more authentic realm, transcending that of the film-within-the-film.

The fact that one of these films revolves around the date celebrated for the signing of the Declaration of Independence reinforces the potential of their events both to question – and to provide opportunity to revive – hallowed American values. Shadows are cast, literally, on Washington's monumental embodiments of these values in *Independence Day*, metaphorically to be lifted in the victorious climax. Foolish or ignorant characters attempt to engage tornado or alien spacecraft without adequate protection, preparation or knowledge. The heroes are qualified to move into the dangerous frontier territory, to take on the deadly force. It is with these characters, of course, that the audience is positioned to identify, in a vicarious experience of what the frontier is supposed to offer.

These films imply that the 'frontier' experience of extremity offers more than just hedonistic thrills for the individuals involved. There is also the possibility of redemption, at both the individual and social levels. The terms of redemption in *Twister* are fairly crude and simplistic. Harding rejoins his old tornado-chasing team when he is about to formalize the end of his marriage to Jo, who is asserted to be the 'right woman' for him. However much they argue, they share the same underlying commitment to the tornado/frontier adventure. He is engaged to Melissa (Jami Gertz), a sex therapist caricatured as incompetent on the frontier terrain, a whining metropolitan creature tied by mobile phone to the impotence of life in the city. It goes without saying that the return to tornado-frontier experience brings Harding back to his senses and the renewal of his relationship with Jo, with whom he can share the conventional heterosexual passions of a literal whirlwind romance – the sequences in which they experience the inside of the tornado together have an increasingly orgasmic quality – in which he remains for the most part the dominant patriarchal figure. The worthy social agenda is provided by a plot mechanism in which the aim of the enterprise is to release into the tornado a recording device capable of giving new information to help in the future plotting and prediction of tornado outbreaks.

Twister also implies that the personal redemption gained by Harding is more generally available to those who regulate their lives according to an honest and instinctive rhythm, redolent of what the frontier stands for in the mythology, rather than becoming mired in the 'decadent' tendencies of the metropolis. His new life with Jo, we are led to assume, will be a healthy and wholesome relationship, sharing the open and hospitable values signified by scenes at the home of Jo's eccentric but adored Aunt Meg (Lois Smith) and the pastoral landscape in which the couple are left at the film's conclusion after the final tornado has passed. The tornado leaves a rambling old farmhouse homestead miraculously intact in its path, an enormously resonant and compacted symbol of the kind of values for which they stand. Their domestic future is prefigured in the image of a couple and their children emerging unscathed from an underground storm shelter, a sequence whose significance is emphasized by its placement *before* we are shown the dishevelled figures of the two principal survivors. The redemption offered by the displaced frontier is a celebration of the nuclear family, particularly the restoration of the father-figure so dramatically plucked from the scene in the prologue, in which Jo as a young girl saw her father carried to his death by a giant tornado.

Twister starts and finishes with a family group seeking shelter from the ultimate 'force five' tornado. In the first case, the father dies. In the second, the family survives intact and the potential of a new family is restored. In the elliptical logic so typical of Hollywood cinema, the future fruits of the successful tornado-monitoring experiment are reaped immediately, by implication, in the emotional pay-off delivered by this rewriting of the tragic prologue. Miller is left dead, and along with him, it seems, the underlying threat posed by the identification between his character and the anonymous corporate forces for which he stands and which have so often been counterposed to the supposedly 'true' American values of the frontier. This theme is not greatly elaborated but does not need to be: the broad implications are implicit and sufficiently familiar in American mythology to stand as shorthand for a whole complex of negative associations. Any more substantial analysis of the relations between corporate capitalism and the realities of daily life in America is effectively short-circuited.

Individual redemption is offered to the leading characters of *Independence Day*. The reluctant genius David Levinson (Jeff Goldblum) is freed from work for a cable television company, enabled instead to put his intellect to the ultimate in worthwhile ends: saving the world. President Thomas Whitmore (Bill Pullman), a former Gulf War pilot, abandons the manipulations of electoral politics to lead a global fight back and takes to the skies himself in the final conflict. Captain Steven Hiller (Will Smith), a black pilot turned down by NASA, flies an alien craft to deliver the crucial blow, while Vietnam veteran Russell Casse (Randy Quaid) recovers from alcoholic haze to die in redemptive kamikaze glory.

The crisis also leads to a revived romance between Levinson and his ex-wife and impels Hiller and his girlfriend to cement their affair in marriage. For all its transgressive potential, the frontier and its analogues remains for Hollywood a place more often associated with the restoration of sexual conformity. On the broader canvas, redemption comes not just in saving the world but through the global unity demonstrated by a world shaking off 'petty' quarrels to come together against the threat of annihilation. At the political level, the President is able to regain power from conspiratorial federal forces that have concealed the truth about alien remains recovered in the notorious Roswell incident of 1947, one of the icons of contemporary American domestic paranoia.

Key elements of frontier mythology are played upon, then, in the dynamics of *Twister* and *Independence Day*. Underlying the confrontations enacted in these films is an opposition between two of the most powerful components of dominant American ideology: the myth of the frontier and alternative myths of technological modernity, according to which America is defined as a model of modernizing progress, whether industrial or post-industrial. The two mythologies are in some respects mutually exclusive. More significant, perhaps, for its ideological resonance in contemporary American culture, is the extent to which the contradictions between the two can be resolved, or at least displaced. This was a central mythic function of the traditional generic western.

Advanced technology is associated with areas of culture – as opposed to the 'nature' experienced on the frontier – which at the very least shade dangerously into the possibility of corruption and decadence. But technology also has a positive role to play, as might be expected of a culture in which the imperatives of the frontier have always existed in a state of tension with celebrations of modernity and progress. From early colonial times to the present, America has often been seen as a place of enlightenment, of new beginnings freed from the inheritances of old cultural baggage and superstitions. In certain manifestations this outlook is consistent with frontier mythology, particularly with conceptions of the frontier as a place of fresh starts, new worlds and escape from the past. If the frontier is viewed as something that played an essential part in the development of a distinctive 'American Way' but that had to pass with the coming of a new 'civilization', then there is no fundamental contradiction: the frontier experience might be seen as having cleared the way for the establishment of a society founded on the enlightened use of technology, for the benefit of all rather than that of encrusted privilege.[3]

Nostalgia for the 'lost' frontier often takes a stronger form, however, as the rosy glow of past reflection is outshone by the active (and often violent) desire to re-create something of the mythic frontier experience in modern life, if only as a substitute for the reality whose existence in the terms promoted by the myth was always in doubt. The tension is manifested at the end of *Twister* in the form of the competing imperatives

Redemptive force from above, II: the tornado as frontier vortex, erupting into the 'tamed' pastoral landscape in Twister, *© Warner Bros. and Universal City Studios, Inc., 1996. Ronald Grant archive*

represented by pastoral landscape – civilized rather than wild, but not decadent either – and frontier vortex. The dangers of the frontier have to be tamed if the pastoral idyll is to be secured. But the continued proximity or possibility of the frontier remains necessary if the pastoral is to maintain its ideal middle position, between two poles, and not to be left open to the corrupting sway of the metropolis.[4] The freedom and vitality of the 'wind' is reconciled with the solidity and settled existence of the 'earth'. That this is all rooted in myth, the shape of the 'original' American frontier often having been structured and organized by events in the metropolis rather than being in any way primal or originary,[5] does little to reduce its ideological impact.

The problem identified by the main narrative movement of *Twister* is not the use of technology itself but an excessive reliance upon it. Miller goes to his death because of his arrogant refusal to take advice from Harding, whose instinctive feel for the movements of tornados has been shown to be superior to Miller's technological and military-style operation. 'The days of sniffing the dirt are over', Miller asserts, although it is clear that he knows Harding's instincts to be reliable. It is through sheer arrogance and disavowal that he is driven to ignore Harding's advice and led to his doom.

Harding's team also uses computerized technology to track the tornados, but it is kept in its place. This is underlined by the fact that it is not Harding himself but other members of the team who are glued to their monitors. Harding prefers to keep his senses alert to the real world, unmediated. Technology is important, but not transcendent. It is also subject to the kind of hands-on improvisation associated with frontier life, where pioneers are supposed to do everything for themselves, to be directly involved in all aspects of life, unlike the narrow specialization of technocratic society. (How closely any of this accords with the harsh rigours of manual labour on the frontier remains questionable.) The device released into the tornado is presented with the full cinematic rhetoric of 'masterful technology', floods of 'vital data' filling computer screens as it flies into action. It is unlikely to work, however, until modified in a moment of inspiration in which fragments of Pepsi cans are used to construct makeshift wings (Jo requests the collection of 'every aluminium can you can find', but only Pepsi seems to exist). Product placement here becomes a source of salvation, the ultimate in positive-vibe positioning for the product involved. Pepsi glitters in the limelight for significant moments, but the placement is firmly integrated into central narrative themes of the movie. It does not 'work against' the narrative, the impact of product placement suggested by Mark Crispin Miller, but gains its resonance precisely from being positioned at a heightened narrative crux.[6]

If the wilderness itself is figured sexually as feminine, the dominant trope in a range of American cultural products, *Twister* proffers its own vivid image in the shape of the vaginal vortex of the tornado, at once hazardous and fascinating, seething and – initially, at least – unknowable. Phallic imagery is also available, the device ejaculating a multitude of sperm-like silver balls that penetrate to the centre of the tornado. The tornado becomes knowable, predictable and at least partially domesticated. As does Jo, whose leadership role in the tornado-chasing team is often supplanted by Harding's return and whose more obsessive attitude toward the tornado seems to associate her with its irrationality.

The most insistent visual signals of the contrasting approaches of the Harding and Miller teams in *Twister* are the convoys of vehicles in which they chase across the countryside. The villains occupy an almost obligatory fleet of anonymous and sinister black vans, signifying the evil forces of centralized regimentation. The good guys are in a motley collection including a battered old motor-home – that modern version of the covered wagon, again – blaring out rock music and generally emanating a spirit of eccentric pioneer individuality. Despite the simplistic mechanics of these kinds of character-oppositions, *Twister* offers some resolution of the competing demands of frontier and technology, although frontier values remain privileged.

A similar dynamic is found in *Independence Day*, in which technology is presented as necessary to survival, but again far from sufficient. A high state of technological readiness is necessary if the aliens are to be defeated, a point that is clearly central to the film's broadly conservative and militaristic stand. As in *War of the Worlds* (1953), on which the film is partly based, it is made clear that the aliens are creatures as feeble physiologically as humans and are daunting enemies only by virtue of technological might. But technology-as-system, part of a giant military–industrial complex, does not work. The full might of jet fighters and nuclear weapons fails initially to make any dent in the alien armour. To break through, the film suggests, something more quirky, human and inventive is required; namely, the computer virus introduced by the maverick genius of David Levinson with a little inspirational help from his father Julius (Judd Hirsch), plus the unconventional aerobatics of Hiller and Casse and the leadership qualities of Whitmore.

The heroic elements essential to success are divided here among several characters. Levinson is hardly a traditional frontiersman, but has some characteristics of the modern counter-cultural equivalent: an environmentalist hostile to the wasteful ways of technological existence. Hiller, Casse and Whitmore (especially once the latter exchanges presidential robes for fighter-pilot outfit) have more conventional frontier traits, as transplanted into the domain of aerial warfare. The jet pilot is privileged as a figure able to maintain heroic qualities of active agency, in control of, rather than determined by, his technology.

A dynamic of progress is partially endorsed, as in the classic western narrative in which the frontier, however much sanctified and privileged, is usually viewed as a state that will pass with the inevitable coming of modern 'civilization'. This is the impression given by the closing images of heterosexual bliss and pastoral tranquillity in *Twister*, the point at which the tornado-wilderness force is about to come under greater control. The final effect is equivocal, seeking to square the values of frontier nostalgia with the hope for future progress, an ambivalence that has always been present in frontier mythology.

The effect of successful popular mythology is precisely to offer such reconciliations, however contradictory their components might appear on closer examination, and however much the analysis of such dynamics in Hollywood might be complicated by consideration of other industrial imperatives. A degree of resolution is provided on an imaginary level for oppositions that cannot be overcome in reality. Issues that raise substantial difficulties for a particular culture, as the inherent contradictions of frontier discourse and modernity do for America, are displaced onto a plane where mythic sleight of hand can offer at least a semblance of reconcilation. A common strategy is to displace difficult thematic oppositions on to conflicts within or around heterosexual couples. These can be given the appearance of reconciliation not only with relative ease but, more importantly, with the delivery of emotional satisfaction that distracts from the existence of other, unresolved tensions. In some cases thematic oppositions are structured explicitly into subsequently resolved character relationships, although the connection is often more elliptical, as it generally seems in *Twister* and *Independence Day*.

It is significant that the troubled romantic couple in *Twister* and one of the couples central to *Independence Day* are existing *former* partners, which gives to the eventual reconciliation a sense of inevitability, a return to an essential unity that has only temporarily been blocked. In *Twister* Harding is associated with the earth, while Jo is closer to the unleashed spirit of the whirlwind. His solidity is needed to pull her back from the brink of an obsession that threatens to run out of control. They are paired as much as opposed, however, both being associated with forces of nature, and Harding – nicknamed 'the extreme' – also possesses a reputation for living on the edge.

Independence Day offers a series of character divisions and pairings that involve some reconciliation of differences, the most prominent being that between Levinson and his former partner, a White House aide heavily implicated in the 'superficial' process of presidential image-mongering. The film is more crude and specific than *Twister*, and more ideologically loaded, in references that assume a familiarity with Hollywood science fiction. A number of swipes are taken against the mushy liberalism of *Close Encounters of the Third Kind* (1977). A spaced-out group of revellers gathers on the roof of a skyscraper hoping for some kind of loving communion with the aliens – and promptly gets vaporized, as does a helicopter sent up to communicate by playing music and flashing coloured lights. The denizens of the rooftop are presented as a fake, metropolitan and decadent version of the kind of redemption that is only really available to those strong enough to engage more violently with the alien. The entire sentimental project of *Close Encounters* is dismissed as firmly here as in the direct reference, in which Hiller punches-out a crash-landed alien, quipping, 'Now that's what I call a Close Encounter'. The joke is guaranteed a laugh, but the politics are more serious in a film that presents the being from another world as a cold, absolutely alien 'Other' for whom all humanity can usefully do is 'die'. This justifies a response of unmitigated violence on the American part that is central to the film's generally reactionary politics.

The evil alien of science fiction that once stood potentially as a metaphor for the Soviet Union is revived here in the post-Cold War era as its ideologically much-required replacement: the Other against which internal unity can be asserted. Complicating factors are removed at a stroke. The effect is much the same as the dismissal of conspiracy theory to which I referred earlier. If one gesture removes the obligations denoted by the benevolent aliens of Spielberg, the other unwinds the entanglements of form and narrative woven by the conspiracy movie subgenre of the Vietnam/Watergate-infected early 1970s. Conspiracy theory is taken on board but only to be disavowed. The threats of both sentimentality and corruption are shuffled off.

A nod to the HAL computer of *2001: A Space Odyssey* (1968) – its sinister red eye and a 'Good morning, Dave' greet Levinson on his computer when he enters the alien spacecraft – seems sufficient to dismiss the burden of Kubrick's tale of the eclipse of human agency by technology. The film embraces ethnic and racial diversity among the central characters, disavowing the existence of internal ruptures along these lines. What is left is a reassuringly simple, binary opposition between Good and Evil, unitary collective Self and absolute Other. The cleansing of American society and the darkening of the Other permit a return to the terms of the pre-revisionist western (or the Cold War) at its most ideologically pure, and a realm in which there is no question other than to kill the alien-Other or be killed.

The version of frontier and technology given in *Twister* and *Independence Day* is more unambiguously celebratory than that found in some earlier explorations of the same mythological landscape. A good point of comparison is *Jaws* (1975), a key film in the development of the contemporary blockbuster format, which negotiates similar oppositions in a more questioning and tentative manner, befitting an era in which the confident assertions of frontier mythology were confronted by the immediate fallout of the Vietnam War and other social and economic upheavals in the early-to-mid 1970s.

The greater stridency of *Twister* and *Independence Day* can be seen at some level as part of a concerted rehabilitation of the myth of the frontier. Frontier rhetoric was mobilized widely during the Vietnam War, but was also damaged by its association with Vietnam. The post-Vietnam era has seen numerous reassertions of the myth, not the least being films about the war and the boom in science fiction from the late 1970s. To suggest a project of rehabilitating frontier-related mythology in this period is not to assume any active conspiracy by those who might benefit from its ideological impact. The ideological work entailed in appeals to the frontier is likely to be pleasing and flattering to much of the audience. These films offer large measures of reassurance. They confront difficult issues but in a superficial manner. Real underlying contradictions remain, at various levels, but the rhetoric of films such as *Twister* and *Independence Day* gives the impression of resolution. This might not always work perfectly, but in general it is likely to offer sufficient pleasure to most audiences for any resort to conspiracy theory to be superfluous. Hollywood's commitment to providing pleasure, its primary route to profit, is enough to account for a reassertion of aspects of frontier mythology, however qualified.

Twister and *Independence Day* appeared at a time when frontier-related values again came up against some awkward realities, however, despite the generally conservative flavour of the political context. The antics of extreme anti-state right-wing militia and bombers might have forced some Americans to confront the darker side of the mythology of frontier violence, redemption and virulent suspicion of state and corporate power. By taking the logical implications of one version of frontier mythology to their violent extremes, these groups have made elements of the mythology potentially less comfortable in the hands of those situated at the more liberal end of the spectrum. They have also been greeted with applause in some circles, however, even if the means are often condemned.

The fervent opposition to the heritage of industrialism and technology expressed by the Unabomber from his *Walden*-esque cabin in the Montana backwoods has wider resonances in contemporary American culture, as is suggested by the iconic adoption of his photofit image (the hooded figure in dark glasses) and by the suspicion of bureaucratic technological dependence expressed in these highly popular movies. Both *Twister* and *Independence Day* play into a context in which they can indulge and offer fantastic resolution to reactionary paranoia about the secret machinations of state or corporate power. This right-wing version of the anti-state/corporate critique serves also to divert attention from what might be far more pertinent questions raised by the left, the alien-conspiracy version channelling such enquiry into the realms of fantasy. A film like *Twister* provides a legitimate and sanitized way of identifying with frontier-type experience. Its setting unambiguously reasserts the mythical 'heartland' resonance of an Oklahoma landscape traumatized by the Oklahoma City bombing of 1995, not to mention its gestures towards the fantasy of *The Wizard of Oz* (1939), whose Dorothy gives her name and homely tone to the technology used to monitor the tornado. (It is notable that the bad-guy Miller version has become D.O.T., the coldly rational Digital Orthographic Telemeter rather than the warm and comforting Dorothy.) *Independence Day* yokes the frontier theme to a barely disguised call for military retrenchment and an implicit celebration of the Gulf War that would not have looked out of place at the height of the Reagan era.

Narrative vs. spectacle

Closures at the formal and narrative levels play an important part in the assertion of imaginary reconciliations in *Twister* and *Independence Day*. In this sense, they fit into the broad category of what have become known as 'classical' Hollywood texts: tightly organized, if not very subtle, cause-and-effect narratives that might not be entirely coherent but leave little room for questioning or doubts that might undermine the mythic resolution. Strong identifications are provided with hero-figures who carry us through the narrative and across any fissures. Our confidence in the abilities of the hero of *Twister* is absolute, whatever setbacks might be faced, simply because of his status as the star of a conventional mainstream feature.

Questions and uncertainties are evoked by some of the central characters in *Independence Day*, but only in order to highlight the final triumph. It is possible to read films such as this 'against the grain' as it were, or to use the flexibility of home VCR or DVD viewing to play around with their temporal organization. The qualities of the texts themselves are not immutable and do not foreclose all possibilities of meaning, but they do shape them quite strongly. Formal closures at the level of *mise-en-scène* and editing tend to tie the viewer tightly into driving narratives that offer big emotional pay-offs as reward. A conscious effort usually has to be made if these pleasures are to be resisted.

The mythic/ideological assertions of these films demonstrate that narrative is in no way surrendered to spectacle in even the more spectacular aspects of contemporary Hollywood. Yet these films do function importantly as spectacle, trading heavily on the appeal of ever grander special-effects sequences that sometimes seem motivated by little more than their own spectacular presence and box-office appeal. Sitting back and simply 'taking in' the spectacle, the impact of 'big' special effects, seems to be as important a source of pleasure in these films as the joys of narrative; perhaps more so, or at least more obviously so for many viewers. The thumping assertion of clear-cut narrative may be an expression of confidence in the values trumpeted, but it may, equally, be a noisy rhetoric overcompensating for underlying doubt, or providing an alibi for the fact that much of the appeal of these films lies elsewhere. *Independence Day* is filled with a particularly over-insistent narrative rhetoric, including 'explosive' sound effects heavily underlining some of the white-out transitions between shots or scenes in the opening sequences.

According to one view, the early history of cinema – American cinema in particular, but also cinema more generally – can be seen in terms of a gradual move from spectacle to narrative. Early cinema, in the 1890s and 1900s, is characterized in Tom Gunning's influential account as a 'cinema of attractions', its appeal based on the direct confrontation and stimulation of viewers rather than their integration or passive absorption into sustained narratives.[7] As Gunning puts it:

> Rather than being an involvement with narrative action or empathy with character psychology, the cinema of attractions solicits a highly conscious awareness of the film image engaging the viewer's curiosity. The spectator does not get lost in a fictional world and its

drama, but remains aware of the act of looking, the excitement of curiosity and its fulfilment.[8]

The focus is on spectacle *as* spectacle rather than as something subordinated to a place within a narrative structure. By the 1910s at the latest, narrative became increasingly important, for a variety of commercial and aesthetic reasons, around which debate continues.[9] 'Classical' Hollywood cinema came to be defined largely by the centrality of linear narratives, to which all other elements are meant to be subordinated.

Some suggest that this central narrative focus has since been lost, especially in the blockbuster productions of what is defined as a 'post-classical' version of Hollywood. Miriam Hansen suggests a number of parallels between the pre- and post-classical, each of which is characterized by 'a measure of instability that makes the intervening decades look relatively stable, by contrast, for they are anchored in and centred by the classical system.'[10] Classical Hollywood is bracketed, Hansen suggests, by 'forms of spectatorship [that] give the viewer a greater leeway, for better or for worse, in interacting with the film – a greater awareness of exhibition and cultural intertexts.'[11]

Early cinema left a good deal of the work of meaning-creation to the exhibitor and the viewer, a process mirrored to some extent by the element of viewer control provided by media such as videotape and DVD. Early cinema lacked a stable home of its own, moving around between venues such as vaudeville and travelling shows. If the 'classical' form established itself in the exhibition context of the dedicated cinema theatre, this has lost its primary position (in numbers of film-watching experiences) to video and the various forms of television.

It might follow – although this is not a point made explicitly by Hansen – that the cinema of attractions, too, has made its comeback, displacing the centrality of narrative. An element of narrative was never entirely absent, however; not even from the earliest Lumiere 'actualities' of the 1890s. And as Gunning suggests, attractions retained their place even when narrative became more sustained and central to the experience. He cites the particular cases of genres such as comedy and the musical. The question is whether spectacular disruptions are merely localized, generically motivated or pulled into line by the melodramatics of plot, or whether they are more central to the dynamics of Hollywood cinema. Moments of spectacle or 'excess' can be seen as intruding into an essentially coherent narrative fabric, a phenomenon often celebrated for what might then appear to be its radical potential; but the fabric may itself be a close weave of both narrative and spectacle.

The latter seems to be the experience provided by films such as *Twister* and *Independence Day*, and may always have been the case in Hollywood.

Any suggestion that narrative has largely been abandoned to spectacle seems a serious overstatement, both of the lack of spectacle in 'classical' Hollywood and of the absence of narrative structure in the 'post-classical' era. This is not to say that the situation is unchanged or unchanging. The balance between narrative and spectacle is dynamic and may shift from film to film, or from one period to another. Good arguments can be made for emphasizing one tendency or the other at particular moments. Spectacle tends to be foregrounded especially during periods of innovation such as the initial use of sound, colour, widescreen or computer-graphics technology. The first sound films tended to be musicals; early colour and widescreen processes were associated with spectacle more than realism. This does not entail an absence of narrative, however, as will be suggested in the case of digital special effects in the next chapter.

There is no shortage of material grounding for the suggestion that spectacle is important in the specific case of Hollywood cinema today. One of Hollywood's key strategies in response to the move of populations to the suburbs, and to competition from television and other forms of leisure activity, has been to use spectacular attraction as the basis of its effort to tempt audiences back into the cinema, playing on the specific qualities of the big screen. This phenomenon began in the 1950s and included experiments such as Cinerama and 3D, both of which originated outside the major studios. The development of CinemaScope by Twentieth Century Fox (first used in the historical spectacle *The Robe*, 1953) marked the movement of spectacular new widescreen formats into the mainstream, where they proved popular and helped, at least temporarily, to stem the post-war loss of audiences.[12] Spectacular cinema underwent something of a decline in the later 1960s, as the studios ran into serious financial difficulties exacerbated by the failure of a few notorious spectacular features, but it returned as an increasingly dominant strategy through the 1970s, 1980s and 1990s.

What Hollywood spectacle offers in some cases is the promise of an experience claimed to have at least something in common with that conventionally associated with the frontier. Spectacle could, in one sense, be seen as the 'moment' of the frontier-type experience offered directly to the viewer: visceral thrills that stand in for the qualities celebrated thematically in the narrative. The levels of narrative and spectacle operate together in a complex pattern of interaction that seems at times to reinforce the inscription of frontier dynamics in the texts. Moments of spectacle often occur on the frontier terrains that are visited.

In *Twister* the spectacle, in the shape of the tornado, actually creates the frontier vortex amid more cultivated open spaces. *Independence Day* offers moments of spectacular engagement set in the landscape farther west, including an exhilarating chase through an iconographic canyon terrain. It is in such a place that the alien can be taken on and defeated by the skills of a pilot like Hiller. The alternative form of spectacle in *Independence Day*, the destruction of the decadent metropolis, also serves to underpin the work of the narrative. The enjoyment of these scenes may include a simple wallowing in the spectacle of destruction, the safely bounded thrill of seeing hallowed monuments blasted to rubble, but this form of pleasure is integrated into the work of the narrative rather than offering merely arbitrary thrills. A key narrative development in *Twister* – the reunion of Harding and Jo – is cemented, or even established, by their mutual experience of tornado-spectacle. Audio-visual spectacle seems to force them back together, again heightening rather than undercutting a narrative crux.

Spectacle is used here in the way that comic moments or musical numbers are used in the more 'integrated' forms of comedy or the musical. Much work on the relationship between narrative and disruptive or spectacular elements has focused on the genres of comedy and the musical, two cases in which narrative seems most obviously to be subject to institutionalized disruption. Comic gags or self-standing comedy performances and musical numbers can disrupt narrative, particularly at the level of linear plot movement (although this does not guarantee any politically or ideologically disruptive effect).[13] But these moments can be a good deal more integrated. Comic or musical performances can be used to convey important story information and to drive the narrative forward. They can also work to underpin narrative oppositions and resolutions. In many comedies, for example, the comic interruption may appear to disrupt story development but fits closely into thematic oppositions such as those between childishness and maturity.[14]

The big production number of the classical Hollywood musical might seem to intrude into plot development but it often plays a key narrative role in asserting the reconciliation of opposites.[15] Spectacle and narrative can work closely together, even in the least likely seeming contexts. Hard-core explicit sex films offer what might be expected to be one of the most extreme cases of narrative subordination to spectacle.

What is the function of narrative in explicit sex films other than as a flimsy excuse, or linking device, for a series of numbers devoted solely to the business of overt sexual display? Even here, Linda Williams suggests, the relationship between narrative and numbers can take a variety of forms, including one in which the sex sequences function 'as resolutions of conflicts stated either in the narrative or in the other numbers.'[16] Even films that go way beyond any Hollywood blockbuster in the extent to which they are designed to appeal to audiences on the basis of (literally) naked spectacular display are capable of combining the narrative and spectacular dimensions. This is by no means always the case, and even where it is, the degree of integration is variable. The same applies to Hollywood films.

Spectacular Narratives argues that a significant degree of interaction between the two is a characteristic of many popular products of contemporary Hollywood. To say this is not to revive a conception of the seamlessly coherent Hollywood text. The fact that spectacle and narrative act in concert in some ways does not prevent them continuing to obey their own logics and appeals in others. Neither dimension necessarily 'contains' or 'disrupts' the other. They operate together in a pattern that displays variable degrees of coherence from one example to another, or from one moment to another in the same film. The logic they obey is less one of coherence/disruption than what Richard Maltby terms a 'commercial aesthetic' attuned to the best way of maximizing profit.[17]

Spectacular cinema is sold partly on the basis of its sheer size and impact, its physical scale of image and multi-channel sound: its function specifically as 'attraction'. Its role in Hollywood is to offer audiences a scale of audio-visual experience that will bring them back into the cinema. Spectacular cinema from the mid-1950s onwards has to be seen in the context of its contrast with television and other home entertainment. The low-level audio-visual impact of television and video is domesticated, literally, by both its small scale and its location among the routines of everyday life. Cinematic spectacle claims to provide something marked as distinct from this quotidian environment, something special, more intense and filled with the large-scale illusion of *presence.*

Big widescreen cinema claims to fill the viewer's vision. Multichannel hi-fi sound, taken up rather more slowly and reluctantly by exhibitors, adds significantly to the impression of immersion in a three-dimensional experience. Viewers are assaulted by a brand of spectacle that might amount to sheer pace and kinetics; to loudness that can be felt as bodily vibration, and brightness that makes the eyes contract. Special effects occasionally become sequences of almost abstract audio-visual 'impact', the specific or detailed motivated realism of which may be less than clear. The viewer is sold the illusion of being transported into the world on-screen, of *experiencing* more directly the moments which, in the films under consideration here, are often those of the frontier or its analogues, moments of direct engagement with extremity for characters within the fiction.

The point was made explicitly in advertisements of the 1950s which repeatedly depicted the widescreen spectator as inhabiting the same space as the on-screen action.[18] As Mark Crispin Miller puts it: 'Just as the theme park promises to take us right "*into* the movies" the movies now fake our integration with the spectacle [...] .'[19] For Miller, this 'series of visceral jolts' is offered '*instead* of narrative'. But the visceral jolts offered to the viewer can also be read as a way of reinforcing narrative dynamics. The experience of watching such movies is sold as a stimulating intrusion into the everyday world of the viewer in a (perhaps rather pale) reflection of the way that the frontier experience on screen intrudes into the lives of the fictional characters.

If the audience of *Twister* is comprised of thrill seekers, in search of better and more exciting spectacular effects, then so are its characters. Whatever the scientific alibi, the chasing of tornados is presented largely in terms of the whooping and the hollering and getting a buzz out of an exhilarating engagement with one of nature's spectacles. There is a parallel between the on-screen relationship of chaser and tornado and that between viewer and cinematic spectacle. The response of the fictional characters to the ever-increasing spectacle of the twister is akin to that of the audience to the special-effects version. Likewise, the giant alien spacecraft of *Independence Day* are as spectacular to those inside the movie as they are to the viewer in the theatre. Much is made of the awesome spectacle within the frame. The mere sight of the spacecraft reduces characters to a state of gobsmacked, eye-popping and jaw-dropping daze, a state in which the experiences of the everyday world are eclipsed.

A similar dynamic underlies the selling of the spectacle *of* the frame, the film itself, which is promoted partly on the basis of effects designed to reduce the spectator to a similar state of awe and wonder in which ordinary life is left behind. The spectator is assaulted by a series of explosive impacts and at times, potentially, overwhelmed. For Peter Biskind, this kind of filmmaking amounts to rendering the viewer passive and childlike, a tendency he finds in some of the films of George Lucas and Steven Spielberg.[20] Pounding forms of spectacle impose themselves forcefully on the viewer and might leave limited space for contemplation or questioning. In this respect, spectacle can have an impact similar to that of driving linear narrative: it has the potential to reinforce, almost physiologically, whatever the narrative asserts. This is not a process likely to leave the viewer entirely disarmed, however, in the manner Biskind suggests. Hollywood spectacle is a powerful medium but far from all-determining even at its most over-insistent.

The formal strategies of *Twister* chiefly involve an alternation between two kinds of cinematography, each of which seems designed to stress a different aspect of the frontier-type experience. In one movement, the film uses airy and exhilarating shots taken from a helicopter, combined with an upbeat score, to underline the freedom, mobility and space within which the heroes move as they race around the countryside, on and off-road, almost unbounded by any restraints.

Alternatively, *Twister* turns to very tightly-framed action sequences, cut and panned rapidly and often using an unsteady camera to create the impression of presence at the heart of the action. This is a form of spectacle, like that found in the explosive scenes of destruction in *Independence Day*, to which I will return in more detail in Chapter 4. What all of this is supposed to offer is an illusion, of course, at both levels, in and outside the space of the narrative. As an experience analogous to that for which the frontier is made to stand, the experience of spectacular cinema may seem pitifully attenuated, and the comparison somewhat stretched. But it is questionable whether this promise of immediacy, intensity and presence is much more artificial and second-hand than any other mobilization of the myth, in contemporary Hollywood or elsewhere. Cinematic spectacle is clearly not the same as anything that the frontier might once have been. But it is sold on the promise of a similar structural relationship, supposedly offering an illusion of authenticity and presence opposed to the heavily mediated and circumscribed experiences of daily life.

The qualities of this illusion have much in common with the utopian qualities of the musical identified in Richard Dyer's suggestive account of some of the specific pleasures offered by Hollywood cinema. Dyer's categories – energy, abundance, intensity, transparency and community – seem to translate readily to the kinds of films examined here. The experience of the frontier is conveyed precisely in these terms. The mythic frontier is a place of energy: 'Capacity to act vigorously; human power, activity, potential.'[21] The characters in *Twister* crash about the countryside, bursting with energy and activity, as generally do those in *Independence Day*. Where constraints exist, it is usually in order for them to be overcome in a demonstration of potential realized in action.

The mythic frontier is also a place of abundance: 'Conquest of scarcity; having enough to spare without sense of poverty of others; enjoyment of sensuous material reality.' This is evoked strongly in the bountiful agricultural landscapes of *Twister* or the geographical expansiveness that provides the crucial breathing space in *Independence Day*. The frontier experience is characterized by intensity: 'Experiencing of emotion directly, fully, unambiguously, "authentically", without holding back.' This is precisely the nature of the experiences generated inside the tornado and in the moments of climactic countdown to destruction in *Independence Day*.

The frontier is also a place where relationships are rendered transparent and where the ambiguities of everyday life are converted into what seem to be clear-cut oppositions. And it is without doubt presented as a place of newly emerging community, purged of the vices of excessive or decadent 'civilization'. So, we have the emerging pastoral family of *Twister* and the post-apocalyptic desert community of *Independence Day*. As Dyer suggests, these qualities often seem to be lacking in the routine experiences of most inhabitants of contemporary western–capitalist society. Some may be found in other popular cultural productions, but few have the scale and impact possessed by cinema that is so important to the rhetorics of energy, abundance and intensity; rhetorics that, in turn, help to assert the qualities of transparency and community.

If narrative offers order and coherence, moments of spectacle may offer an alternative, the illusion of a more direct emotional and experiential impact. In terms of the mythology, perhaps, narrative is the domain of 'civilization' (organization, structure, routine) and spectacle that of the frontier (uncluttered engagement, presence). Like the mythology of the frontier, Hollywood cinema tends to offer a dialectical interchange between the two, an attempt to play on the appeal of each and to go some way at least towards resolving some of their contradictory imperatives. To return to the level of Hollywood institutions, there may also be some approximate match between two more or less historically paralleled pairs: the 'classical' version of frontier mythology and the 'classical' studio system, on the one hand, and new reassertions of frontier mythology and elements of the 'new Hollywood' of the 'post-studio' era, on the other.

The heyday of the studio system was a time when cinema-going was an institution central to the life of many Americans. It would be expected to be more or less centrally located in terms of the materials of its movies, largely tending to reflect, mobilize or negotiate around dominant ideologies, although not without the ambiguities likely to result from any attempt to produce popular cultural products that draw on a potentially disparate and sometimes contradictory range of popular discourses. The 'post-studio' era began in part as one of change, of challenge to old industrial practices and values. It opened up new possibilities, both in content and formal strategies, partly as a result of the diminution of cinema's previously more central role as a cultural institution. Frontier mythology came under question in some films, as did the way Hollywood operated as an industry. New voices were allowed to some extent – from counterculture to 'blaxploitation' and the influence of European art cinema – in an attempt to cut costs and to find new audiences, especially in view of the financial collapse that hit many of the major studios in the late 1960s and early 1970s. Classical Hollywood narrative style was among the practices to be questioned by some innovators, although the extent of this can easily be exaggerated.

More familiar practices have been asserted, however, at more than one level. The mythology of the frontier has been strongly reasserted in many films, along with something close to 'classical' narrative form, despite all the problems entailed by the use of that term. So has the dominance of the majors. The legally-enforced removal of the major studios from the sphere of exhibition merely demonstrated the centrality of distribution, a sphere they continue to dominate. The central place of the cinema itself has also been reasserted, to a significant extent, in relation to media such as television and video. Television and video screenings may have become more important in terms of the ultimate revenue earnings of movies, but cinematic exhibition remains a key marketplace, the location at which future values tend to be set for circulation in subsidiary channels. The centrality of spectacle or a narrative based on loud rhetoric played an important part in the rebirth of the specifically *cinematic* experience in the 1980s and 1990s, moving towards a renewed emphasis – although not always achieved – on the quality of the audio-visual experience.

Each of these oppositions can easily be overstated and some caution is needed in asserting any sweeping changes, one way or the other. The 'break' that occurred in the later 1960s and early 1970s was far from total, for example, many films continuing to be closer in spirit to earlier Hollywood product than to the more eye-catching examples of the 'Hollywood Renaissance'. It would be wrong to suggest that the mythology of the frontier simply 'died' and was reborn. All of these issues are complicated by the fact that sales to television meant that 'classical' films had a continued presence on the cultural scene. Significant changes did occur, but they were relative rather than absolute and do not always map onto so tidy a framework as suggested above.

At the level of form, some contradictory imperatives appear to be in play here. Products designed for the big screen and influenced by thoughts of suitability for exploitation as computer games or theme-park rides may not appear to sit so happily on the television screen (via broadcast, cassette or disc). What kind of aesthetic most effectively bridges the gap? Mark Crispin Miller's answer is that Hollywood movies have come to look and sound like television commercials. The source of such a change, he suggests, can be found in the influence of product placement strategies and reciprocal movements of creative personnel between cinema and advertising. Contemporary Hollywood movies work,

> without, or against, the potential depth and latitude of cinema, in favour of that systematic overemphasis deployed in advertising (and all other propaganda). Each shot presents a content closed and unified, like a fist, and makes the point right in your face: big gun, big car, nice ass, full moon, a chase (great shoes!), big crash (blood, glass), a lobby (doorman), sarcasm, drinks, a tonguey, pugilistic kiss (nice sheets!), and so on.[22]

This may be true of some films, or sequences within them, including to some extent the close-framed action sequences of *Twister* and some of the explosive conflagrations in *Independence Day*. But it does not account very well for the more expansive visual style used in these and other contemporary spectaculars. More than one style of spectacular imagery is available, as will be seen in subsequent chapters. These are sometimes combined in the same film, a fact that might reflect the importance of both cinematic and televisual consumption. The full potential of the widescreen frame tends not be realized in the contemporary blockbuster because of problems in transition to the small screen. *Jaws*, for example, makes far greater use of the margins of the frame than *Twister* or *Independence Day*, a fact that can at least partly be attributed to the establishment of video as a economically central format in the intervening decades.

Today's blockbusters continue to offer the spectacle of large-scale imagery to a far greater extent than suggested by Miller. They tend to be framed, however, in such a way that they can be edited or scanned into television format without causing damage noticeable to many viewers. This is true even of a massively spectacular event such as the sinking of the ship in *Titanic* (1997). It might be argued that some movies are designed for big-screen blockbuster appeal and others for smoother transition to television and video – if it were not for the fact that the biggest hits on both television and video are usually those which made a big splash in the cinema. The effects-led cinema blockbusters are the films that tend more than others to fill whole walls in video rental outlets. Peter Kramer offers one of the more lucid explanations of this phenomenon:

> Big screen spectacles rely for their revenues on small screen media, and these in turn rely for their appeal on movies which, when replayed on domestic small screen media, carry with them the grandeur and mystique of cinema. The theatrical presentation of expensively-made movies to paying audiences who willingly and wholeheartedly submit themselves to the power and excesses of big screen spectacles remains an important cultural experience which is able to infuse the more mundane and casual use of domestic technologies with special meaning.[23]

New developments in domestic television and digital video technology may go some way towards narrowing the gap between the cinematic and small screen experience. Widescreen digital television, DVD and surround-sound systems are sold with the promise of creating a 'home cinema' effect capable of doing greater justice to the qualities favoured by the big screen. How widely these will be taken up remains to be seen. As primarily domestic media, television and video are consumed in ways often very different from the cinema, allowing all sorts of distractions and other simultaneous activities. The difference is considerably more than one of technological fidelity, and the market for more 'cinematic' home systems may be limited to certain niches. The driving force behind such developments has less to do with questions of cinematic or television aesthetics than economic motivations: the creation of new opportunities to sell into what have become relatively saturated markets for existing hardware. The relative importance of theatrical and domestic consumption contexts has important implications for the formal qualities likely to be favoured by Hollywood spectaculars, but these are not easy to untangle from a number of determinations.

Back to the frontier

The films considered here demonstrate the continued saliency of aspects of the particular narrative complex associated with frontier mythology – complete with its various complications and resolutions, its thematic concerns and blend of narrative and spectacle – in contemporary Hollywood cinema. The ideology of the western was always riven by tensions, most notably between the rival values of wilderness and civilization, which became increasingly explicit in the post-war period. The subsequent wholesale revisionism of westerns of the Vietnam and immediate post-Vietnam eras made sufficient inroads into the classical mythology substantially to reduce its acceptability to both industry and audiences. The westerns of the last decades of the twentieth century tended to be one-off affairs, frequently posing as 'alternative' in ideological stance, rather than a central thread in the familiar Hollywood fabric.[24] The more straightforward version of frontier mythology that animated the classic western has been transposed, in part if not wholesale, to a number of alternative domains.

A parallel might be drawn between the status of the western at the end of the twentieth century and that of the frontier itself in the late nineteenth century. The apparent closing of the historical frontier, announced in 1890, was greeted with dismay, just as the demise of the generic western might be mourned by some today. But substitutions were found in both cases. The loss of the actual historical referent has been seen by some as reducing the importance of frontier themes to the American imagination.[25] If anything, the opposite might be the case. The loss of the actual frontier has been no bar to the maintenance of the mythology, but has left it all the more free to be expanded and developed. The traditional concept of the frontier was always rooted more in myth than reality, although it was also capable of *creating* reality through the acting out of the myth. The passing of the historical experience from which frontier mythology was extrapolated has helped to remove from view some of the contradictions it contained from the start.

Mythology tends to be strengthened rather than weakened as its immediate – or, rather, always *imagined* – relation to experience is reduced. The loss of the actual generic western today has been equally little bar to the maintenance of significant elements of frontier mythology in Hollywood cinema. It has enabled the mythology to be developed and reinforced, in some cases imposed with a force that would not be possible within the original generic confines. To adopt Rick Altman's terminology,[26] certain of the 'semantic' elements of frontier mythology – the basic units of meaning – may have changed (as in the case of the Native American 'Other' replaced in *Independence Day* by the alien) while others have been retained (open western landscapes, for example, as signifiers of frontier virtues). More significantly, the basic 'syntax' – the underlying structure of oppositions – often remains largely intact. This is not to suggest an a-historical reading of structured oppositions but rather to provide a framework within which both change and continuity can be charted within the mythic/ideological landscape. Continuity is more the outcome of active commercial and ideological projections and interventions with their own specific histories than a reduction to any timeless realm of universal myth.

Frontier mythology tends to be politically reactionary in form, often blatantly elitist, racist, sexist or homophobic. In theory, the frontier, as a place 'outside' or on the edge, opens up the possibility of a subversive blurring of boundaries. More often, in Hollywood, it provides the opportunity for a re-establishment of dominant structures; an appeal, to be expected in much of popular culture, to that which is already comforting and familiar. The frontier-type landscape is often presented as a place of male activity and leadership, for example, a location in which male dominance can be made to appear 'natural' rather than culturally constructed. Manifestations of the frontier beyond the confines of the western are sometimes able to get away with repressive ideological content that few would dare to attempt any longer in the original genre. The frontier can be a place of radical critique, implicitly or explicitly condemning aspects of contemporary culture, politics, ideology or society. Any such criticism is usually approached from a broadly right-wing perspective, however, asserting the 'freedom of the individual' in a way that fits both conservative ideology and the industrial investment of Hollywood in an individualist and star-based narrative scheme.

2

Digital Dinosaurs: From T-Rex to Titanic

> [...] the most astonishing special effects of this nature in cinema history: the dinosaurs seem *alive*. The story can't bear such close scrutiny, but while this thrill ride is going, you won't be bothered with such details.
>
> Leonard Maltin[1]

> It is every bit as hard to imagine a movie without spectacle or performance, without special effects or a star, as it is to imagine a movie without a narrative. This has important implications for critical practice. Rather than being a passive subject formed in the imagination of the movie-as-text, in this account the moviegoer actively constructs his or her own satisfaction by choosing to concentrate on some aspects of a movie and avoiding others.
>
> Richard Maltby[2]

Extinct dinosaurs bestride the earth and sea. Tyrannosaurus rex and velociraptor menace the heroes of one film, while RMS *Titanic* is raised from the seabed to steam towards its doom in another. *Jurassic Park* (1993) and *Titanic* (1997) were received to a large extent – although not exclusively – in terms of their spectacular effects. The latest 'magic' created by computer-based imaging was either celebrated, for its incredible 'realism', or denigrated, as a distraction from any concern with character development or narrative. On the one hand, the impression given is that there are few technical limits to what can be depicted in convincingly spectacular detail and texture on screen in the digital age. Narrative, on the other hand, is often found wanting, subject to severe constraint amid flamboyant displays of cinematic technology. *Jurassic Park* and *Titanic* are good examples of the kind of Hollywood blockbuster accused of offering nothing *but* the spectacular attraction of its special effects. Such films are often ridiculed for a lack of credible storyline, character or depth. But *Jurassic Park* and *Titanic* combine their spectacular 'thrill rides' with strong narrative dynamics, each drawing at least partly on myths and ideologies associated with the American frontier. This chapter will examine their appeal in both dimensions, including a closer textual analysis of the relationship between spectacle and narrative.

'Something you don't see every day'

Films such as *Jurassic Park* and *Titanic* are, undoubtedly, sold to a large extent on the basis of spectacular attraction. The scale and quality of spectacle is a major factor in the advertising, promotion and journalistic discourses surrounding their release. The dinosaur special effects were singled out as the main selling and discussion point of *Jurassic Park*. *Titanic* first entered general public awareness in reports of its escalating budget and the delay of release from summer to Christmas 1997. What started as potentially negative associations were exploited by the filmmakers as a key marketing angle: a celebration of the grand quality of spectacular entertainment resulting from such lavish spending. The romance narrative was also sold but television and print advertising and the film's website all included a strong emphasis on the scale and spectacle of the ship.[3]

Jurassic Park and *Titanic* also foreground the spectacular nature of the attractions within their own fictional frames, as we saw in *Twister* and *Independence Day*. This is particularly clear in the case of *Jurassic Park*, the premise of which is the creation of a giant entertainment park in which the dinosaurs are designed to be the ultimate in spectacular attractions. There is an element of self-consciousness about the film's own status as spectacle, including the shots of merchandising products on sale in the park shop. The whole process comes profitably full-circle with the opening at Universal Studios of a theme-park ride based on the movie *about* a theme park, a ride that delivers the visitor conveniently to its retail outlet. As the chaos theorist Ian Malcolm (Jeff Goldblum) complains, Jurassic Park represents the power of genetic intervention 'packaged, patented' and 'sold', in much the same way as this kind of film is packaged and pre-sold to audiences. The first sight of the dinosaurs leaves the principals, paleontologist Alan Grant (Sam Neill) and paleobotanist Ellie Sattler (Laura Dern), in the characteristic blockbuster-movie state of open-mouthed amazement. The sequence is worth closer analysis. It plays an important part in the establishment of audience identification with the characters, at this point specifically as viewers of the on-screen spectacle, but also highlights our own experience of the spectacle of the movie itself.

Grant and Sattler's jeep comes to a halt. Grant peers out towards the front and screen-right as the camera dollies in and along to him, taking us closer to his position, but denying the reverse-angle shot that would reveal the object of his attention. We cut to a high angle shot through the roll bars of the jeep. Maintaining his gaze, Grant stands, the camera moving up with him into a medium close-up. He pulls off a pair of sunglasses to reveal eyes wide and popping. The reverse angle is again teasingly conspicuous by its absence. Grant reaches down, without relaxing his look, and turns Sattler's head to face in the same direction, forcing her to share the object of his gaze. Her jaw drops, shades are once again removed and she stands, the camera rising to couple the pair in a two-shot. It is only at this point that we are shown the object of their attention, although the sequence assumes our prior knowledge of the kind of spectacle involved. We can take pleasure from both the delaying of the moment of revelation to us and from witnessing the astonished reactions of Grant and Sattler. We get the best of both worlds, sharing to some extent the amazed reaction of the pair but also enjoying the sense of superiority established by our ability to smile knowingly at their response. There is, in fact, a three-level hierarchy of looks and knowledge at work: Grant is the first to see, and is thus able to steer Sattler's attention; we are the last to *see*, but first to *know* what is being seen – and hence clearly privileged above Grant – having almost certainly been tempted to the screen by the promised spectacle.

Up to this point the sequence obeys the usual continuity conventions of Hollywood editing regimes. Throughout the different shots, Grant, Sattler and the dinosaur are kept in the same positions relative to one another (Sattler on screen left, the dinosaur off to the front and right). When the anticipated reverse-angle cut is made, however, one of the key conventions is bent slightly if not broken. The 180° line is crossed.[4] We are given the jeep and its occupants in the right foreground with the huge figure of a brachiosaur slowly pounding its way past and behind them, moving from left to right. The positions of Grant and Sattler are reversed, the camera having jumped to a position behind them. If this shot had not included the two characters in the frame, its spatial relationships would seem more conventional, approximating their point of view. It is quite usual for the 180° line to shift position as one sequence gives way to another, but a striking effect is created by doing so at such a key moment: just as the dynamic established in the previous series of shots is consummated in our first sight of the special-effects creations around which revolve so many of the expectations brought to the film.

The effect is to underline the significance of the cut, giving it an added impact. Grant and Sattler end up positioned as small figures in the left-hand lower corner of the frame, looking up as the giant figure passes behind. They occupy the position, almost, of two more cinemagoers, watching the spectacle as if from the audience, an effect maintained to some extent as they dismount from the jeep and walk along the lower edge of the frame pointing at the dinosaur in a state of continued awe. For Grant and Sattler, the moment of seeing is defined immediately as one of 'knowing'. Unlike us, they might not have known in advance what they would find at Jurassic Park, but they have barely recovered from the initial shock before they are counting off the various speculations about dinosaurs that visual evidence can place as either myth or reality. Seeing is believing, it seems, on both sides of the screen. If the 180° line is crossed in a movement into a new sequence, a new set of shots around another point of equilibrium, then both characters and audience have been led into a spectacular new vision of the world.

Grant and Sattler's position in the foreground, as surrogates for the audience, is replicated to some extent during the spectacular sinking of the ship in *Titanic*. 'Now there's something you don't see every day', says Molly Brown (Kathy Bates) from one of the lifeboats. In the previous shot the lifeboat sits in a foreground behind which both she and the viewer can see the gigantic ship sitting in the water at a magnificently unhealthy angle. Our first sight of the *Titanic*, both as a wreck and in its former glory, is mediated by looks from within the fictional world. The first glimpse is of the wreckage, seen from a salvage submersible and recorded on video footage replayed at several points in the film. Some of this is presented in point-of-view shots that align our initial experience with that of the salvage experts. The intact ship is also presented in terms of spectacle to the hordes crowding the quayside before the maiden voyage. There is a familiar pattern of faces looking up at the spectacle, with the exception of Rose DeWitt Bukater (Kate Winslet), whose role is structured to reject the appeal of such showy displays.

What of the direct relationship between the viewer and the spectacle? What is our experience of the spectacular set-pieces of these films? Are we pulled into the narrative space of the text – the 'diegetic' universe of the world on screen – or do we sit back at a greater distance, enjoying the spectacle in its own right? It is not easy to answer in any definitive manner. Different viewers may respond in different ways and none of these are easy, if possible, to access, through empirical research or any other method. Even if measurable, it is doubtful that the various levels of audience response could be reduced to any single essence. We can attempt some informed speculation, however, based initially on the organization of the text. Textual material does not entirely determine meaning. Viewers are likely to bring a range of different orientations, and blockbuster films are designed to accommodate these as far as possible. The enormous box-office success of *Titanic* has been attributed by many commentators to its ability to offer multiple points of audience access. But films such as these are carefully structured to have a specific range of impacts, particularly in the point-of-view and editing regimes, and the potency of the medium itself should not be ignored, even if other factors also have to be taken into account.[5] So, what should we make of the way these two films are structured? A closer look is needed at some of the key set-piece sequences.

The central set-piece in *Jurassic Park* is the attack of the T-rex on a pair of automated landcruisers engaged in a trial tour of the attractions. The party is comprised of Grant, Sattler and Malcolm; three scientists whose endorsement the park's owner Hammond (Richard Attenborough) is seeking to satisfy the concerns of investors represented by the lawyer Gennaro (Martin Ferrero). Also along for the ride are Hammond's grandchildren, Tim and Lex, 'our targeted audience' as he calls them. The appearance of the T-rex, one of the most anticipated features of the movie, is delayed in order to build our anticipation and that of the characters. Our first full view is introduced by a sequence in which the camera cranes up from behind one of the landcruisers. We get a blurry perspective through the rain-spattered window and sunroof of the vehicle, akin to a point-of-view shot from the characters within, before the camera moves back to give a more 'objective' and clear view of the head and neck of the T-rex, filling the centre of the frame. It turns to look menacingly in our direction, before we cut to something like its point of view looking at Gennaro, who flees, abandoning the children. A series of shots follows, taken from inside the two vehicles, in which the fence is being destroyed but the dinosaur is not in view.

A longer shot shows the T-rex step back into central frame as it emerges through the fence and pounds its way between the vehicles and out towards the audience, roaring and opening its jaws towards screen right. We cut to close shots of Malcolm and Grant in one cruiser, gazing at the T-rex, then have a reverse-angle from the back seat, looking over their shoulders and through the windscreen at the passing beast. Another two-shot of Malcolm and Grant is followed by a shot from the inside of the other cruiser, in which Lex gets out a large flashlight. As she shines the beam at the T-rex (guaranteeing its unsavoury attentions) we return to the perspective from the back seat of the other vehicle. The next series of shots comes from inside the children's cruiser, and from a position just outside, as the T-rex subjects them to growls and a close-up eyeball inspection, before launching an attack on their vehicle. This is constructed mostly from closely framed shots of the children, the dinosaur and the watching Malcolm and Grant, who eventually get out of their cruiser in an attempt to distract the dinosaur. This sequence includes several more shots in which the T-rex stands full-length and centre-frame: chewing the tyres off the vehicle, moving towards Malcolm and Grant in turn, and finally plucking Gennaro from the toilet seat where he has sought shelter.

The whole sequence can be divided, approximately, into two kinds of material. One series, which accounts for the majority of the set-ups, keeps our attention focused closely on the characters and their relationships to the T-rex. The other series is comprised of the shots that give us a clearer view of the T-rex itself, as it bursts through the fence, attacks the underside of the children's cruiser, follows Malcolm and Grant and eventually eats Gennaro. It is the latter series that offers the greatest sense of sheer spectacle in terms of the display of the dinosaur *to us* in its full computer-generated glory. In most of these cases the T-rex dominates the frame and is available directly to the gaze of the viewer. It is at these moments that we can look closely and marvel at how real it appears. We are able to inspect the detail up close, the texture of the creature and how well it moves. We may adopt a relatively detached approach at these moments, examining and probably admiring the quality of the spectacle itself.

The first series of set-ups gives the sequence a rather different emphasis. They seem designed to integrate the spectacle of the special-effects dinosaur with the immediate narrative situation: the imperilment of the characters, especially the children. We are given approximations of the perspectives of the characters. Our experience of the T-rex is strongly filtered through theirs. We watch not so much the T-rex as the 'dinosaur as threat to the characters'. The overall impact of the sequence seems to favour this kind of experience. Even when the T-rex dominates the frame it is rarely seen alone rather than in terms of its relationship to the on-going drama. When it raises its head above the fence for the first time, our experience of the dinosaur is related closely to the position of the car. When it bursts through the fence, a clear spatial relationship is maintained between the dinosaur and the two vehicles. And, of course, in the shots of the beast threatening or attacking the adults, our experience of the spectacular creation is tightly integrated with the fate of the protagonists. The camera does not dwell excessively on the T-rex. None of the full-frame shots lasts more than a few seconds before cutting back to a strict regime of surrounding viewpoints and reverse-angles. To the extent that viewers are 'positioned' by the text in this sequence, the pace of the

The T-rex confronts Alan Grant (Sam Neill) and *the viewer: spectacular creature effects on display, but integrated into narrative space and relationships with character in* Jurassic Park, *© Universal City Studios, Inc. and Amblin Entertainment Inc., 1992. Ronald Grant archive*

editing plays a important role, leaving relatively little time or space for the attentive viewer to pursue alternative orientations. The viewer who wants simply to concentrate on the direct spectacle of the dinosaur is treated to a teasing selection of viewpoints, a process figured within the fictional world in the image of Malcolm straining to peer through a clouded windscreen.

The spectacle of the T-rex attack is integrated into the narrative momentum of the sequence, which should really be no surprise given the status of emotional identification with character as one of the basic tenets of Hollywood cinema. The point can be underlined by imagining the opposite situation, in which special-effects spectacle alone was dominant; if, for example, we were given a long sequence of lingering shots of the T-rex, something the standard of special effects might allow here if not in many earlier monster movies, where the editing regime was to a greater extent an act of disguise. The brevity of some of the dinosaur shots in *Jurassic Park* is governed partly by the huge cost of the effects, but also driven by their insertion into a narrative dynamic. The conclusions to be drawn here depend on how exactly we choose to define 'spectacle', however. It would be quite reasonable to describe the whole of the T-rex attack set-piece as spectacle: the spectacle not just of the dinosaur but of the entire scene of noisy action into which it is carefully inserted. A similar question can be asked about the use of 'narrative' in this context. If we think of narrative in the sense of the larger story told across the duration of a film, a sequence such as this could be seen as a counter to narrative development. Any larger-scale narrative movement appears to be halted while this quite prolonged sequence unfolds.

Michele Pierson suggests that this is precisely the case with *Jurassic Park* and numerous other Hollywood science fictions in which 'the presentation of key computer-generated images produces a distinct break in the action'.[6] The dinosaurs, Pierson suggests, are 'displayed as objects of aesthetic contemplation, bracketed off from the temporal and narrative space of the action'.[7] This is in my opinion a fairly standard misinterpretation of the way many of these films work. Pierson's chief example is the sequence I have already considered in which the brachiosaur makes its first appearance. The brachiosaur is presented rather more than the T-rex as an object for our contemplation, but it is not bracketed off from the narrative space of the action for the precise reason that our contemplative gaze is motivated by that of the protagonists, getting their first stunned sight of the recreated dinosaurs, a moment loaded with narrative resonance.

The T-rex is not remotely 'bracketed off' from the narrative space of the action in the sequence described above; it very physically inhabits that space on the screen. It might still be argued that there is a temporal bracketing, given the length of the sequence. That would presuppose that the action sequence did not contain any developments of importance to the larger arc of the narrative. In this case it does contain such developments, as I will suggest below, in terms of both the linear cause–effect narrative of *Jurassic Park* and the underlying narrative structures of the film. Pierson makes the useful point that: 'Even within the same film, several modes of presenting special-effects imagery will often be in evidence'.[8] But this is a qualification that does little to prevent the exercise of rather sweeping generalizations. She suggests that there was a move in the late 1990s away from the less integrated display of computer-generated attractions, but does not provide very convincing evidence for either the change or the original situation described.

Titanic indulges in sheer spectacle a good deal more than *Jurassic Park*, but it is still closely integrated with the fate of the central characters. From quayside to disappearance beneath the waves, the ship is displayed

Big *screen spectacle: the camera lingers on the full glory of the sinking ship in* Titanic, *© Twentieth Century Fox and Paramount Pictures, 1997. Ronald Grant archive*

regularly for its spectacular impact on the viewer. The camera lingers on the vessel on numerous occasions, providing spectacle that goes beyond the requirement of the story. The extent of this spectacular 'surplus' was emphasized by many critics through a comparison with the treatment of the ship in *A Night to Remember* (1958), a version of the story customarily admired for its 'restraint', which provides respectable special effects but does not dwell on such images.

The viewer of *Titanic* is sometimes offered the spectacle on two levels: the spectacle of the Titanic itself and the spectacle of the special effects camerawork that can be achieved using computer-generated digital images and miniature models. This is particularly the case in a couple of sweeping movements across the length and breadth of the ship. The most notable example comes after the young Jack Dawson (Leonardo DiCaprio) declares himself 'king of the world' while exulting in the experience of standing at the bow as the ship speeds through the water. The camera performs a grand sweep back along the full length of the superstructure, past the funnels, across to the other side and then pauses, leaving the ship to steam away. This is a bravura sequence, shot from a computer-controlled camera rig. It is built from a combination of digitally created elements and designed to mimic the helicopter-based shot that would be used to display a real ship. The effect might be to make us think the ship is real, a giant reconstruction or stand-in, or to take its status for granted: 'convincing' special effects sometimes serve a negative purpose, ensuring that our attention is not drawn to the fact that any trickery is involved. Or we might admire the state-of-the-art special effects that allow such an illusion to be created.

A range of different responses are available. The image has a hyperreal quality, an almost impossibly perfect cleanness of line and a sheen that perhaps betrays its graphic character. The status of the effects as high-end, detailed and 'convincing' computer-generated animation is established partly by contrast with the sketchy computer graphics version of the sinking of the ship deployed earlier, when a simulation is shown within the film by the salvage team diving on the wreck.

A similar point of contrast is inserted early in *Jurassic Park*, a 'cartoon' animation used to show visitors how the dinosaurs are created from fossilized DNA. 'Realism' is an entirely relative concept: the presence of 'crude' animation in both films establishes a gap between this medium and the key special effects sequences, thus heightening the apparent 'reality' of the latter, an effect akin to the destruction of the drive-in screening of *The Shining* in *Twister*.

The key special effects sequences in *Titanic* depict the prolonged sinking of the ship and it is here that spectacular attraction is at its most powerful, providing one of the strongest box-office draws of the picture. The sinking builds up an ever more spectacular series of visions of the foundering leviathan. These are, undeniably, the 'money shots' of the film, the sequences that justify the huge budget and form a key part of the advance publicity expectations built around the film. What is offered is a truly massive spectacle, the combination of scale and detail that can only really be achieved on the big screen. The liner's bow submerges to the point at which the stern points upwards, its massive bulk raising the propellers clear of the water. The spine of the ship is fractured by the strain, sending the stern crashing back into the water, only to be lifted again as the bow is submerged further. The detail and texture in all this is highly impressive, tiny human figures spiralling to their death and even the water – along with fire, a traditional bugbear of special effects – appears to maintain the appropriate scale. There can be little question that much of this has physically been recreated in full. This can only be an artificial spectacle, to be viewed in terms of awe and wonder at how the effects were achieved.

Or is that really the case? Again, it is hard to be sure how audiences experience this kind of thing. It is quite possible that the realism of the spectacle is sufficient to ensure suspension of disbelief by many viewers, as is surely one intention of the filmmakers. In line with more general principles of 'classical' Hollywood filmmaking, the act of creation, of artifice, is concealed in order to carry the spectator into the world of the story. This is a dominant strain in the history of Hollywood cinema: the attempt to establish an 'invisible' style that does not draw attention to its own process. The romance plot of *Titanic* is designed partly to reinforce this effect through emotional identification with character. But there has always been a counter-tendency in Hollywood, to exhibit and celebrate the sheer spectacle of the musical, the big star performance, the epic, or today's special-effects blockbuster. The romantic narrative itself is caught in this twin dynamic: built around identifications that project viewers into the diegetic space, but also founded on extra-diegetic factors such as star-spectacle, especially in the case of Leonardo DiCaprio as a major draw for the young female audience credited with so much of the film's box-office success. *Titanic* may be a product of the particular blockbuster-centred regime of the Hollywood of the late 1990s, but it is also a manifestation of the blend of narrative-led invisible style and up-front spectacle at which the industry has long excelled.

The spectacular element is very strong, especially during the sinking of the ship, but even here it remains integrated with our focus on the fate of the principal characters. There are moments when we can sit back and take in the vast spectacle unfolding on the screen and for rather longer than is the case in *Jurassic Park*, but we are constantly returned to the plight of Rose and Jack. Their movements are closely tied in with the broader historical epic, an obligatory feature of classical Hollywood narrative structure. Mainstream films that tackle material of large scale and scope are invariably structured around the fate of a small number of individuals and, usually, a heterosexual romance. It should be no surprise that physical consummation of the love between Rose and Jack coincides closely with the decisive encounter of the larger story, the moment the iceberg hits. The implications of this juxtaposition will be considered below in terms of narrative structure. From this point on, there is an oscillation between two points of focus: the story of Rose and Jack and the broader tragedy unfolding around them. The fate of the fictional protagonists might be a sideshow but it is interwoven with the bigger picture. So, when the ship's stern is raised spectacularly for the final stages of the sinking, Rose and Jack are immediately on hand. The space that has become a key location in the historical event is domesticated as the privileged place where the paths of the lovers first crossed. As Rose reminds Jack at the time, 'this is where we first met'. The appalling scenes of mass death and destruction are salved to some extent by the romance, the smile that breaks out on Rose's face and the upbeat swirl that comes over the music track.

Shots of Rose and Jack are intercut with the broader spectacle of disaster throughout the final stages of the sinking. The camera lingers on painful shots of doomed passengers sliding and clattering down the ship, but there are always Rose and Jack to whom we can be returned on a more comforting scale. This can be illustrated by listing the shot sequence in the final movement of the sinking. It starts with a spectacular series of shots of the broken-backed Titanic, the bow starting to go back under the water, sea pouring into the cleft amidships and the propellers rising clear of the water for a second time. We then have a close two-shot of Rose and Jack in an embrace and holding onto the stern railing. Another longer shot depicting all of the ship that remains above water is followed by a medium shot of a section near the stern, a closer shot of passengers tumbling down the deck towards and past the camera, a quick head-and-shoulders close-up of Rose and Jack and then a mid-shot of them beginning to climb over the railing as the angle of the ship increases. This is followed by something like a reverse-angle shot from sea-level of the stern beginning to tower above the water and a medium-long shot from behind Rose and Jack, further establishing their position at the stern in the context of the movement of the ship and the plight of other passengers. The next three shots focus our attention more exclusively on the romantic pair: Jack climbing over in mid-shot, a loose approximation of Rose's point of view as Jack reaches down to pull her over the rail, and a shot of Rose's head as she is about to be pulled over; again, not really Jack's point of view, but from a position just off to his side and a typical example of Hollywood cinema's use of viewpoints that put us alongside the central protagonists without confining us entirely within their subjective position.

The next image is a medium shot of the stern as it moves towards the upright from an angle of about 45°. This is followed by another shot of Rose that seems slightly closer to Jack's point of view than the previous example, as he pulls her towards him; then an answering shot of Jack filling the height of the frame and taken close to Rose's viewpoint. We are pulled in a degree closer to fleeting positions of identification as the principals establish the location from which they will initially go down with the ship. Next we have a general shot from above the stern, a medium shot closer to the stern rail, now draped with struggling bodies, and a closer shot that frames only Rose and Jack on the stern. This is followed by a big spectacular long shot of the entire rear end of the ship upended vertically, then a shot from above the stern framed to concentrate on Rose and Jack. A similar pairing follows: a big shot, this time taken from alongside and slightly to the front of the broad spectacle of the ship, followed by another closer shot of the scene at the stern that focuses on Rose and Jack but does not exclude all others.

Next comes another big spectacle shot, taken from high and directly above the stern, followed by a medium shot that starts mostly on the protagonists but pans to reveal the spectacle down the length of the superstructure. A close two-shot of Rose and Jack is followed by another pair of medium shots that focus on the whole of the stern and falling passengers. There is then a series of closer shots of passengers crashing down the ship, the last of whom exchanges a look and a pair of shots/reverse-shots with Rose before falling to her death. A second pair of shots, in which Rose exchanges looks with another passenger who has climbed to the high side of the rail, is followed by the beginning of the ship's vertical descent into the waves. This sequence is again constructed from a mixture of general spectacle and close focus on the two protagonists, the final moments dominated by two-shots of the latter as Jack gives Rose instructions on what to do and she expresses her trust in him.

A detailed examination shows that the sequence has been structured to integrate the broad spectacle of epic event with the fictional romance, very much in a manner that might be expected from a 'classical' Hollywood text. There is a constant and fairly rapid pattern of editing, moving between the 'big' shots of the spectacle and the closer framing of the principals. The relationship between Rose and Jack and the broader action is kept clear throughout. The viewer is offered a combination of moments that invite admiration of the grand spectacle in its own right and moments that tie us into patterns of identification with the experience of two individual characters. Exactly how viewers take pleasure in one aspect or the other cannot be determined by textual analysis alone, but it can indicate likely tendencies. It can suggest some of the appeals on offer, even if it cannot guarantee a full account of how these are negotiated. Viewers might choose to adopt a position of distance from the somewhat cheesy romantic narrative and the perspectives of Rose and Jack, but short of averting their gaze they would find it hard to avoid being pushed into some degree of identification. For many, pleasure might be found in an immersion in the narrative, being 'carried away' by the melodrama of the events. For others, sitting back and admiring the spectacle *as* merely a spectacle might be more important. Or the two dimensions might offer a combined pleasure whose precise delineation at any moment may be impossible to measure.

Commenting on Hollywood films more generally, Richard Maltby puts it like this: 'The two elements of story-telling and spectacle are held in essential tension, and the movie exists as a series of minor victories of one logic over the other.'[9] Maltby's analysis of this relationship is generally a fruitful one, but his metaphor here may be rather too combative. Should spectacle and narrative be seen as essentially at war with one another, or as working in concert? From the point of view of the industry there is much to recommend a more or less harmonious (if not necessarily 'coherent') combination of the two, a point suggested by Kristin

Thompson in relation to animation. On the one hand, Hollywood films have long been structured to naturalize the world on screen as part of the process of drawing viewers into the narrative. But, she suggests, 'the idea of films as magical, extraordinary things is valuable.'[10] This was true of the early films of the 1890s and 1900s, of the classical era of the studio system, and is certainly the case today when Hollywood is keen to present its product as something special and out of the ordinary. As Thompson puts it: 'This conflict between the impulse toward naturalization of films on the one hand and the desire to retain their novelty effect on the other confers a considerable value upon the animated film.'[11]

Animation served an important function for Hollywood, making cinema a perpetual novelty. It could do this without threatening the basis of a more naturalized 'classical' cinema, founded on an ideology of realism, because it was restricted mostly to the non-prestigious ghetto of children's comedy, a defence against its disruptive implications. Animation ceased to perform this function, in Thompson's account, when its audience was lost to television in the 1950s. But, she suggests, it may have been replaced by the later trend towards special-effects films: 'Interest in the cinema as a technical marvel has again been renewed, to Hollywood's greater financial advantage.'[12] The computer-animated special effects of films such as *Jurassic Park* and *Titanic* create the same kind of effect. They highlight the aspect of Hollywood cinema that stresses the magical and extraordinary capabilities of the medium. These qualities can hardly be said to have been restricted 'safely' to the margins of contemporary Hollywood. On the contrary, they play an important part in many of the most industrially 'prestigious' productions. 'Magical' spectacle is in the foreground of these texts, and Thompson's account perhaps underplays its importance throughout the history of Hollywood cinema. Again, an account based on notions of 'excess' and 'disruption' might be replaced by one in which the two components of narrative and spectacle are more closely, if not always evenly, interwoven. The careful integration of spectacular attraction and its relationship with characters and on-going action may prevent the spectacle from overwhelming narrative or audience identification with characters. But the relationship between the two elements is a good deal less hierarchical than is suggested by terms such as 'disruption' and 'containment'. Thompson implies that magical spectacle was hived off into animation, a realm in which it would not contaminate mainstream production. This does not appear to be the case in Hollywood today and it is doubtful that it applied very generally to the 'classical' era.

Special effects of the kind used in *Jurassic Park* and *Titanic* offer one way of bridging the opposition between the dimensions of narrative and spectacle. On the one hand, they seek to offer a 'photorealistic' effect designed to help us to suspend disbelief, to lose ourselves in the world of the fictional narrative.

Acute attention was paid to textural detail in the construction of the dinosaur effects in *Jurassic Park*, including technologies developed to create the sense that skin and muscle moved realistically in relation to the skeleton of the animals and that the flesh appeared to expand and contract to simulate the appearance of breathing.[13] The stated aim was to make the dinosaurs appear as real as if they had been photographed in the wild. A literal 'photorealism' meant simulating the impression of photography as much as of the dinosaurs themselves. The unnaturally clean and 'perfect' images generated by computer were deliberately blurred to increase the impression of photographed reality, while artificial film grain effects were added to give the pictures a more organic and 'natural' look.[14] The aim here was to make the dinosaurs achieve the same level of reality as the rest of the film, as much as any exterior reference point of 'reality', to integrate them seamlessly into the fictional fabric. These are effects that, on one level, aspire to the status of naturalistic 'invisibility' rather than the more overt 'flashiness' of the computer-generated effects found in a film like *Terminator 2: Judgement Day* (1991).

The distinction between visible and invisible effects is not so stable, however. The effects in *Jurassic Park* and *Titanic* also invite our enjoyment and celebration of their power *as* spectacular and contrived special effects. The integration of the dinosaurs into the cinematic reality does not entirely conceal their illusory status. It invites us to be impressed by the effect at the very moment that the effect is meant to disappear into transparent illusion. The point at which the quality of special effects renders the 'seams' invisible might be taken as the moment when we are taken entirely 'into' the diegetic universe of the film; from a position of contemplating spectacular attraction to absorption within the excitement of the narrative situation. But the process may be more complex than this suggests. In the promotional discourse surrounding a film like *Jurassic Park* it is the very 'seamlessness' of the effects that constitutes the attraction to which our attention is drawn. Exactly on which level these effects are experienced is not easy to determine, but one possibility is that the enjoyment lies in a combination of these two experiences.[15]

For Don Slater, this kind of confusion is precisely the basis of the appeal of the modern magic trick, a phenomenon he examines in the context of visual spectacles ranging from the nineteenth-century diorama to contemporary science fiction cinema. Magic offers the 'pleasure of being deceived, or taken in' by an experience of constructed reality: 'We know what we are seeing to be impossible and yet the pleasure of the experience is in seeing – before our very eyes – the most realistic staging of something which cannot happen.'[16]

Slater explains this in terms of the broad context of the development of the modern world. Modernity, he suggests, 'chases magic from the world'[17] in a project of scientific disenchantment. The world is reduced to the realm of empirical facts determined largely on the basis of vision. A version of modernity that bases 'believing' on 'seeing' – rather like Grant and Sattler's experience of the brachiosaur – finds itself in a contradictory position, however: 'it must constantly generate visual spectacles which inspire belief.'[18] The scientific demonstrations of the eighteenth century, for example, depended on producing wonder in order to attract audiences: 'in the very process of making public the disenchanted facts of the world, they can be re-enchanted through visual spectacle.'[19] For the audience, such spectacles are experienced as quasi-magical, rather like cinematic special effects. The powers of science and technology appear to be a new form of magic. Whether these phenomena can be attributed so sweepingly to as broad a category as 'modernity' raises as many questions as it answers, but the general shape of Slater's argument about the way magical spectacle works seems applicable to cinematic special effects. They are invariably described in terms of 'magic' and can be seen as demonstrating the specific powers of cinematic science and technology.

Special effects-laden films like *Jurassic Park* and *Titanic* are, at one level, celebrations of the capacities of cinematic technology, even while their narrative dynamics often question the role of technology. The enjoyment of special effects lies, perhaps, in allowing ourselves to be deceived while knowing that this is not entirely the case. Advance publicity or word-of-mouth is likely to ensure that most viewers of *Jurassic Park* or *Titanic* know that pleasure is expected to be taken from the spectacular effects as a form of 'magic'. We can let ourselves go, surrender to the 'wonders' of convincingly-rendered dinosaurs or ship, but at the same time retain an element of distance and control through our awareness that we are *allowing* ourselves to delight in an illusion; and, further, that we are delighting in it precisely because of its quality *as* illusion. We are able to stand back just far enough to be able to enjoy both halves of the equation.

'Just head out for the horizon'

If the spectacular dimension of *Jurassic Park* and *Titanic* is often closely integrated with narrative developments at the local level, the appeal of these films also needs to be examined in terms of the 'deeper' structure of the narrative. The 'quality' or subtlety of the story frame may be questionable. Some plot developments might not be as convincing as the digitally rendered spectacle, but narrative weakness at this level should not be mistaken for a lack of narrative dynamics. Each of the films considered in this chapter has a carefully organized and orchestrated linear narrative dynamic, along with underlying narrative structures that can be read at least partly in terms of discourses that play on the resonances of frontier mythology.

Titanic can be read as a manifestation of frontier-related mythology in one obvious way: the epic, but doomed, journey of hundreds of European migrants to the new opportunities of America. This is conventionally interpreted as a journey from the restrictions of Europe to the freedoms of the New World. *Titanic* steams westward, repeating the basic spatial dynamic of frontier lore. There are complications, however. For the 'huddled masses' below decks, it is meant to be a voyage to freedom, but as Rose makes clear: 'To me it was a slave ship taking me back to America in chains', an evocation of a very different dynamic and one troubling to the dominant ideal American self-image. The film shakes off these negative associations, however, insisting that the journey for Rose will be one of freedom, as a result of her involvement with Jack. *Titanic* sets up a series of (not very subtle) thematic conflicts that play on the basic opposition between 'decadence' and 'over-civilization' and an 'authenticity' that is figured in tropes redolent of the mythical frontier. The excessive opulence of the *Titanic* is contrasted with the stark elemental sea in which the crossing ends. The hubris of those who believe the ship to be unsinkable is set against those who, by implication, are more in touch with the elements. The arranged marriage planned between Rose and Cal Hockley (Billy Zane) is contrasted with the 'spontaneous' individual emotion between Rose and Jack. The repressive formal dinners and restrained music of the first-class dining rooms are countered by the more 'honest' and 'authentic' abandon of the lower elements enjoying themselves below decks. The cowardice or ineffectuality of some in the face of the disaster is compared with the heroism or stoicism of more favoured characters.

Jack is marked as the key representative of the frontier tradition. Much is made, however unconvincingly, of his life as a free spirit, not just as a roughneck but also as a talented artist and all-round sensitive individual. He lives beyond the confines of an imprisoning society, but is not 'uncivilized', a fact marked by the emphasis on his caring qualities. Rose's mother, the architect of her marriage of convenience, asks sneeringly if he finds his rootless existence appealing. 'Yes, ma'am, I do', he replies, proceeding to deliver a paean to frontier values: 'I've got everything I need right here with me. I've got air in my lungs and a few blank sheets of paper. I mean, I love waking up in the morning not knowing what's going to happen, who I'm going to meet, where I'm going to wind up.' Rather crass, maybe, but the stuff of ideal American self-images, if not actual aspirations. 'You can just call me a tumbleweed blowing in the wind', he says earlier, acquiring the aura of a fully-fledged Huckleberry Finn. 'Why can't I be like you, Jack; just head out for the horizon whenever I feel like it?' asks Rose. He promises that one day they will ride horses in the surf: 'But you'll have to do it like a real cowboy, none of that side-saddle stuff.'

In any approximation to reality it is clear that Rose cannot be like Jack for very good reasons to do with wealth, class and gender, and other powerful social determinants (not to mention the fact that what he is 'like' is a fantasy in the first place). She is tied into a socially determined fate as constricting as the corset her mother straps her into during a scene in which the reason for her marriage is revealed – the fact that her mother has been left a penniless widow. But the film allows her to make the transformation she desires. Jack ends up drowned, but his example provides the leverage for Rose's character to reconcile the real social contradictions in a classic example of popular myth-making.

Each of the two main characters demonstrates the ability to move in the world of the other. Jack is able to bluff his way through a formal dinner; Rose escapes briefly to play a full part in the revels of the lower decks. She shakes off the constraints of class and 'breeding', performing a dance routine she has not done in years, the kind of self-expression she has been denied since childhood. This point is underlined when we share her observation of a young child being taught to sit up straight and to place a napkin delicately on her lap with lace-gloved hands in the style of the 'refined lady' she is also destined to become. Jack's world is presented as one of freedom, instinct and spontaneity. The film suggests these qualities are present in Rose but have been forcibly suppressed. She senses the special qualities in the paintings of Picasso and the French impressionists, for example, works scorned by a creature of convention such as Hockley. This is a rather cheap narrative device designed to align us with Rose on the basis of our superior knowledge of what history's verdict will be on such artists. Today's received wisdom is used, somewhat contradictorily, to assert the openness of Rose to the non-conventional. Jack's role in *Titanic* is structured to enable him to help Rose to bring out her 'instincts', to free them from conventional repression. The scene in which she witnesses the training of the young child follows immediately from her rejection of Jack's impassioned advances. The next sequence finds Jack at the bow of the ship, the place of freedom and exultation, the sharp edge cutting its way towards the New World. Rose appears behind him, saying she has changed her mind, and he guides her up onto the bow-rail, her arms stretched wide, to share the freedom, the feeling of flying and a passionate embrace.

I want to return here to the moment that Rose and Jack make love below decks. This comes after he has sketched her naked, stripped of all finery to her 'natural' state (apart from a giant diamond around the neck, an index perhaps of a flawless and irreducible natural purity). The moment of climax follows a head-on shot of the ship steaming towards the camera and scenes between two lookouts at the crow's nest and the watch on the bridge. The viewer is meant to anticipate an imminent sighting of the fatal iceberg (we have already been informed that the vessel will not see daylight again). The collision does not come until shortly afterwards, when Rose and Jack are enjoying a mutual post-coital glow on the forward deck and when Rose says she will be disembarking with him when the ship docks. It doesn't make any sense, she adds, 'that's why I trust it'. Instinct is privileged over reason or the kind of socially-determined and dominant notions of 'sense' that threaten her with lifelong imprisonment. 'Sense' here means preconceptions supposed to come between us and the authentic experience of reality; the kind of 'sense' that conditions the reactions of Captain Smith (Bernard Hill), who we are told has '26 years of experience working against him', assuming from unexamined past experience that anything big enough to sink the ship could be seen in time for it to turn safely. The embrace of Rose and Jack is witnessed by the two lookouts in the crow's nest, just seconds before their gaze is shifted by the spectacle of the iceberg looming ahead. It is hard to avoid making some kind of thematic connection between the two events, the physical consummation between the two principals and the less joyful coming together of the *Titanic* and the iceberg. It is possible to read each, in this juxtaposition, as an outbreak of elemental force, a 'natural' challenge to dominant or oppressive values and institutions. Jack eventually dies in the freezing ocean, leaving Rose free to pursue the lifestyle of her choice. Something like a montage-sequence of Rose's life after her return to America is supplied towards the end of the film in the form of a pan across the various photographs that the elderly Rose has at her bedside. We can see that she has pursued the life of a frontier adventurer, posing in the pictures with a game fish, a biplane and on horseback: cowboy-style, naturally.

Strong narrative themes in *Jurassic Park* draw in a similar way on elements of frontier mythology. Alan Grant and Ellie Sattler are found near the start of the film on their home ground, out in the frontier Badlands of Montana. He is wearing a cowboy hat, neckerchief and plaid shirt; she is in jeans. They are introduced with close-ups of hands-on work uncovering a fossilized dinosaur from the dirt. Frontier credentials are established, as with Bill Harding in *Twister*, through direct engagement with the earth and through a distrust of technology. Grant's first line is 'I hate computers.' Colleagues are using a radar device to find buried fossils. 'A few more years' development and we won't even have to dig any more', says one. 'Where's the fun in that?' asks Grant. The picture on the screen flickers as soon as he touches it, confirming his aversion to technologies that threaten to come between him and direct experience of the world.

Like *Titanic*, *Jurassic Park* offers a cautionary tale about the dangers of hubris, of assuming that the fruits of science and technology can lead to mastery of the natural world. Arrogance underlies both the creation of the giant ship and the recreation of the dinosaurs. The heroes of the films are those who question this stance rather than insisting on the infallibility of the Promethean creations. The dinosaurs of *Jurassic Park* are meant to be under strict control, kept from breeding by the creation of an all-female population. But, as Malcolm suggests, Hammond and his team are dabbling with an awesome force and such control is impossible to guarantee. Life will not be contained, he asserts. 'Life breaks free, it expands to new territories and it crashes through barriers, painfully, maybe even dangerously.' He is proved right when it turns out that the dinosaurs have adapted. Nature has taken its course and they are breeding in the wild. If the T-rex is not at first tempted to put itself on display to the tour party, resisting the appetising prospect of a chained goat, Grant is unsurprised: 'T-rex doesn't want to be fed, he wants to hunt. Can't just suppress 65 million years of gut instinct.'

In this way, *Jurassic Park* shares a fundamentally reactionary ideology with *Titanic*, a focus on the forces of 'nature' and 'instinct' that effectively denies the socially constructed nature of the realities we inhabit. In *Titanic*, what is validated is a notion of the individual as some kind of pure or 'natural' essence that can be either repressed and imprisoned or allowed to flourish. Class seems to figure quite centrally in the film, with its scene-shifts between different social levels, but this is something of a façade behind which social determinants are dismissed as essentially secondary. Class is present as something to be overcome, a rhetorical strategy that is in some ways more powerful than merely ignoring the class dimension. It is possible to read the film differently, as a demonstration of blatant class discrimination, but it is structured to encourage an individualist approach. Rose is presented as a free spirit, by nature, whatever her class or background (her lack of freedom as a woman is alluded to at one point by her mother). She awaits only the catalyst that will enable her essence to be expressed.

Jurassic Park promotes a similar view of the world. Natural drives and instincts are privileged. Malcolm's speech about life expanding to new territories and crashing through barriers may seem to be an apt response to those who think they can exert godlike control, but it could also be read as an attempt to vindicate movements such as the original American frontier expansion, to justify such colonial endeavours through an appeal to 'nature' that removes them from the realm of politics or culture.

A key element of this ideology as it operates in Western capitalism is the ideal of the nuclear family, a social and historical construction constantly sold in terms of its supposedly 'natural' basis. It is here that *Jurassic Park* might be engaged in its most sustained narrative 'work' as a cultural product. The entire discourse of the film around issues of nature/authenticity vs. hubris and over-reliance on technology revolves around a project focused on the construction or reconstruction of the nuclear family. It bears a striking similarity here to *Twister*, particularly in its effort to restore the figure of the father. Just like *Twister*, the narrative dynamic involves the restoration of an idea of the nuclear family that initially seems to be under implicit threat. It is tempting to read this theme in terms of the authorial voice of Steven Spielberg, executive producer of *Twister* and director of *Jurassic Park*. Harding and Grant join a long list of actual or displaced fathers established or redeemed in Spielberg's films. The issue may be of particular concern to Spielberg as a result of his own childhood experience[20] but its prominence in his films – hugely successful as most of them have been – suggests broader resonance in a cultural context in which a particular version of 'the family' is treated as a special realm that should exist beyond the 'intrusions' of the social sphere. A host of contentious issues are in this way removed from what is seen as any legitimate arena for political intervention.

In *Twister* the threat to the formation of the nuclear family comes in the form of Harding's pending divorce from Jo. In *Jurassic Park*, the problem is Grant's dislike of children, clearly expressed from the start. He is hostile to the attentions of a group of children present at the Montana dig. He tries to avoid Tim and Lex when they set out for the tour of Jurassic Park. He seems to have eluded Tim only to be confronted by Lex, who grins and quips: 'She said I should ride with you because it would be good for you.' Sattler gives an indulgent smile and Grant nods in resignation. The implication is that Sattler wants children, Grant does not – and that Sattler's wishes are likely to prevail. By the end of the film this has been achieved. Grant and the two children are firmly bonded. As the survivors make their escape from the island by helicopter, Sattler and Malcolm sit on one side of the passenger compartment with Grant opposite, the children asleep in his arms. Sattler smiles contentedly, catching his eye and glancing down at the children. He repeats the gesture, looking from the children to her. The entire wordless sequence imposes a 'happy ever after' defined in terms of the establishment of a nuclear family. Tim and Lex may not be Grant and Sattler's children, just as the family that emerges from the storm shelter at the end of *Twister* is unrelated to the protagonists of that film. The rhetorical implication is clear, however. Grant and Sattler will go on to bring up children of their own, but the economies of Hollywood narrative demand that Tim and Lex act as proxies, offering an immediate emotional fulfilment for the viewer.

How, then, does *Jurassic Park* achieve the transformation of Grant's attitude towards children? It is through an excursion on to a 'frontier' terrain. Bonding occurs through the shared experience of hazard out in the wilds of the park. This process begins with the T-rex attack. The sequence plays an important part in the linear movement of the film, subjecting the children to danger and forcing Grant to make a commitment on their behalf. He enters into a sustained period of engagement with the children, eventually leading them to a place of safety in the tree-tops. The three are made into a unit by their experiences and the fact that their travails in the muddy landscape leave them the same shade of dirty-brown. As Grant settles down to sleep he is briefly discomforted by an object in his pocket that turns out to be a fossilized velociraptor claw, an object he used earlier to intimidate a boy who had not treated his comments with due respect. He throws it away. With great narrative economy, again, the film suggests a changed attitude towards children, a discarding of his old enmity. The point is made rather less subtly in the accompanying dialogue. 'What are you and Ellie going to do now if you don't have to pick up dinosaur bones any more?' asks Lex. 'I don't know – I guess we'll have to evolve, too,' Grant replies as gently soothing music builds and he laughs indulgently at Tim's dinosaur jokes. The change is naturalized again, a move towards the nuclear family associated with evolution, progress, inevitability and general saccharine cosiness.

If a move onto the frontier-type landscape of *Jurassic Park* is the catalyst for the establishment of a proxy nuclear family, an important dimension is provided by the role of technology or its absence. The theme park is heavily dependent on computer technologies, but the systems expert Dennis Nedry (Wayne Knight) is not to be trusted. It is no accident that it should be the computer expert who has become corrupted. Nedry – a caricature figure, the ultimate in greedy, overweight, untidy and generally 'disgusting' computer 'nerds' – is being paid to steal samples of dinosaur DNA. He represents the worst excesses of over-reliance on the products of 'civilization', technology, consumerism and fast food. When he loses his way to the dock with his samples, and crashes his jeep, he proves entirely unsuited to any kind of practical or survival skills and does not last very long. It seems fitting that he should be killed by a dinosaur that finishes off its prey by spitting gobs of corrosive liquid. Nedry has switched off many of the computer systems in order to cover his moves, and it is this that causes the débâcle in the park, including the freeing of the T-rex.

The electric security fences are switched off, endangering everyone. The loss of power also creates the frontier opening in the film, however.

It is only when no longer immersed in the protective and artificial technological web that Grant undergoes his transformation, with all its social and political baggage. The spectacular moment of the confrontation with the T-rex occurs not just at an important moment in the development of the linear narrative but also provides a vital crux in the underlying narrative dynamic, the oppositions established between 'frontier' and technological realms. It is Grant's engagement with nature, unmediated, that brings out what the film implies to be his 'natural' role as parent. The products of technology are destroyed, forcing him onto a terrain where he has to depend on his own instincts and abilities. The cinematic impact of the T-rex sequence plays a direct part in Grant's transformation. It is the audio-visual spectacle, the pounding and howling of the T-rex and the screaming of the children, that provides the force to lever Grant into a new position. He is changed through an emotional assault of a kind that the cinematic apparatus seeks to enact simultaneously on the viewer. The spectacular qualities of the sequence heighten the narrative dynamic rather than undermining it, as we saw with other examples in the previous chapter. A similar process is found in one of the key moments of *Titanic*: a spectacular vision of the central characters at the ship's prow underlines emotionally the point at which Rose makes her commitment to Jack.[21]

The T-rex attack sequence is fully integrated into the narrative of *Jurassic Park*, in terms of both forward-movement of plot and the development of central underlying themes. If the degree to which spectacle and narrative are integrated is variable in the contemporary Hollywood blockbuster, this is an example at the more integrated end of the scale. It fits the definition of the 'truly integrated' given by John Mueller in the context of an analysis of the musicals of Fred Astaire. In the integrated musical, Mueller suggests, the musical numbers advance the plot by their content: 'During these numbers something happens which changes the characters or the situation, and a test of integration in this sense would be whether the number can be cut out of the musical without leaving a noticeable gap.'[22]

The T-rex sequence as spectacular special-effects 'number' passes this test. Its removal would leave a noticeable gap as it plays a key part in motivating and establishing Grant's commitment to the children and in developing the theme of bonding through the experience of the technologically 'unmediated' frontier realm. Full integration is only one of six possibilities suggested by Mueller, others of which might be applied variously to sequences in contemporary non-musical spectaculars. Mueller's first category is the number completely irrelevant to the plot, a quality a good deal less common than is sometimes implied. Even the most 'bracketed' of special-effects extravaganzas are likely to contribute to plot at some level. They might fit into Mueller's second category: numbers 'which contribute to the spirit or theme'[23] rather than to specific developments of plot. This might be the case with those parts of the tornado-chasing spectacle of *Twister* in which a general sense of freedom and excitement is generated more than anything concretely tied to plot or thematic development.

Mueller offers three additional categories to fill in more of the ground between the extremes of full and non-existent integration. Numbers might enrich the plot without advancing it, he suggests, deepening knowledge of situation or character without actually changing anything. This category might apply to the sequence in *Jurassic Park* in which Grant and the children are almost trampled by a stampeding herd of ostrich-like gallimimus that are being chased by the T-rex. This was a ground-breaking special effects achievement at the time, the dinosaurs appearing to move past and between the human characters, creating the impression that they share the same space.[24] It is a spectacular sequence, partly designed to show off this effect, but not without narrative resonance. The plot does not move forward in any significant manner, but the sequence contributes to the progressive bonding of the trio in the wilderness and to the delineation of each character. Grant remains fascinated and distracted by the observation of real dinosaur behaviour, 'just like a flock of birds evading a predator'. Lex is nervous, keen for reassurance that gallimimus is a safe 'vegi-saurus' like the brachiosaur, and eager to get away after the appearance of the T-rex. Tim gets to show off his dinosaur knowledge (correctly identifying the variety), his wit (a quip, in answer to Grant's ponderings, that 'er, they're flocking this way') and a boyish fascination with the quantity of blood that appears when the T-rex brings down and eats one of the flock. Conventional gender roles are confirmed, in other words, as far as the children are concerned.

Two more categories suggested by Mueller are similar to one another, although with different emphases that pick up further nuances. These are: numbers 'whose existence is relevant to the plot, but whose content is not' and those 'which advance the plot, but not by their content.'[25] In each case the precise content of the 'number' is not crucial to the plot, in the way it is to the 'truly integrated' sequence, although the existence of the sequence is of a greater or lesser degree of relevance to the broader progression of the narrative. There is plenty of scope for debate about which of these categories might be most appropriate for any individual sequence. We might imagine a reading of the T-rex attack in a rather different version of *Jurassic Park*.

Say, for the sake of argument, the theme of Grant's attitude towards children, with all the baggage that carries, was absent from the film. In this case, the T-rex attack might fit into the latter of Mueller's categories. The sequence would be important to the advancing of the plot of an action-adventure spectacular about the threat posed by escaped dinosaurs, marking the key moment when the security fences are breached and one of the most dangerous beasts is let loose. In this case, however, the specific detailed content of the sequence – its focus on the children and the levering of Grant into making a commitment – might not be so vital to the plot. What Mueller offers is a useful continuum of possibilities that underlines the variable nature of the precise relationship of any spectacular sequence to narrative dimensions and is a good deal more nuanced than the either/or extremes implied by many commentators on contemporary Hollywood.

In both *Jurassic Park* and *Titanic* a 'natural' realm associated with the frontier is juxtaposed to a complex made up of a mixture of artifice, fabrication and technology: a set of more or less negative values that does not necessarily add up to an entirely coherent package. The 'natural' is strongly favoured but it is important to note that technology is not entirely rejected. The narrative seems to work towards some kind of reconciliation of the opposition between the two. *Titanic* celebrates the technological wonder of the ship rather than regarding it as sheer folly. The spectacular display of the vessel is strongly implicated in this celebration, in the sweeping visions of *Titanic* at full speed and the pounding spectacle inside the engine rooms. At the same time, this is tinged with the lurking sense of doom based on our knowledge of the ship's fate. The result, potentially, is a mixture of feelings that itself seems to blend a sense of technological marvel with an awareness of its limitations: a reconcilation of the opposition, perhaps, at an emotional level. What is questioned by both *Titanic* and *Jurassic Park* is not so much modern technology itself as those who treat it with an overbearing arrogance or hubris. In *Titanic* it is the *assumption* that the ship could *not* sink, rather than the sinking itself, that is blamed for most of the deaths; otherwise more lifeboats could have been provided. It is the pressure on the captain to go faster, to push too hard to arrive ahead of schedule and make the headlines, that seals the vessel's fate. The suggestion is that the problem lies not with the ship itself but with the arrogant desire to push to extremes, to satisfy pride and ambition at the expense of maintaining any respect for nature.

This is precisely the arrogance of which Malcolm accuses Hammond in *Jurassic Park*: a 'lack of humility before nature'. But competence in the realms of technology is not entirely rejected in *Jurassic Park*. The figure of Nedry as computer 'nerd' extraordinaire (his name an anagram of 'nerdy') has to be balanced against that of Lex, who turns out to be a computer buff and whose skills come into play in one of the climactic confrontations when she is able to re-boot the computer system just in time to restore the door locks. A significant moment of negotiation occurs earlier, out in the park, when Tim calls Lex a computer 'nerd'. She rejects the term, defining herself as 'a hacker', and thus establishes a position opposed to that of Nedry. The term 'hacker' has much more positive connotations, those of the unregulated outsider capable of making raids on established computer systems; a term with associations closer to those of the frontier pioneer, as in the 'cyber-cowboys' of William Gibson's influential novel *Neuromancer* (1984).

Oppositions between 'frontier' and technological realms in these films are often underlined by the projection of the respective qualities on to individual characters. But this personalization of the underlying issues can also be used in the process of reconciliation. It is significant that the designer of the *Titanic*, Thomas Andrews (Victor Garber), is portrayed in a highly sympathetic manner, as noble and honest. The narrative design is careful to place him on several occasions in close contact with Rose – and so with us – confirming her suspicions about the impending fate of the ship and eventually donating his lifejacket. It is not the designer who pushes the captain to increase his speed, but J. Bruce Ismay of the White Star Line (Jonathan Hyde), the figure who had the grand idea for the ship. Andrew designed it in detail and oversaw the construction, and so is associated with real hands-on knowledge and ability. Ismay's was the pride and arrogance, the determination to build something so big 'its supremacy would never be challenged'. Andrew goes to his death with dignity. Ismay sneaks, shamefaced, on to one of the lifeboats with the women and children. Separating out these two characters, and their respective attitudes and fates, seems an important rhetorical strategy. It enables us to share in a celebration of 'frontier' virtues while retaining a good measure of faith in the 'civilization' and 'technology' capable of a feat such as the construction of the *Titanic*.

A similar effect might be found in *Jurassic Park* in the opposition between Hammond and Malcolm. The rhetoric of the dialogue exchanges between the two seems strongly to favour Malcolm's position. He puts his finger on weaknesses in Hammond's project that events will confirm. He adopts the position of 'nature', casting Hammond as arrogant opportunist. But elements such as casting and performance complicate the picture. Malcolm, as played by Goldblum in a familiar unconventional scientist mode (a role he has adopted in a number of films including *Independence Day*, *The Fly*, 1986, and *Life Story*, 1987), is certainly the more 'hip' and sexy of the two, but he is also a rather cold and distant creation. Richard Attenborough's incarnation of Hammond is cuddly and avuncular, and the audience appears to be intended to share his reaction to some of Malcolm's irritating mannerisms. He comes over as genuinely 'well-meaning' and is prepared to learn his lesson. Again, what reads at one level as a simple binary opposition is broken down, to some extent, in a process that might offer some kind of reconciliation.

These films allow us to have the best of both worlds. We can enjoy both the thrills and spectacle *and* buy into the endorsement of 'nature' or the 'frontier' experience. The spectacular dimension is dependent upon the 'arrogance' of those who create the leviathans, not to mention the technological achievements of Hollywood special effects. Without Hammond and Ismay there would be no *Jurassic Park* or *Titanic*, no magnificent spectacle for us to enjoy. The underlying narrative dynamics tend to celebrate nature and the frontier. The combination of spectacle and narrative might itself play a part in the broad process through which the underlying oppositions are given some kind of imaginary reconciliation. If cinematic spectacle can sometimes offer a vicarious equivalent of the frontier experience, the relationship between spectacle and narrative may also become implicated in the treatment of the underlying thematic oppositions of the texts.

The positioning of the spectacular effects sequences as 'special' has implications that cross over into the narrative realm of these films. As Michael Stern argues, everything in a film is an 'effect', 'something fabricated, made', and the act of assigning a special status on some effects has an ideological impact in tending to naturalize all of the others.[26] Drawing attention to the 'amazing' dinosaur or ship artefacts has the effect of rendering 'ordinary', banal or invisible much of the narrative content. The spectacular strategies of films like *Jurassic Park* and *Titanic* reinforce a narrative dynamic that revolves largely around the naturalization of particular social and cultural structures. As I suggested in the Introduction, critical approaches that describe these films in terms of spectacle that overwhelms or evacuates narrative can reinforce this sense of the 'emptiness' of texts that are in fact heavily freighted with myth and ideology.

It is no small irony that the financial success of all of the films considered so far in this book is to a large extent due to the kind of dependence on 'state-of-the-art' technology that is questioned by the dominant strain of the narrative. The experience that stands in for that of the 'frontier' is often a product of the very system from which the narrative asserts the possibility of escape: technology, giant business oligopoly, and so on. This is not an accident. Large-scale spectacular effects play an important part in helping the Hollywood majors to retain oligopolistic control of the industry. New effects technologies can be used to reduce costs, particularly in the case of 'invisible effects' such as the digital removal of unwanted items or the addition of background elements such as landscapes or crowds. These technologies are often celebrated as offering the potential to increase access to more pluralistic and lower-budget kinds of filmmaking. Keeping up with the latest technologies is generally expensive, however, and can be seen as part of Hollywood's traditional strategy of maintaining or raising 'barriers to entry'. Despite periodic calls for cost-cutting and savings, it has generally suited the majors for the costs of production, distribution and marketing to remain high because this prevents anyone else from getting a foot in the door. Once a certain level of special-effects technology has been deployed it creates a demand that other films match the same expensive standard. Issues of 'quality' and 'standards' such as this have long acted as a cover for the enshrining of just one – expensive, Hollywood – way of operating, when others, which do not have access to the same promotional resources, might be equally valid.[27] Competitors often attempt to emulate Hollywood spectacle, without having the resources to do it properly, thereby seemingly proving the maxim that 'nobody does it like Hollywood', a self-fulfilling prophecy.

Based to a significant extent on the success of a large number of small, independent houses – in addition to the market leader, Industrial Light and Magic – the digital effects business might be held up as exemplifying a move in 'post-studio-era' Hollywood towards a decentralized or 'post-Fordist' production system. There has been a clear move away from the Fordist mass production-line system that characterized the heyday of the studio era. But this is another change that can easily be overstated. Moves towards what post-Fordists term 'flexible specialization' in the production process – the general shift to an environment in which film packages are assembled on a one-off basis with different elements of each package supplied by a large number of small providers – have not been matched by any such decentralization at the crucial levels of finance and distribution.[28] There have also been moves towards some re-centralization at the production and post-production level. As far as digital effects is concerned, the majors have begun to take over: 'To date, the studios have chosen either to buy established entities outright (Sony with Imageworks, Disney with Dream Quest); take substantial stakes (Fox with VI Effects, DreamWorks with PDI [Pacific Data Images]); or form their own in-house divisions (Warner Bros.).'[29] As ever, the majors are happy to leave the risks of innovation to outsiders (the same pattern was seen in the case of the development of sound in the 1920s and of widescreen processes in the 1950s), moving in to reap the benefits at a later stage when potential profitability has been demonstrated.

3

The Final Frontier: Space Fictions

What are ya, some kind of half-assed astronaut?

Quint to Hooper in *Jaws*

For 30 years they questioned the need for NASA. Today we're going to give them the answer

Executive director of NASA in *Armageddon*

The astronaut of real-world space exploration is an ambiguous figure: a pioneer of the ultimate 'new frontier' and one of the heroes of the modern age; yet, at the same time, enmeshed into a web of technology that makes acts of individual agency increasingly hard to distinguish. Precisely such an opposition forms the underlying structure of *The Right Stuff* (1983), the story of the first American astronauts, which gains much of its resonance through a comparison between the Mercury seven and a group of military test-pilots from whose ranks some of them are drawn. The astronauts are depicted as struggling to maintain a sense of individual heroics in the face of mediation by technology and the press hullabaloo that surrounds their every move. The experience of the test pilot, the film suggests, is more authentic, at a cutting edge where the skills of the individual are still more important than the technologies of the aircraft. *The Right Stuff* will be situated in this chapter, thematically more than historically, between two opposite extremes manifested by the speculative projections of *2001: A Space Odyssey* (1968) and the *Star Wars* cycle (from 1977).

In *2001: A Space Odyssey* humanity seems already to have been eclipsed by the machine. The *Star Wars* films herald a brash return of individual heroics on the space frontier. A similar dynamic underlies the use of spectacle in the two films. In *2001* conventional linear narrative drive is almost entirely abandoned to the unfolding of slow, contemplative spectacle. The spectacle of the *Star Wars* films is very different: fast, furious, and reattached to something much closer to 'classical' narrative. The use of *Star Wars* as an exemplar can hardly be questioned, given its continued influence on contemporary science fiction cinema. *2001: A Space Odyssey* was also influential, setting new standards in the realm of special effects. It is considered in this chapter, however, less in terms of its influence than the pole it represents in its treatment of the relationship between spectacle and narrative. I am not suggesting that *2001* is typical or representative of a wider movement in the way *Star Wars* might be. It is in many respects something of a one-off; not entirely isolated from broader social, cultural or industrial contexts, but the work of a maverick filmmaker, Stanley Kubrick, operating on the margins of Hollywood. It offers a good example of the use of one variety of spectacle and the use (or absence) of particular narrative forms.

The huge commercial success of *Star Wars* marked the start of a sustained boom in Hollywood science fiction, the centrality of which can be explained in terms of both narrative and spectacle. From a narrative point of view, science fiction is well equipped to explore and offer some imaginative resolution to a number of pressing social issues, including the broad issue of the relationship between 'humanity' and that for which science, technology and rationality are deemed to stand. More particularly, science fiction offers an ideal location for the articulation of discourses that draw on the mythology of the frontier. The terrestrial frontier in America may have been declared closed more than a century ago, but in space the frontier can, in the imagination, be extended towards infinity. Space offers a domain in which complaints about the oppression of deserving Others, such as Native Americans or other victims of colonial policies, can be avoided. In space, as Richard Maltby and Ian Craven put it, playing on the poster tag-line for *Alien* (1979), 'no one can hear you scream about misrepresentation.'[1]

If the popularity of science fiction can be explained in part by its ability to negotiate important narrative themes, it can only fully be understood within the industrial context of contemporary Hollywood. Science fiction, with its scope for the imagination of all sorts of new worlds, technologies and beings, is the ideal arena in which to highlight the spectacular characteristics of big-screen entertainment. This goes a long way to explain the importance of a genre formerly restricted mostly to low budget 'B' movies. Given the prevalence of science fiction in contemporary Hollywood spectacle, including a number of examples considered elsewhere in this book, the focus of this chapter will be limited to one branch of the genre, that which is set in space. It will also include films such as *The Right Stuff* and *Apollo 13* (1995), based on factual developments in space, and *Armageddon* (1998), which inserts an element of 'real' space travel into a work of spectacular fantasy.

Space odysseys: from *2001* to *Star Wars*

What is missing from *2001: A Space Odyssey* is most of the history of humanity itself. It is lost in the transcendent match-cut in which a flying bone thrown into the air by an ape that has learnt the use of tools is transformed into a spaceship on the way to an orbiting station and an antiseptic future of artificial landscapes in space. Humanity, by this stage, seems to be hanging by a thread. A few banal exchanges of dialogue are all that exist to bring any life to Dr Heyward Floyd (William Sylvester) and his colleagues on the moon base where a new discovery will propel a further generation of space travellers towards and beyond 'the infinite'. There is little sense of frontier adventure or redemption in any of this, and no impression of speed or boldness. In our first sight of the *Discovery* spacecraft, taking the first manned mission to Jupiter, it moves slowly into the frame from above left. The shot is held until it gradually fills the screen. The next shot is a three-quarter view from the front and side in which the camera pans along with the ship, reducing its movement within the frame to almost nothing. An extreme long shot from the side follows in which the *Discovery* stretches its frail and spindly length across the widescreen expanse. A melancholic piece by Khatchaturian creates an atmosphere of bleakness and loneliness in the cold outer reaches of the solar

Stasis in the void: the Discovery barely moving in the frame in 2001: A Space Odyssey, *© Turner Entertainment Co., a Time Warner Company, 1968*

system. The sense of going nowhere is heightened by a cut to the figure of the astronaut Frank Poole (Gary Lockwood) jogging and shadow-boxing endlessly around the ship's giant centrifuge, an image of futility and disorientation rather than an evocation of any exciting sense of pioneer spirit. The motif of circular movement occurs regularly during the film, including a giant space station revolving above the Earth, and is also reflected to some extent in the larger events of the film, which appear to trace a movement from the 'dawn' of humanity to some strange kind of rebirth.

If human history has been lost in *2001: A Space Odyssey*, so to a large extent has 'classical' Hollywood narrative. The film unfolds extremely slowly in lengthy segments: the 'Dawn of Man' sequence on Earth, the journey to and events on the Moon, the Jupiter mission and 'beyond the infinite'. The first section presents nearly fifteen minutes of wordless performance by a group of ape characters. Narrative development does occur during this sequence. It tells a story of bands of apes that argue and fight with one another, are victim to predators, and some of which learn the use of weapons after the appearance of a strange black monolith. None of this is made explicit, however. There is no user-friendly narrative voice-over or exposition, beyond a title reading 'The Dawn of Man', to ensure that we get the point. The connections between the different segments of the film are at first far from clear. The match-cut from flying bone to spaceship is stunning in its narrative economy, but the act of temporal compression is so extreme as to leave the viewer to do the work and make the connection between what appears to be the initial 'gift' of technology and its eventual fruition in space travel.

Floyd's flight to the space station and docking takes far longer than necessary from the point of view of narrative exposition, a period during which we are given no indication of who Floyd is or what might be going on. A narrative tease is introduced on the space station, when a Soviet scientist quizzes Floyd about strange developments at an American base on the Moon. A trap is laid for the viewer when Floyd stonily refuses to be drawn to comment on rumours about the outbreak of an epidemic of unknown origin. The implication is that the rumours might be true, although we find out during a briefing scene on the Moon that they have been carefully planted to conceal the reality. A partial answer to the mystery is provided during the briefing, when Floyd refers to a discovery on the Moon 'which may well prove to be among the most significant in the history of science'. Some minutes later we are introduced to the black monolith that has been unearthed, but we are told that it remains a 'big mystery'. As the monolith is inspected it lets out a piercing signal and we see a conjunction of the monolith, the sun and the Earth similar to an image accompanying the monolith that appeared in the 'Dawn of Man' sequence. We then cut to the title 'Jupiter Mission, 18 months later', a positively effusive example of nondiegetic narration as far as this film is concerned. A television report watched on board the *Discovery* fills in some immediate background but tells us nothing to connect with the preceding events. A few hints are dropped some thirteen minutes into the Jupiter Mission sequence, when the computer HAL remarks on some 'extremely odd things about this mission', including strange stories about something being dug up on the moon. But it is not until nearly an hour into the Jupiter Mission that we are given the full background: that the monolith found on the moon emitted a radio beacon aimed at Jupiter, prompting their mission to follow up this first sign of intelligent life elsewhere in the universe.

The gradual supply of information and the use of devices such as the television broadcast are familiar Hollywood narrative conventions, but strung out in *2001* to a point at which the film risks many viewers falling through the gaps. The narrative structure is linear, but lacks anything like the relatively or seemingly tight plotting of cause-and-effect characteristic of classical Hollywood. Mystery stories, of which this is a celestial variety, are granted more leeway in this respect. Generic motivation allows for audiences to be teased and led astray rather more than usual, but any such pattern in *2001* has been stretched temporally to a point at which the difference outweighs any similarities. By the latter stages of the film, when the surviving astronaut Dave Bowman (Keir Dullea) travels through a strange gateway into another dimension, we have been provided with a good deal of background, but the narrative becomes even more enigmatic. Bowman's entry into the 'star gate' is not depicted in a clear, literal manner. We see another monolith out in space with the *Discovery*, Jupiter and other planets or moons. One of the ship's exploratory pods comes towards the camera. There is a conjunction of planets and the monolith. The camera tilts upwards and the special-effects sequence of the journey begins. As a point of contrast, it is interesting to note that in the book, written by Arthur C. Clarke in conjunction with the screenplay co-written by director/producer Kubrick, the entry into the 'star gate' is figured more explicitly: Bowman's pod heads towards the monolith which seems to invert itself and become the entrance to a tunnel. The film seems deliberately to avoid such literal narrative clarity in points of relatively minor exposition, let alone the 'big' questions raised by the events. The 'star gate' lightshow is extended for some nine minutes before Bowman lands up in a period-furnished room. In a series of visions of himself, he ages, eventually seeming to be reborn in the form of a foetus which, in the closing images of the film, sits in orbit above the Earth. As with the rest of the film, it is perfectly possible to construct narrative explanations for all this with the aid of the novel, repeated viewings or the many critical analyses that have been produced. In the film itself, however, especially on a single viewing, any overt explication is conspicuous by its absence.

The viewer of *2001* is encouraged to sit back and admire the spectacle, while being given ample time to consider what it is all about. It is no surprise that the film had a release in the Cinerama format, the widest of widescreen processes geared more to the provision of spectacle than narrative. *2001* is an extreme case of a tendency towards a portentous, slow-moving epic style that began in the 1950s, a tendency pushed to the point at which linear narrative often seems largely suspended. *2001* offers a form of contemplative spectacle that might be described as 'bracketed off from narrative concerns' in this sense, to use Michele Pierson's phrase. A measurement of the difference between *2001* and *Jurassic Park* underlines the extent to which the concept of 'bracketing off' does not apply to the latter without a severe flattening of perspective. *2001* provides plenty of spectacle for viewers to enjoy at their leisure. The spacecraft move ponderously, the camera lingering over each manoeuvre. The shuttle to the space station drifts languidly across the frame while a pen floats lazily in zero gravity at Floyd's side. The arrival at the space station is extended to give time to explore the wealth of detail in the widescreen frame, where tiny figures are visible through windows inset above and below the docking bay. The spectacle is at times breathtaking: for us, that is, but not generally for the protagonists.

This is a notable difference between the presentation of spectacle in *2001* and that of films discussed previously, where our thrills were mediated through the reactions of the characters. So, in *2001*, while we admire the gliding shuttle and its balletic interaction with the space station, our hero, Floyd, is asleep. While Floyd sits in a video-phone booth to call home, the dizzying view out of the window behind is of the Earth appearing to rotate around the frame, a spectacle to which he remains oblivious. The one occasion in which an awed response is shared by both viewer and protagonist is the 'star gate' sequence, perhaps the definitive example of special effects as an abstract display of sound and light into which the viewer is projected. A fast-moving kaleidoscope of lights and images comes towards the camera, passing on either side, the first example of any such rapid motion in the film. The display is intercut with images of Bowman's face, looking into camera, and a series of extreme close-ups on his eyeball. We are given his point-of-view on the lightshow, the length of which is disorienting to the viewer as well as to the fictional character. Speed and identification with the perspective of the protagonist might seem to make the 'star gate' sequence closer in structure to the spectacles examined in the previous chapter, but this is not the case. The result is more likely to be an extended sense of disorientation. What is not offered is any even balance between 'subjective' and 'objective' perspectives. We spend most of the film situated outside the action, quite coldly withdrawn. Then, at the climax, we are overwhelmed by an intense identification. Neither is particularly comfortable compared with the structure of more conventional Hollywood products.

The *Star Wars* films could hardly be more different. They offer a brand of spectacle that is hyperkinetic, flashy and bright. Space is presented not as the distant void invoked in *2001* but as something to be traversed rapidly and with style. The exploration of space in *2001* is presented as an activity that has necessitated the immersion of humanity in a technological web. In the *Star Wars* films space is enabling. Humanity is not overwhelmed by the scale of the universe but empowered by its ability to cross it at speed. The spaceships of *Star Wars* can zap into 'light speed' and streak across the universe at a velocity that reduces passing stars to a spectacular blur. Conflict also obeys an aesthetic of the 'zap', provided by laser-type weapons that fire bright beams of energy and appear to kill quickly and cleanly. Even some the transitions from one scene to another are characterized by this dynamic energy. A range of different wipe techniques is used, in homage to an earlier generation of action-adventure cinema, including one variety in which the wipe moves laterally across the screen to the accompaniment of a screaming Empire fighter.

The zap aesthetic: bright lights and kinetics flash across the screen in Star Wars, © *Twentieth Century Fox Film Corporation, 1977. Ronald Grant archive*

The *Star Wars* films also offer a return to something closer to the 'classical' Hollywood narrative structure built around individual heroics, pressing deadlines and a dash of romance. In this respect they can be contrasted not just to *2001* but to a number of films that explored more complex forms of narrative in the relative freedom allowed to some film-makers when the major studios were trying to find their way out of the financial crisis of the late 1960s and early 1970s. If one aspect of this 'New Hollywood' was represented by the 'modernist' tendencies of *2001* or the films of Robert Altman, the dominant version was marked by the appearance of 'blockbuster' attractions such as *Jaws* and *Star Wars*, films that offered a combination of spectacle, driving narrative and mythic or ideological recuperation. It was this combination, with its blend of appeals, that appears to have been responsible for much of their huge success at the box office.

Star Wars opens with a chunk of preparatory exposition, in the form of a lengthy post-credit crawl. The viewer is then plunged into the ongoing action-spectacle, as the spaceship of the rebel Princess Leia (Carrie Fisher) enters the frame from above, followed with much audio impact in the cinema by a pursuing Empire vessel. We are supplied economically with both the necessary background and the immediate thrill of action spectacle, left in no doubt as to what is happening or who are the good or bad guys. The action is fast-paced from the start, any more 'serious' and mystical material about the 'Force' balanced by doses of comic by-play. *Star Wars* departs from any 'pure' notion of classical structure, having internalized the repeated cliffhanger/resolution pattern of the adventure serials to which it pays homage. Complications are also introduced in subsequent films by their own on-going serial status. But, as has already been suggested, that which passes for 'classical' Hollywood has always embraced a range of diversions and other formal components and is not a tradition from which *Star Wars* is radically separate.

Despite all their differences there are some overlaps between the *Star Wars* films and *2001*, particularly in their treatment of the relationship between 'humanity' and technology. For all its withdrawal from a commitment to a driving linear form of narrative, *2001* has a strong underlying thematic dynamic. What emerges from the film is a grand evolutionary tale in which humanity appears to be little more than a passing epiphenomenon. The presentation of the spectacle as something generally unrelated to the perspective of the protagonists is in keeping with this thematic concern, as is the way the narrative and spectacle are structured throughout to avoid any strong sense of viewer identification with the characters. Floyd is our first human point of contact, but he remains aloof and noncommittal, as does the camera. He is rarely pictured in close-up and there is no conventional Hollywood sense of being given special access to his thoughts or feelings. The death of Poole, one of two possible points of identification during the Jupiter mission, is understated and oblique. He is killed by HAL while engaged in a mission outside *Discovery*. What might have been a moment of melodrama is reduced to a shot of a pod approaching the camera, a series of rapid cuts in to HAL's electronic eye and a glimpse second-hand on a monitor of Poole as a tiny figure spinning away into space. As Bowman sets off to recover the body, HAL kills the three remaining members of the mission by switching off the systems that sustain them in hibernation. Their death is registered only in fading graphic read-outs and a couple of warning lights. They die without ever having been alive as far as the viewer is concerned; much the same could be said for the emotional blank that is Poole.

The *Star Wars* films share to some extent the negative view of the impact of science and technology found in *2001*. The mysticism of the 'Force' is favoured over the technocratic evil Empire. The hero Luke Skywalker (Mark Hamill) is encouraged to switch off his computer guidance system in the climactic battle. 'Use the Force, Luke; let go', urges the disembodied voice of the mystic Jedi knight Obi Wan Kenobi (Alec Guinness). Luke switches off the system and allows the Force, or his instincts guided by the Force, to take over, duly proceeding to hit the target and destroy the enemy Death Star. The 'dark side' of the Force is represented by Darth Vader, who cautions his allies in the Empire when one declares the Death Star 'the ultimate power in the universe'. 'Don't be too proud of this technological terror you have constructed,' says Vader. 'The ability to destroy a planet is insignificant next to the power of the Force.'

To prove his point when challenged, Vader begins to strangle his adversary purely by an act of will. Technology might be questioned at the thematic level, but much of the appeal of the film is based on a celebration of space-age technology and, by implication, of the cinematic technology that makes such visions possible. It is the technology that provides the excitement and kinaesthetic action on which the spectacle of all the *Star Wars* films is founded. An evil and oppressive technology might be in the hands of the Empire, but technological devices are also embraced by the heroic rebels, providing the means for exhilarating instances of effective individual agency: precisely what is denied in *2001*. Han Solo's Millennium Falcon has special modifications that make it one of the fastest craft in the galaxy, capable of spectacular manoeuvres, as are the X-wing fighters used by the rebels.

The original *Star Wars* and, to a greater extent, *Return of the Jedi* (1983) climax with major space-battle sequences in which the heroes demonstrate their ability to use technology to their own ends. The latter also features a lengthy terrestrial chase on 'speeder' bikes in which the good guys manage to out-manoeuvre the imperial stormtroopers, a sequence that uses the hyper-speed blur aesthetic that characterizes the pod-race in *The Phantom Menace* (1999). The winner of the pod-race, the young Anakin Skywalker, is revealed as a prodigy, capable of fixing any kind of technology. As might be expected, however, this high level of technological facility is tied up with his ambivalent status, intertextual knowledge establishing that Anakin will turn to the 'dark side' of the Force and become Darth Vader. The problem, again, is not technology itself but the use to which it is put. *Star Wars*, like so many Hollywood films, has it both ways, questioning and celebrating advanced technologies and in the process offering the element of reconciliation that seems far from available in *2001*. If there is one icon that figures this reconciliation it is the light-sabre, the weapon of the Jedi knight that neatly combines the qualities of mythical sword and hi-tech buzz. It is not just the technology of the heroes that is appealing in the *Star Wars* films. The Empire still has most of the best techno-toys, from screaming tie-fighters to the giant imperial walkers of *The Empire Strikes Back* and the unfurling battle and destroyer droids of *The Phantom Menace*. These provide much of the fun and fascination, even if they are a threat to the sympathetic characters and end up being put out of action. Like the villains in these and many other films, the threatening products of technology are often more seductive than the good; our enjoyment of the spectacle provided by these devices and by their destruction is another way perhaps of helping to reconcile some of the contradictions involved. Either way, space in the *Star Wars* films is exciting and invigorating for fictional characters and viewers alike. The spectacle provided is of a kind that backs up the tone of the narrative, as in *2001*, but to very different effect.

The narrative of the original *Star Wars*, as many have pointed out, owes more than a little to the western frontier tradition. The young hero is called away from a pastoral life to do battle on the high frontier. He resists at first, but his mind is made up for him when he returns home from an encounter with Obi Wan to find his relatives dead and the place smouldering. Part of the plot is a mission to rescue a captured princess, a version of the 'captivity narrative', one of the earliest American literary genres, which told of the capture of white women by 'savage' Native Americans. The presence of the captivity narrative, and the smouldering desert home, brings associations from *The Searchers* (1956). The idealism and *naïveté* of the hero of *Star Wars*, however, compared with the bitterness and alienation of the Ethan Edwards character in *The Searchers*, is one indicator of how much more freely elements of the frontier myth can be reasserted in the guilt-free realm of outer space. A more cynical and wise-cracking version of the frontier hero is represented by Han Solo (Harrison Ford), who appears in a parody of the saloon bar confrontation scene wearing a western-style gunbelt and waistcoat. The appropriately named Solo enacts the classic role of the unattached frontier individualist who eventually makes a commitment to the cause of the good community.

The initial *Star Wars* project appears to have been a conscious attempt by George Lucas to revivify not just a particular blend of spectacular narrative but also the frontier myth damaged by the repercussions of the Vietnam war and other events in the late 1960s and early 1970s. Lucas himself had given a grim portrayal of the relationship between humanity and technology, and a more detached kind of spectacle, in his first feature, the dystopian *THX 1138* (1971). *THX 1138* has far more in common with *2001: A Space Odyssey* than with the *Star Wars* cycle. A bleak, computer-monitored future world is figured in sparse widescreen compositions that isolate the title character (Robert Duvall), imprisoning him in frames within the frame. *THX* is a slow-moving, contemplative work, its images often verging on formal abstraction. The figure of *THX* is squeezed to the margins of the frame, a decentring that reflects the wider fate of humanity in the film. *Star Wars* makes very different use of the widescreen image, sometimes using the width to create its kinetic impressions but usually keeping the principals carefully centred in the screen, just as 'the human' is restored to a central place of effective agency. Lucas is quoted as declaring an intention to move from *THX* deliberately to offer a replacement for the lost mythical structure of the western:

> After I finished *American Graffiti* [his second feature], I came to realize that since the demise of the Western, there hasn't been much in the mythical fantasy genre available to the film audience. So, instead of making 'isn't-it-terrible-what's-happening-to-mankind' movies, which is how I began, I decided that I'd try to fill that gap.[2]

John Hellman offers a suggestive reading of the initial *Star Wars* trilogy in these terms in the aftermath of Vietnam. He reads *Star Wars* as a relatively untroubled shift of the syntactic relationships of the western into space. The darker tone of *The Empire Strikes Back* (1980), in which an unprepared Luke discovers the dark side of the Force, is seen as placing elements of the mythology under question. The viewer is left, Hellman suggests, in a position analogous to that reached in the moment of negative insight found at the end of Vietnam war films such as *The Deer Hunter* (1978) and *Apocalypse Now* (1979). This involves a discovery of the central character's own uncomfortably close relationship to an evil previously seen as Other. The third film, *Return of the Jedi* (1983), 'moves forward from traumatic self-discovery to energizing triumph.'[3] A suitably chastened Luke is able to confront the dark side and prevail once more over the Empire. Some of the dynamics of the Vietnam conflict are inverted in a film that ends with a battle on a forested planet in which the Empire represents the force of technologically-equipped oppression while the rebels join a band of Ewoks armed with 'primitive' technologies such as the bow and arrow.

Space 'realities': from 'right stuff' to wrong

The Right Stuff assumes neither the cold technological determinism and detached vistas of *2001* nor the spectacular comic-book heroics of *Star Wars*. It dramatizes instead something of the opposition between aspects of the two, filling in elements of the history, culture and politics occluded at each of the extremes. *The Right Stuff* is partly about the way space travel is translated into the realm of heroic myth and spectacular attraction. The American space programme, the film suggests, was conducted largely for purposes of spectacular display rather than in the interests of 'rational' science or discovery, and there is plenty of historical material to back up such a suggestion.[4]

The early years of the space race between the United States and the Soviet Union is placed in the context of a Cold War setting in which each power sought to use achievements in space to support its claim to be the more progressive. Kennedy only gave his approval to the Apollo Moon project once convinced of its merit in symbolic rather than practical terms. Public support, and hence the political will to provide funding, also appears to have depended upon the appeal of spectacle and heroism. The Mercury astronauts of *The Right Stuff* play on this to demand some of the trappings necessary to maintain their self-image as skilled pilots, with some control of their mission, rather than mere test specimens. They secure the addition of a window to the capsule and a hatch that can be operated from inside. For the test pilot there is a dimension of hands-on control and improvization. Thus, when the doyen of test pilots, Chuck Yeager (Sam Shepard) falls from his horse and injures his ribs on the eve of an attempt to break the sound barrier, he is helped to find a makeshift way of locking down the door of his experimental aircraft and goes on to make history. The only use we see of the astronaut-operated hatch on the spacecraft is rather less fortunate. Gus Grissom (Fred Ward) loses his capsule when he appears to panic and open the hatch in the sea after splashdown. Direct control offers the test pilot a resourceful inventiveness to overcome adversity. For the astronaut, cocooned within a much deeper technological web, it offers the chance to 'screw the pooch', as the lingo has it.

The structure of *The Right Stuff* makes much of this opposition. The test pilots are presented as the true heirs of the frontier tradition. The astronauts are enveloped in a vast mass of technology and bureaucracy. Their world is dominated by bright, clinical and shiny surfaces. The test pilots occupy a frontier realm in the high desert of New Mexico, a landscape of Joshua trees and scrub, picked out in elegiac autumnal colours suggestive of late frontier era. Yeager is presented as a daring horseman, the film drawing a parallel between his feats of bare-back riding and taming the latest experimental aircraft bronco. The test pilot remains in touch with elemental force, the film suggests, while there is little the astronaut can do to avoid being engulfed by the technology.

The domain of 'real' space travel was sold to the public in terms of the 'new' or 'high' frontier, but Hollywood representations have not very often made the connection stick. Successful space missions are, ironically, all too like some aspects of *2001: A Space Odyssey*: mostly rather dull and tedious and featuring protagonists whose personalities rarely capture the imagination. The terms of the epigraph to this chapter from *Jaws* speaks volumes on this point. The astronaut is used as a figure through which Quint, characterized as the frontiersman, castigates the scientist Hooper for his reliance on a heap of technological equipment. It is only when things go wrong in space, it seems, that a frontier-style opening is recreated. Hence the fact that the only real Apollo mission made into a Hollywood feature is Apollo 13, 'the one that went wrong'. An element of pioneer heroics is restored after a technological fault threatens the lives of the crew in *Apollo 13* (1995). A life-saving replacement air filter is constructed when a team of technicians on the ground improvizes its components from an assortment of objects available in the spacecraft. Hands-on human ingenuity overcomes the limitations of technology and bureaucratic institutions. If stories of real events in space travel often lack sufficient emphasis on such acts of heroic human agency they are also more limited in the dimension of spectacle.

The Right Stuff and *Apollo 13* have their moments of spectacle. As Scott Bukatman suggests, in the flight sequences of *The Right Stuff* 'movement is linked explicitly to transcendence and implicitly to the spectacularity of cinema.'[5] The film opens with actual and mock-historical newsreel footage of a test flight shot in black and white with a narrow aspect ratio of 1.33:1. The jet loses control and crashes, the image bursting into a blaze of widescreen colour as the aircraft explodes into a fireball on the ground. Vivid spectacle is thus directly associated with the capacities of contemporary big-screen entertainment.

Numerous other instances of 'historical footage' are presented in the 1.33:1 format, establishing implicitly an opposition between spectacular cinema and its more impoverished forerunners. The heroes appear in both places, however, suggesting that the film aims to create a balance between the rhetoric of fictional spectacle and authentic 'reality'. In the fictional reconstructions, the flights of the X-1 test jet create an impression almost of pure speed as the aircraft catapults repeatedly across the wide screen in very rapid montage sequences. The film also shifts register, briefly, in key transcendental moments such as immediately after Yeager breaks the sound barrier, using prism- or vortex-like imagery designed by the experimental filmmaker Jordan Belson. As Bukatman puts it:

> If, in the narrative, [this] represents a utopian transcendence and the penetration of a new frontier, as filmmaking it presents a utopian transgression of the realist, representational codes that dominate narrative cinema. The film viewer – this one, at least – is swept away into an aural and visual crescendo. The technological, indeed technocratic, system of the postwar, postclassical Hollywood cinema has produced an emotionally moving evocation of temporary transcendence, a sublime but ephemeral movement beyond its own boundaries.[6]

Such moments are relatively rare in films based on real events in space, which are generally constrained by a requirement to remain within the bounds of what is recognizable as reality. This means little more than flying into orbit or to the Moon, and spacecraft that offer something closer to the generally ponderous movements found in *2001*. *Apollo 13* has the spectacle of launch and vistas of the Earth and Moon as seen from space. Significantly, however, its most spectacularly dramatic moment takes the form of fantasy rather than reality, when the astronaut Jim Lovell (Tom Hanks) has a nightmare in which things go wrong in a fashion that more closely resembles the action of space fiction. In general, *The Right Stuff* and *Apollo 13* rely less on spectacle than on the working out of narrative dynamics. In the case of *The Right Stuff*, the demands of the lengthy and quite complex narrative probably helped to account for its failure at the box office. Science *fiction*, in contrast, is free to create spectacles of almost limitless variety, special-effects technologies permitting, which is one obvious reason why the fictional version so heavily outnumbers the factual in Hollywood. The spectacular dimension of space fictions also adds to their ability to invoke potent associations with the experience of the frontier.

There is another option, located somewhere between outright exercises of the imagination and fidelity to the limited scope of real space travel. Approximately realistic versions of space flight can be introduced into imaginary situations that owe more to science fiction than fact. *Mission to Mars* (2000) displays a solidly realistic aesthetic in its construction of a flight dated just 20 years in the future. The spacecraft appear to be plausible extrapolations from those of today. In design, action and narrative premise, *Mission to Mars* is in some respects a domesticated version of

2001. The principal Mars mission spacecraft combines characteristics of the real world space shuttle and the *Discovery*, including a giant centrifuge set-piece at its heart. Emergency extra-vehicular activity by the astronauts obeys the space 'realist' convention of ponderousness.

This is not pursued to the same relentless degree as the pod sequences in *2001*, however, and is combined with an element of hands-on action-heroics and a strong dose of emotional melodrama. The male half of a husband-and-wife astronaut team sacrifices himself heroically, floating off into space, to prevent his partner putting her own life at risk in an attempted rescue: a sequence far removed from anything conceivable in the emotion-drained universe of *2001*. The enigmatic and implicit back-story of *2001* is replaced here by a dénouement that provides clear-cut answers: the ingenuity of the protagonists enables them to discover the truth of humanity's Martian ancestry. *Mission to Mars* seeks to remain within the bounds of near-contemporary plausibility, constraining itself both in action and hardware, in order to lend some substance to a work of fantasy. As with many predecessors, including some of the space science fiction of the 1950s, the most spectacular exercises of the imagination are reserved for the domain of the alien, the otherness of which is partly a function of its contrast to a more quotidian construction of the future.[7]

Some similar strategies are found in *Armageddon*, along with a great deal more in the way of action heroics. Earth is threatened with imminent destruction by an asteroid on collision course. The only way to stop it, assembled experts conclude, is to send a mission to land on its surface to destroy it by planting a nuclear device underground. More fanciful proposals are initially suggested by the NASA boffins. But, they are told, 'we've gotta come up with something realistic here', a statement that might also be read to some extent as a comment on the film itself. The tools to be used in this endeavour are, therefore, more or less contemporary. The mission is to fly in two space shuttles: recognizable as a familiar product of our time, although advanced just enough to make a spectacular bumpy landing on the asteroid almost plausible. The secret X-71 model, we are told, has an impenetrable titanium alloy skin cover that makes it 'the toughest, meanest, most sophisticated space vehicle man has ever made'. It needs to be, if it is to stand up to the rigours of this action spectacular. The occupants of the shuttles also need to carry out their mission like proper action heroes, rather than bouncing around feebly in low gravity as Neil Armstrong is shown doing on a tape of one of the Moon walks. To this end we are introduced to the Directional Accelerant Spacesuit, which gives the occupants more control over their movements.

The slight pushing forward of the technology involved in these details is mentioned during the preparations for the mission but not made an issue during the action itself. The point seems to be to clear away some of the limitations posed by the world of 'real' space. The new elements are not very important in a positive sense, merely as devices that enable the viewer to suspend disbelief at some of the more unlikely heroics. Ideally, once introduced, they can be taken for granted and then forgotten. Their function is to allow us not to be worried by such issues. This achieved, *Armageddon* can proceed to offer satisfaction at the levels of spectacle, excitement and frontier heroism. The protagonists of *Armageddon* are rendered equal in heroism to those of an all-out science fiction such as *Independence Day*, a status marked by the rhetorical insertion into both films of an almost identical image: the statue of marines planting a flag on Iwo Jima, shot from a low angle against a golden sky: a definitive American icon of heroic endeavour.

Armageddon is an extremely big and noisy example of contemporary Hollywood spectacular. It offers a brand of spectacle different from that found either in *2001* or the *Star Wars* films, a version to be examined in detail in the next chapter. For the moment I want to focus on what it offers primarily at the level of narrative structure. *Armageddon*, like *Jurassic Park* and *Titanic*, is the kind of film often accused of sacrificing plausible or sustained narrative to the demands of a constant supply of spectacular set-pieces. It does batter the audience with a surfeit of spectacular action. It may seem crude and manipulative in many respects, but judgements such as this can overlook the fact that the narrative is carefully constructed, full of checks and balances that offer a wide range of potential reconciliations of various issues. Of particular interest in this chapter is the negotiation offered between the astronaut and NASA, on one side, and a more traditional version of frontier heroics on the other. The heroes of *Armageddon* are a motley crew of roughnecks, led by Harry Stamper (Bruce Willis). They occupy a classic instance of the displaced frontier domain, a hazardous oil-drilling operation on a rig in the South China Sea. Stamper is a tough self-made man whose role as owner of his own business does not prevent his 'hands-on' involvement in the action. His crew are a disparate bunch of eccentrics but apparently expert at their work. Stamper is recognized as 'the world's best deep core driller' and, inevitably, recruited to take his team on the mission to save the world.

Armageddon begins by establishing an opposition between the roughnecks and NASA. A good deal of fun is had with the contrast between the two, and between the treatments offered by *Armageddon* and *The Right Stuff*. The roughnecks undergo tests similar to those experienced by the astronauts in *The Right Stuff*. The Mercury astronauts are cast as a group of individuals not easily handled by NASA. This is taken considerably further in *Armageddon*, the tests appearing largely irrelevant and failed miserably. The NASA astronauts with whom the roughnecks are first confronted appear pasty and distinctly non-macho in their matching green jumpsuits. The response of the astronauts to their new colleagues is an obligatory: 'Talk about the wrong stuff!' NASA is a government agency and stands for doing things carefully and by the book, its astronauts highly trained and disciplined. The roughnecks are a loose-knit but emotionally close bunch of mavericks. One option for the film is to cast NASA as the 'bad' bureaucracy to which the 'good' guys are opposed, and elements of this are established. NASA appears to be part of a network of potentially sinister state forces, the favourite demons of the contemporary frontier tradition. It has been able to obtain from the patent office the design for Stamper's drilling rig; in other words, it is able to override the freedom of the individual entrepreneur to protect his own property, a hefty offence against the idealized 'American Way'. There are a number of dark hints suggesting how the initial suppression of knowledge about the asteroid is achieved. An amateur astronomer who claims the rights of discovery is traced by the FBI. One of the requests made by the roughnecks as part of their payment is: 'You guys wouldn't be able to tell us who actually killed Kennedy, would you?' It is answered with a blank look, but the joke is based on the lingering suspicion that these kinds of state institutions have access to such knowledge. But the narrative of *Armageddon* works to reposition NASA within this discursive structure. A series of manoeuvres enables NASA and its representatives also to be celebrated, and some of the differences to be reconciled.

The smoothing over of structural oppositions between NASA and the roughnecks is achieved partly through the working out of tensions among the latter. The early stages of the film find Stamper hostile to one of his men, the impetuous AJ (Ben Affleck), because he is in love with his daughter Grace (Liv Tyler). AJ is painted by Stamper as too young and immature, not to mention being a mere roughneck unfit for his daughter. AJ's shortcomings are demonstrated by a foolhardy decision, on the basis of a 'hunch', to restart a drilling operation Stamper had shut down for safety reasons. AJ's action provokes a dangerous incident in which a damaged drilling rig hits a gas pocket. This detail is built upon at crucial moments later in the film.

A similar situation develops when the roughnecks are working on an underwater simulation. AJ's team is tested when the computer simulates the drill hitting a gas pocket followed by a hard layer of iron. Stamper and another member of the team warn AJ to slow the drill. AJ refuses (and is promptly dubbed 'space cowboy' by one of the NASA men). Stamper repeats his warning, AJ pushes ahead and the simulator declares the transmission wrecked. AJ complains that the NASA computer was 'just playing it safe'; the rig, designed by Stamper, would have worked. Stamper's reply seems to shift the location of his character somewhat in the dynamic previously established. 'Those men in that room have zero tolerance for showing off, hot-dogging, going by your gut instinct or you trying to be a hero', he barks. He appears to side with the NASA position, to some extent, and against the perspective behind which the film puts its considerable weight.

Armageddon is, after all, precisely about 'showing off', 'hot-dogging', celebrating 'gut instinct' and creating heroes. The roughnecks do all of these things, and so does the film itself. It certainly 'shows off' its own loud special effects, it 'hot-dogs' and it sets out to create heroes – and its makers would doubtless claim to go by their 'gut instincts' rather than following computer programmes. So why should Stamper make such a speech? It seems to have two effects. One is to bridge the gap between Stamper and NASA to some extent, to help to 'save' NASA for the good side of any oppositions that are going to be asserted. The other is to begin to reconcile a dynamic the film establishes around the issues of youth and maturity and the break-up and reconstruction of family loyalties.

At the start of *Armageddon*, Stamper is accused by Grace of being immature. He loses his authority as a father figure, having to resort to his power as her boss to order her off the rig and away from AJ. Stamper is established as a less than satisfactory father, in conventional terms, having raised his daughter in a world of oil rigs and roughnecks. The film eventually seeks to reconcile these difficulties. Part of Stamper's problem, his men tell him, is a failure to recognize that Grace has now grown up and has a life of her own. The same goes for AJ. In the first gas pocket incident AJ is clearly in the wrong. The same seems to be the case in the second occasion, although the narrative appears to position itself equivocally. Yes, Stamper appears correctly to read the situation, but AJ also has a point. His words carry a good deal of weight in a film in which viewers are likely to expect a celebration of individual heroics and gut instinct rather than the calculations of computers. And if Stamper designed the rig, and he is the hero played by Bruce Willis, surely we can expect it to work triumphantly. Some kind of balancing act occurs in this sequence, also indicated by the terms in which Stamper makes his point. It is 'those men in that room' whose 'zero tolerance' he evokes, rather than exactly his own. He also proceeds immediately, against the strong wishes of NASA, to insist that his men be given the following night off – the eve of the mission. The extent to which he is identified with the perspective of NASA is hedged.

The third occasion in which AJ is in charge of a drill threatened with 'blowing' seems more conclusive. This is the real thing, on the asteroid, and the last hope of the mission. One team has already been lost to an explosion. The drill is going to blow again, warns Stamper, but this time he leaves AJ to 'make the call'. AJ pushes on and reaches the required depth for the successful destruction of the asteroid. Stamper relinquishes his authority to AJ, an 'Oedipal' transfer finalized when he sacrifices his life, forcibly taking AJ's place as the one who has to stay behind to set off the explosive. Stamper gives a final speech in which he says he always thought of AJ as a son, is 'damned proud' to have him marry Grace, and so on. Terrible clichéd stuff, of course, as is the final tear-jerking reconciliation between Stamper and Grace before he goes off to do his decent thing. Familial reconciliation is also offered in a more marginal detail, but packing an emotional punch, in the form of another member of the crew who becomes reunited with his estranged wife and son. We know from an earlier glimpse that relations between the couple are such that the mother has obtained a court order to keep him away; once he has become established as a global hero, however, any such realities appear to be wished away in tearful embraces.

On one level this is all 'dreadful Hollywood nonsense', but it merits close examination rather than dismissal because these kinds of magical reconciliations appear to be a significant aspect of the appeal of a film like *Armageddon*, along with its noisy spectacle. Magical reconciliation offers the prospect of having it all ways, a major characteristic of mainstream Hollywood production. The figure of Harry Stamper alone embodies a number of contradictory appeals. He is the wealthy owner of a company, but also a 'frontier' individualist. We are introduced to Stamper hitting golf balls at a Greenpeace vessel, but at the same time he says he gives the group $50,000 a year in donations. He can be immature, foolish, comic and heroic, but also responsible and heroic.

AJ is young, impetuous and foolish but also heroic and romantically locked into an embrace with Grace at the end of the film. Even the sleaziest of the roughnecks, Rockhound (Steve Buscemi), a source of much of the off-colour humour in the film, turns out also to be an unlikely 'genius' who obtained a double doctorate from MIT at the age of 22. Unlikely hero though he might seem, the increasingly crazed Rockhound represents the combination of qualities upon which the mission depends: the 'genius' expected of NASA (which turns out to be limited in scope) and the practical know-how and idiosyncrasy of the roughnecks. The entire spectacle of *Armageddon* can be taken at face value or, at times, as an overblown parody of the genre, complete with a joke about its summer 1998 rival *Godzilla* and references to other films including *Star Wars*, *Pulp Fiction* (1994) and *Dr Strangelove* (1964).

Some viewers might take pleasure in the reconciliation of one or another of these contradictions, or the whole bunch. It is a luxury to be able to have it all ways at once, with no responsibility for worrying about real issues that might remain on closer inspection. Alternatively, viewers are free to choose from a multitude of different entry points to the film.

A range of appeals are on offer and it is not possible to say with any certainty which might be picked up, in exactly what manner, and by which 'kinds' of viewer. As Edward Branigan puts it: 'Normally, the classical narrative does not give the impression of ambiguity, nor does it encourage multiple interpretations, but rather, like the chameleon, it is adaptable, resilient and accommodating. It will try to be what the spectator believes it to be.'[8] The existence of a range of potential attractions is an essential component of a blockbuster strategy that seeks to maximize the audience for each of a relatively small number of 'big' films.

Armageddon seems to offer something that can be described as a 'dominant reading'. Its gender politics, for example, is mostly comprised of macho posturing. If the 'dominant reading' is partly a move towards the reconciliation of contradictions, however, this involves an openness to identification with more than one side in some of the issues raised. It is not a question of a complete or total reconciliation of the various oppositions put into play. Instead there is a wealth of reconciliatory material, some elements pushed harder than others, and much of the effect is achieved simply by the pace, overwrought emotion and noisy spectacular impact with which the whole thing moves.

If *Armageddon* seems to move away from support for Stamper's partial identification with the NASA position midway through the film, this does not really matter because a number of other devices are brought into play to secure NASA's place among the heroics. The film adopts a strategy found widely in films that set up oppositions around issues of freedom/individualism vs. oppressive institutions. It inserts a third element, usually a specific part of the institutional complex, that prizes open a gap and allows another part to cross over to the other side. In this case, and it is hardly unique, it is the military and a bunch of not clearly identified 'presidential advisers' that perform the job. NASA may have its reservations, but it is the senior military presence in the film, General Kimsey (Keith David) who is most hostile. This is a theme that bubbles away beneath the surface but comes to a head when it turns out that there is a secret 'secondary protocol' for the mission. A series of mishaps mean the drilling operation on the asteroid is behind the clock and radio contact may be lost. The President and his advisers rule that the secondary protocol be put into operation, a plan according to which the military takes charge of the mission and explodes the nuclear weapon remotely on the surface. This is clearly a mistake: it will not work, a privileged NASA expert has informed us. More to the point, it cannot possibly be the right course of action in a Hollywood blockbuster if it wipes out the stars.

The executive director of NASA, Dan Truman (Billy Bob Thornton), establishes the institution's credentials as primarily on the side of the good guys by arguing against the secondary protocol with both the general and the President, although to no avail. The general gives his orders, with some reluctance. A group of burly men in berets march into Mission Control to take over. Truman quietly instructs one of his operators to kill the up-link through which the missile timer is being controlled, a development which distracts the military/astronaut commander of the mission Colonel Willie Sharp (William Fichtner) sufficiently for Stamper to overwhelm him. The link is soon re-established, but the move buys Stamper just enough time to convince Sharp to switch off the device. In proper pioneer style, Stamper makes his case in terms of the judgement of those on the spot rather than 'listening to someone that's 100,000 miles away'. Truman, for good measure, tells Stamper earlier in the film that he always wanted to be an astronaut himself, to wear a mission patch. The senior NASA man, shown to have some kind of disability, wants to join the frontier heroics. In return for Truman's help, one of Stamper's last moves is to tear off one of his patches for AJ to present to the mission controller on his return. This interaction is in keeping with many rhetorical flourishes throughout the film that give heroic status to the space programme.

Elements of this are also found in *The Right Stuff* and *Apollo 13*. The narrative spine of *The Right Stuff* may be structured around an opposition between test pilot and astronaut, but at the end, Yeager, the closest thing to the conscience of the film, concedes that the astronauts also have some of what it takes. The heroics of *Apollo 13* are shared between the three astronauts in space and the mission controllers at Houston. The chief controller is a former astronaut, a fact suggested intertextually by the casting of Ed Harris, who played John Glenn in *The Right Stuff*.

Armageddon starts with a space shuttle exploding after being hit by fragments of the asteroid (with possible echoes of the *Challenger* disaster), but ends with the shuttle presented as a symbol of triumph and hope. Children race through the street in carts rigged up to resemble it; others run with model shuttles held aloft in some unidentified run-down townscape where a wall displays a fading portrait of President Kennedy and the words 'Peace' and 'Life', an image that re-establishes the original idealistic 'new frontier' rhetoric. The troubled Hubble telescope also has a brief moment of stardom, flashing down early images of the asteroid with stunning cinematic speed and efficiency. One or two cynical notes are struck – Rockhound observes just before lift-off that 'we're sitting on 4 million pounds of fuel, one nuclear weapon and a thing that has 27,000 moving parts built by the lowest bidder' – but on the whole the film bathes the space project in an ecstatically heroic glow. *Armageddon* ends up as a public relations exercise for NASA, a factor not unrelated to the administration's cooperation in the making of the film. NASA occupies a position that can be described as contradictory or as reconciling oppositions, as it has often been situated in reality: an institution that is both technocratic bureaucracy and an embodiment of 'frontier' virtues. *Armageddon* helps to establish a sense that something resembling 'real' space travel can be reconceptualized in terms of action spectacle, frontier heroics and reconciliatory narrative dynamics.

4

Maximum Impact: Action Films

KB:	So what kinds of things do you like then, in a film, what would make you choose ...?
John:	Lots of blood.
Martin:	Yeah.
Lee:	Explosions.
Martin:	Good effects.
John:	Dead bodies.
KB:	Anything else? Plot, anything like that?
Martin:	We don't watch it for that! We watch it for the Action, well I do anyway.

Martin Barker and Kate Brooks[1]

> The success of American motion pictures lies in the greatest common measure of film-ness, in the presence of maximum movement and in primitive heroism, in an organic relationship to contemporaneity.

Lev Kuleshov[2]

The countdown timer of a bomb attached to a fuel tanker reaches zero. A quick shot of the injured body of the henchman who planted the device. He lies on the top of the tanker as it bursts into flames that shoot up, through him, towards the camera and fill the entire screen. In long shot from the side, flames blossom from the underside of the tanker, which has crashed onto a bridge. The flames take up most of the screen. Cut to a head-on shot of the bridge, flames and debris spreading to fill most of the frame. Another head-on shot shows flames bursting through the roadway. Cut to a closer shot focusing on the detail, flames once more dominating the image. From another angle flames continue to burst up through the road, sending cars and other debris flying. The screen is almost entirely filled with billowing flame. The car carrying the heroes speeds head-on towards us at the lower edge of the frame. A medium shot from the front shows the three occupants, two adults and a child. Flames and flying cars are visible behind through the rear window. Cut to a long shot of the bridge, dissolving in flame. A huge fireball and debris blasts out towards the screen and screen-right, almost entirely filling the frame. An extra-long shot shows the whole structure from the side, the huge explosion bursting towards the camera and magnified by its reflection in the river below. A overhead shot fills the screen with flames and dislodged sections of bridge/roadway which disintegrate as the flames roil upwards towards the camera. The tiny figure of a helicopter visible at the start of this shot is caught in medium shot as it is blown apart, filling the screen yet again with fire and debris. One large piece of wreckage cartwheels towards the camera, just missing to screen right. In long shot, the car drives at the camera, missing to the left, most of the screen filled with the flames that pursue the car.

A series of shots from inside the car include the flames behind, moving rapidly towards both vehicle and viewer. A long shot is filled mostly with flame and flying cars. A head-on perspective establishes the position of the car with the boiling fireball even closer behind, sending two burning cars high into the air, disappearing from the top of the frame. A long shot from the side shows the car approaching a toll booth, pursued closely across the frame by the fireball, the massive scale of which is clear as it passes, carrying two blazing cars above its leading edge. Head-on to the toll booths, we see the car carrying the heroes framed in the space of the centre booth, against a background inferno. The two flying vehicles veer off at angles above. The car shoots through the booth, which explodes almost instantaneously in its wake. The fireball – bigger than ever – takes over almost the entire frame. In medium-long shot from head-on the car is framed for a second time, an instant later, in the structure of the toll booths, which erupts into flames again. A series of shots show the two airborne cars plunging from the sky and the startled reaction of the occupants of the lead car. One flaming car flies directly over the top of their vehicle, the woman turning to watch its progress through the back and then the front window. The car lands, bursting into flames in their path and is only narrowly avoided. A big close-up shows the front wheels of their car driving into a wall of fire. A long shot from head-on resolves into a mass of flame as the falling car bursts into explosion. Close-ups of the occupants frame each against the inferno as the car swerves to avoid the falling debris. The car continues to move towards the camera, in medium-long shot, passing to screen left as the fireball appears to recede. An extra-long shot of the bridge from the side repeats an earlier view, but the flames are fading. Dissolve to a shot of the car driving towards the camera then passing to screen left, the inferno reduced to a dull glow in the distance.

Pause for breath! A sequence like this loses much of its impact when reduced to prose. On screen it zips by in some 49 'action-packed' seconds. According to my count there are 42 shots, not all of which I have listed separately. The sequence comes near the end of *The Long Kiss Goodnight* (1996), a climax that provides a good illustration of what is offered by the most frenetic examples of the contemporary Hollywood 'action' film. The kind of 'impact' provided here is found more widely in contemporary Hollywood, to varying extents, including many of the films already discussed in this book. Films that might be distinguished from one another according to generic characteristics have a good deal in common in this respect. The action movie has also established a category in its own right, however, recognized by both industry and viewers. This chapter will consider how exactly these films are structured, in terms of both spectacle and narrative.

Spectacle of a particular kind is clearly a central component of action films, although precisely how it works needs to be considered in greater detail. Some commentators, particularly Martin Barker and Kate Brooks, have argued that narrative is of little if any significance to the appeal of these films. Barker and Brooks stress the importance of taking account of what actual viewers *say* they get from action films, which produces an emphasis on the spectacular dimension. This is of interest in itself, but narrative is also important, even if its role is not usually acknowledged by viewers. It is important to the moment-by-moment experience of the films, including the experience of spectacle itself. It is also important in terms of underlying thematic oppositions similar to those I have already explored. This chapter will begin with an examination of what exactly is offered by the spectacular dimension of action films, before going on to explore how this can be related to narrative concerns.

'A series of blows to the consciousness and emotions of the audience'

So what exactly is the appeal of an action sequence such as the one from *The Long Kiss Goodnight* described above? Big explosions are very much the stuff of contemporary Hollywood action movies and have been at least since the establishment of the James Bond cycle in the 1960s (and perhaps a good deal further back). Bond movies often climax with the empire of the villain being consumed in vast conflagration. The scale of the explosive highlight of *The Long Kiss Goodnight* is rather smaller, but it is also from one perspective a more dynamic cinematic experience than that usually found in the Bond films.

How exactly is the sequence from *The Long Kiss Goodnight* constructed in relation to the filmgoer? Two major ingredients are apparent. First, the editing is extremely rapid. The shot succession is such that, at full speed, many individual images can barely be distinguished. Second, the dynamic of individual shots and montage effects often involves a rapid movement towards the camera. The car and, to an even greater extent, the fireball, are constantly thrust out towards the space occupied by the viewer. The frame is repeatedly filled or filling with a mass of flames that threaten to burst out from the screen. The effect is akin to that of films made in 3D, in which the audience is characteristically assaulted by a series of objects that appear to be projected into the auditorium. One of the most obvious examples is the chunk of helicopter debris that flies out towards the camera, missing closely on one side, to be followed the next instant by the car missing on the opposite side of the screen.

The sequence offers an 'in your face' experience, the effect established largely by the rapid pace of editing. Cuts tend to be made on movement, particularly the movement of the fireball, and serve to magnify its impact. Overall, the sequence is rapid and compressed, but individual moments are extended in time by the editing regime. The initial explosion of the tanker and its impact on the bridge is rendered in a quick-fire series of shots from different angles and positions that seems to present it happening more than once. Up to a point, this is standard procedure in the analytical editing patterns for which classical Hollywood is renown, offering a variety of perspectives on the action. The speed with which this is done here, together with the element of temporal overlap, creates an effect in some ways closer to the brand of montage celebrated by Soviet filmmakers and theorists such as Sergei Eisenstein, from whose writing the quotation used for the heading of this section is taken. The result of the editing is greater than the sum of the parts. Few Hollywood features present a literally full and complete view of the action. Conventional editing regimes offer a compressed and stylized perspective that actively constructs as much as it records events in front of the camera. An illusion of an 'ideal' and approximately 'objective' viewpoint is created, largely through the sheer familiarity and 'invisibility' of continuity editing patterns. The climactic explosion sequence of *The Long Kiss Goodnight* takes this form of stylization a significant step further, however. The distinction is not absolute, but the speed and design of the editing works with movement towards the camera to create a dynamic that seeks to recreate cinematically the very 'explosiveness' of the on-screen experience.

Another example of a departure from 'classical' editing continuity is found in the shots of the car framed in the gates of the toll booth. The destruction of the toll booth is depicted twice, in extremely rapid succession, although exactly what happens in the second shot is impossible to isolate at full speed. In a strict form of classical continuity editing this should be forbidden. An ability to avoid such overlappings has been identified as a key marker of the move from early to 'classical' Hollywood style, although even here continuity is often established impressionistically rather than through a literal adherence to the verities of time and space. The fleeting overlap in this case is clearly not a mistake but used to get the dynamics of the editing 'into' the action, to heighten the explosive impact for the viewer. The dynamics of the movement of the car and fireball towards the audience is increased through the use of the cut and the instant blur of repetition. Constant shifts of perspective are used throughout the sequence at a pace that keeps the viewer on edge and in some cases taken by surprise.

A similar effect is achieved in the rapid succession of the shots of helicopter debris and car coming out at the screen and passing the camera on either side. A particular kind of spectacle results from this explosive-impact editing. The explosion and fireball is not rendered as the kind of spectacle we are encouraged to sit back and admire from a distance, an option sometimes used in action spectaculars such as the Bond films, which are often keen to linger on the spectacle provided by expensive sets, stunts, physical effects or footage of 'exotic' locations. The first Bond film, *Dr No* (1962), ends with a big explosion, but shot in a single take from high above, a style typical of many Bond set-pieces. Rapid editing and elements of discontinuity are found in some fight sequences in the early Bonds, including *Thunderball* (1965) and *On Her Majesty's Secret Service* (1969), but such techniques are used sparingly.[3] The climax of *The Long Kiss Goodnight* is constructed to draw the viewer further into the experience. The protagonists are pursued and assaulted by the fireball and so, in a sense, is the audience; it is worth noting again how often the frame is more or less filled with boiling flames that appear to confront the viewer directly. The protagonists are being assaulted from all angles, constantly forced to shift their gaze one way or another, and so to some extent is the viewer.

The basis of these different kinds of spectacle can be analysed at a number of levels. There is a long history of debate in film theory about the relative merits of creating effects through montage assemblage or by using longer shots that seek to establish the more solid reality of the events unfolding in front of the camera. In André Bazin's classic account, this is a question of the very essence of the 'cinematic'. He argues against those who celebrate the 'essentially' cinematic qualities of montage:

'Essential cinema, seen for once in its pure state, on the contrary, is to be found in straightforward photographic respect for the unity of space.'[4] If the aim is to persuade the viewer of the material 'reality' of the staging, if not of the narrative events, impressionistic montage might not be the most effective strategy. A James Bond film wants to convince us that the filmmakers have visited its locations, have really gone to great lengths to build elaborate sets such as the artificial lake and underground volcano complex of Blofeld in *You Only Live Twice* (1967) and to perform hazardous stunt sequences before the camera. The use of a more contemplative form of spectacle here might be understood in Bazin's terms: 'It is simply a question of respect for the spatial unity of an event at the moment when to split it up would change it from something real into something imaginary.'[5] To create an effect through rapid editing is to risk destroying any sense that the action involved was actually played out at some level of reality. It is sometimes the signature of lower budget films. A more 'literal' staging preserves a measure of reality in the 'pro-filmic' event – although the difference is relative rather than absolute – and can be a way of calling attention to lavish expenditure, a key ingredient in the selling of the Bond cycle as big-screen spectacle. This is the particular strategy the Bond films have tended to adopt. They offer a version of spectacle based on the presentation of lavish plenitude, in both production design and 'exotic' locations, the appeal of the latter located initially in the historical context of the beginnings of the package holiday boom in the 1960s. Consistent commercial success kept the recipe largely intact to the end of the century.

What is at stake here is not any abstract 'essence' of cinema but a number of different approaches that might be used to a greater or lesser extent or favoured in one context or another. The explosive montage-based approach is used sparingly in some Hollywood action features, as in *The Long Kiss Goodnight*, which reserves it primarily for the climactic conflagration, and more heavily in others. Explosions that propel flames, vehicles and other debris at the viewer are widely used in *Independence Day*, for example, but only occasionally in *Twister*. *Jurassic Park* deploys a combination of styles, moving between the big emphatic, rapidly-edited close-up approach in some instances – largely confined to a few moments of intimate engagement with attacking dinosaurs – and more distanced framings that serve to increase the illusion of the 'pro-filmic' reality of the dinosaur effects. The fact that the dinosaurs occupy an entirely illusory space encourages a visual style rhetorically associated with the assertion of apparently solid reality before the camera. A similar sense of materiality is established by the contemplative extreme found in *2001: A Space Odyssey*. *Armageddon*, in contrast, offers an unremitting battery of impact effects (see Chapter 6).

Another variation is found in Hong Kong action films, which have often influenced their Hollywood counterparts. The pleasure of this form, for David Bordwell, is based on a combination of exaggerated expressive qualities and a more clearly delineated sense of the actual moves of performers than is offered by the Hollywood variety.[6] A classic martial arts film such as *Enter the Dragon* (1973) makes expressive use of sound and slow-motion, but usually holds a single-shot perspective on fight sequences to demonstrate the real capabilities of the star, Bruce Lee. *Police Story III: Supercop* (1992) offers a mixture of techniques. Editing is used to heighten fight and other action scenes, but the camera is also allowed to dwell on the performances of the stars, Jackie Chan and Michelle Yeaoh. A series of big explosions midway through the film displays a montage-based structure similar to the action sequences of *The Long Kiss Goodnight.* Like Hollywood, Hong Kong action has moved towards increasingly 'cinematic' or montage-based effects, a tendency that shifts the centre of marketing attention towards 'auteur' directors such as John Woo, who has also broken into the Hollywood mainstream, and away from the authenticity of on-screen performance. *Legend of Fong Sai Yuk II* (1993), directed by Corey Yuen, is just one of numerous films to have largely abandoned an emphasis on the integrity of performance in favour of the full panoply of montage effects including rapid cutting and emphatic temporal overlaps.[7]

Explosive editing provides a powerful source of impact that fits with the continued desire of Hollywood to offer large-scale spectacle to draw audiences to the cinema. It also seems consistent with Mark Crispin Miller's claim that some products of contemporary Hollywood have adopted the rapid, flashy and 'shallow' imagery of the television commercial or music video. Spectacular effects created by rapid editing and the movement of objects towards the camera may translate from big to small screen more effectively than forms of spectacle based on a more contemplative gaze at large-scale images such as the sets and locations of the latest Bond movie or a sinking *Titanic*, which might explain their prevalence in the contemporary Hollywood blockbuster. Any tendency towards a shift in this direction is clearly not absolute, given the existence of prominent examples of 'grand' spectacle such as *Titanic* and the complex overlaps between cinema and televisual media identified by Peter Kramer. Additional complications result from the association between the more contemplative or leisurely form of spectacle and 'pro-filmic reality', an association that makes this approach attractive when an effort is made to convince audiences of the 'reality' created by special effects. Neither could any movement towards more rapidly cut action spectacle be reduced to a single cause. If the increased commercial centrality of television and video is a significant factor, so too is the development of the very particular editing regimes of advertising or MTV, an aesthetic that makes the early Bond films appear pedestrian even if they were cut faster than normal for mainstream productions at the time of release.[8]

Today's action cinema is encouraged to adopt a frenetic approach if its impact is to be maintained in this cultural context, especially given the overlap between its audience and that of formats such as music video. These tendencies might account for a degree of movement back towards some rapid action-sequence editing in recent James Bond films, although the extent of this remains limited. An aesthetic suited to the small screen may be of particular relevance to the less expensive action film, a form, like horror, that has historically had a higher than average reliance on productions designed primarily for the home video market. The perceived importance of this kind of spectacle in the contemporary landscape of the industry might be one reason why the action format – like science fiction, traditionally the stuff primarily of cheaper 'B' movies – has moved into the big-budget mainstream in recent decades.

The effect of montage-based spectacle has much in common with the concept of 'attractions' developed by Eisenstein, the source of the term used by Tom Gunning in relation to early cinema. An attraction is defined by Eisenstein as 'any aggressive moment [...] that subjects the audience to emotional or psychological influence, verified by experience and mathematically calculated to produce specific emotional shocks in the spectator in their proper order within the whole.'[9] The purpose for Eisenstein is to wake the audience into an active engagement that can bring to the surface the contradictions of capitalism; effectively, to batter the audience into some kind of new dialectical synthesis. Hollywood's motives are very different, of course, but Eisenstein's prescription for a brand of cinema that works as 'a series of blows to the consciousness and emotions of the audience'[10] fits quite closely with the comments of action-movie fans interviewed by Barker and Brooks. One of the central pleasures of action films identified by their respondents was what Barker and Brooks describe as 'the joys of being "done to" by a film':[11]

> One whole way of talking about films describes a wish to be physically affected by them: typical (wanted) experiences are 'being knocked out of my seat', 'making me jump', 'hitting me between the eyes'. This is driven by a demand for 'pace'. A bad film is a 'slow' film, that 'sends you to sleep'. A good film of this kind doesn't just keep you awake, it *shocks* you awake repeatedly.[12]

The sequence from *The Long Kiss Goodnight* would meet with approval according to these criteria. It offers exactly the kind of impact or 'being done to' desired by the action fan, an effect found wanting in some examples of the genre. These viewers are not seeking to be awoken to some new understanding of the world, as Eisenstein might have hoped, but to be stimulated physically for its own sensuous pleasure. They want, as Barker and Brooks put it, 'to *participate* in the film',[13] to be directly acted upon by the film, an effect defined more than anything in terms of the pace at which the action proceeds, a quality that again makes the climax from *The Long Kiss Goodnight* seem a model example.

More instances of the 'impact aesthetics' offered by this sequence are not hard to find. They have become the staples of the contemporary action cinema. A good example is *The Rock* (1996), produced by Don Simpson and Jerry Bruckheimer, two specialists in the noisy action blockbuster. One of the biggest action sequences in *The Rock* is a car chase that ends in the obligatory orgy of destruction. The hero Stanley Goodspeed (Nicholas Cage) in a bright yellow Ferrari joins dozens of police in pursuit of escaped prisoner John Mason (Sean Connery). Pace again is the dominant effect for which the sequence strives. The chase includes extremely rapid editing, especially at the numerous moments of physical impact. Shots of the drivers of the vehicles are unsteady, giving the impression of having been grabbed with difficulty during real conditions of high-speed pursuit. Numerous objects come flying towards the camera. The illusion of speed is created primarily through editing, although other devices are also used. One is a variation on the trick of shooting moving objects through intervening structures such as fence poles or trees, which create a stroboscopic effect heightening the impression of speed. An extreme example is used in *The Rock*. As Goodspeed resumes his pursuit of Mason midway through the chase we are given what at first appear to be three extremely rapid shots of the Ferrari, little more than a yellow blur moving from right to left accompanied by three bursts on the soundtrack of the Doppler-effect noise made by a racing car passing at top speed. The car is moving fast across the frame, but the 'cuts' give the impression of greater speed that might literally be depicted. They create an illusion of high speed while freezing the action momentarily in a manner that renders the speed visible: real high speed shot in real time from a single camera would pass too quickly to register as anything other than a single blur. A closer analysis frame by frame shows that in fact no cuts have been used at all. There is just one shot, a fast pan from right to left. The Ferrari comes into the frame from the right but disappears behind a blue car moving in the opposite direction. It reappears as the blue car passes only to be obscured again, twice, by two white cars. The Ferrari leaves the frame on the left just as a red car enters from the same side. The effect is an impression of extreme speed, heightened by the motion of the other cars in a direction opposite to that of both the Ferrari and the panning camera.

In typical action film style, the scale of thrills and destruction increases with delirious implausibility as the chase proceeds. The climax comes when Mason's vehicle crashes into a San Francisco cable car that is forced downhill out of control. Close head-on shots of Goodspeed at the wheel of the Ferrari are intercut with what appears to be his point of view: a pair of unsteady shots of the road and cable car immediately ahead that swerve to match squealing-tyre noises on the soundtrack, offering the viewer a perspective in the middle of the action. The next series of shots focuses on the cable car and its operator. A number of rapid cuts include several impressions of the cable car coming towards the screen. This segment climaxes with an image that starts with the centre of the frame occupied in long shot by a parked car. The lower edge of the cable car is visible in the upper right-hand corner of the screen, scraping past the car and heading directly for the camera. The cable car appears to be about to pass closely on screen right, but a jagged section on the near side keeps coming directly at the screen until a blurry mass fills the entire right side. Only then, when it seems that it cannot miss, does this object suddenly veer away as the cable car passes in a low angle that finishes in such extreme close-up that the frame is filled by a blurred image of its side. When this sequence is viewed at full speed the edge of the cable car appears to smash directly into the screen, accompanied by a loud crash.

Explosive action: the fireball signature of the action movie sends a cable car into the air in The Rock, *© Hollywood Pictures Company, 1996. Ronald Grant archive*

The precise content of the image that follows in the next instant is impossible to discern even with the aid of a freeze-frame. The effect is an 'in your face' impact even greater than those already described. Not that the film wastes any time dwelling on such moments: the chase and progress of the cable car continues immediately, building to the inevitably fiery crescendo as the cable car slams into a group of cars that burst into flames, sending cars and entire cable car into the air. The cable car falls to the ground and comes sliding downhill towards Goodspeed's vehicle and, of course, towards the lap of the viewer. Goodspeed gets out just before the car is crushed and in time to round off the sequence with a witty one-liner, another typical characteristic of the form.

Another sequence from *The Rock* further confirms this impact-aesthetic, based to a large extent on pace and motion towards the camera, and helps bring out an additional feature common to each of these examples. Goodspeed and Mason, now well on the way to becoming action-movie buddies engaged in a dangerous mission on Alcatraz, are in a network of tunnels under the prison. An incendiary device is dropped in an attempt to flush them out. A long shot down one tunnel shows a fireball heading towards the screen. Cut to Goodspeed, who appears to have heard something in the distance. Cut back to the fireball coming closer until the flames fill our vision. Several more angles on the fireball follow, dividing approximately into shots in which it passes more or less across the field of vision and those in which it heads for the screen. The last part of the sequence starts with Goodspeed and Mason running towards the camera in two-shot, the fireball approaching from behind. At first they move in slow motion. Closer shots focus on their legs and then their mid-body sections, by now reduced to little more than silhouettes against the ever-encroaching fireball. This set of shots ends extremely rapidly and it is not clear exactly what happens even when it is viewed in still frames. The last couple of shots appear to be speeded up, or there may be a jump cut. At one moment two figures are in the frame; an instant later, there is only one. The screen then fills with flames. The effect is similar to those examined in *The Long Kiss Goodnight.* Normal continuity conventions are superseded by other techniques in the construction of moments of extreme impact. Anything like a strictly logical shot-sequence gives over into impressionistic effects designed to give the viewer some kind of vicarious experience of the explosive events on screen.

Each of these examples from *The Rock* and *The Long Kiss Goodnight* makes use of images in which aggressive movements assault the viewer head-on. But it is important to note that these movements are usually intercut with other images in which the dynamic of the impact is more lateral, across the screen rather than towards it. The movement of the out-of-control cable car in *The Rock* obeys this logic very clearly. One moment it is coming straight at the viewer, out from the screen, but an instant later it is slamming across the screen from one side to another. The effect is to give the viewer the thrills associated with direct assault but to ameliorate this with ostensibly more 'objective' perspectives. An entire sequence of action coming out at the viewer might be too much even for the devoted action fan, creating a chaotic and disorientating effect. To have a clear impact the assault requires a point of contrast, just as most action films are structured overall to move from periods of high intensity 'noise' to quieter and more reflective interludes. The mixture of more 'objective' and more 'subjective' viewpoints found in these films does not in fact differ greatly from the norms of 'classical' Hollywood construction, as we saw in *Jurassic Park* and *Titanic*. As Thomas Schatz puts it: 'The ultimate power of the cinema, particularly in the classic Hollywood tradition, is this tension between subjective identification and objective detachment, between participation in the action and the observation of it.'[14]

Another common factor in each of the action sequences discussed so far is the 'explosion and fireball', an essential ingredient in the recipe. No self-respecting action movie is complete today without at least some exploding fireballs along the way, whether they result in climactic conflagrations or just spice up the action along the way. Why fireballs so often? The fireball, it seems, offers one of the easiest ways to render visible the kinetics out of which action sequences are constructed. Unlike bullets, for instance, which are fired aplenty, usually from loud and flashing automatic weapons, a fireball has the virtue of being clearly visible. Bullets and other weapons can be slowed down, but to do so more than fleetingly is to risk losing the vital element of pace. The emphasis in big action shoot-out sequences is usually on the loudness of the gunfire, the brightness of muzzle flashes and the resulting impact of bullets, rather than the projectiles themselves. Fireballs can move quickly, but can also be rendered convincingly at speeds that provide time for the action that often occurs in their glowing paths. The fireball is all the force and intensity of the ideal action sequence compressed and made visibly manifest. Consideration of its qualities might also help to explain exactly *why* the impact aesthetic of the Hollywood action blockbuster is so pleasurable. Close textual analysis of action films helps to reveal how exactly viewers are given the impression of being 'done to' that they desire. But why should they desire such a thing? What kind of context might explain the appeal of action films?

It is useful here to return to the list of qualities drawn up by Richard Dyer in his work on the Hollywood musical. Many of these qualities – energy, abundance, intensity, transparency and community – are offered by these action sequences. They are overflowing especially with energy and intensity, in both the actions of the characters and the dynamics of cinematography, editing, music and other sounds. The fireball appears to be a burst of pure energy and intensity. The appeal of such characteristics, for Dyer, lies in the contrast they offer to the daily lives of most cinemagoers. The energy of the films can be seen as offering an escape from the exhaustion or pressures of modern life. Their intensity can be appreciated in contrast to the relative dreariness and monotony of everyday existence. Abundance – provided in the action film partly through an abundance of objects spectacularly to be consumed in flames – is a substitute for the scarcity that dominates real life for many people. Transparency and openness might be contrasted with the manipulations often involved in ordinary life and relationships, while the celebration of community can be seen as a substitute for the fragmentation so often seen as characteristic of the modern world. In Dyer's account the identification of such qualities, and their contrast with quotidian reality, is a way of analysing how entertainment products respond to real needs or shortcomings at a social level, even if they do this in a distorted manner.

This remains a very generalized explanation and raises many questions about the political or ideological significance of the films to which it has been applied. Dyer's account could easily be viewed from a Marxist perspective in which the films are seen as serving an ideological purpose by offering superficial satisfaction to needs or desires that might otherwise lead to demands for real change in social or economic relations. If life under capitalism (or patriarchy, neo-imperialism, or whatever formulation we use) is necessarily dull and oppressive for many, then offer them short-term stimulation and 'escape' at the movies. It would be wrong to dismiss this perspective entirely, but there is a danger that such analysis can fail to take into account the precise nature of the pleasures offered by this kind of cinema, and too easily assume that all such enjoyment has to be lined up unambiguously on one side or the other of a strict ideological equation. To dismiss these pleasures as merely involuntary complicity in the work of oppression is a one-dimensional approach. Audiences respond in differing ways, none of which are likely to reduce to simple accounts of ideological oppression or freedom to use materials in any way they choose. Responses are structured in various ways, including textual cues, social background and promotional discourses that shape audience expectations.[15]

Valerie Walkerdine suggests that action films such as Sylvester Stallone's *Rocky* and *Rambo* series, often dismissed as 'macho, stupid and fascist', are better seen as 'fantasies of omnipotence, heroism and salvation. They can thus be understood as a counterpoint to the experience of oppression and powerlessness.'[16] An attempt is made to locate 'the specific conditions of the formation of pleasures for particular groups at a given historical moment',[17] in this case the experience of a working-class masculinity for which fantasies of escape tend to be rooted in achievements centred around bodily rather than mental feats. Class, gender and other social dynamics are heavily involved in the production of particular kinds of pleasure in and for particular audiences, but in complex ways. These need to be examined within specific social and historical contexts, which can supply persuasive arguments.

Hollywood action films of the 1980s and 1990s have often been interpreted in terms of negotiations around the status of contemporary masculinity. Approaches based on social–historical context do not guarantee the security of single or definitive readings, any more than those founded on textual analysis, industrial strategy or interviews with audiences. A combination of such approaches is the best we can offer in the hope of providing a firmer foundation, especially where the findings at one level appear to confirm those of another, which seems to be the case in the contemporary action film. If the impact of the cinematic experience of action offers an escape from everyday life, it is significant that a similar juxtaposition is found in the narrative themes of many of these films. They often address, quite explicitly, the tensions between 'normality' and the world of action and spectacle.

'I don't use guns and I don't kick down doors'

Stanley Goodspeed is no conventional action man. He is employed by the FBI but as a chemical and biological weapons specialist rather than a field agent. Goodspeed is called on to help tackle a group of renegade Marines who threaten to unleash rockets loaded with nerve gas on the population of San Francisco if their demands are not met. Contrary to his expectations – although not those encouraged in the audience – he is required to join a team of commandos on a mission into the island stronghold. 'I'm just a biochemist,' he complains. 'Most of the time I work in a glass jar and lead a very uneventful life. I drive a Volvo, beige one. But what I'm dealing with here is one of the most deadly substances the earth has known.'

The reference to his car – a watchword, of course, for 'safe but dull' – is repeated later and plays an important part in the construction of his character. The juxtaposition between Volvo/safety and 'one of the most deadly substances' establishes a dynamic that runs through much of this film, and many other examples of the action genre.

The protagonist of the action film is sometimes a pure creature of action and adventure, a thoroughgoing professional at the game. James Bond is an obvious example, usually lacking the slightest semblance of a domestic life. But in many cases the hero is positioned more ambiguously, straddling the line between action-adventurer and something closer to 'normality.' So, if Goodspeed says he drives a Volvo, and we are to take this as symptomatic of his usual routine, it is not safe pottering about in a beige Volvo that we see, but the extreme antics of high-speed chase in a bright yellow Ferrari. He makes his work sound dull, a conclusion supported by our first glimpse of him fooling around in the laboratory to pass the time. Seconds later, however, an alert sounds and Goodspeed is fighting in his sealed glass chamber to defuse a bomb before it sets off a package of explosive and lethal sarin nerve gas.

These might be seen as symptoms of incoherence, of the narrative weakness of which action films often stand accused. 'Incoherence' in itself makes a certain sense in popular cinema, or any other cultural product aimed at large and potentially diverse audiences. It may be a symptom of 'offering something to everyone'. This is always worth bearing in mind when we engage in ideological readings of Hollywood films. The elements do not necessarily 'add up' to a single detachable meaning.[18] But many of the contradictions within the films considered here seem to map into a reasonably stable pattern. What appears to be offered is not just random and contradictory items but some kind of *negotiation* between the two extremes. Goodspeed is cast as a relatively ordinary character, but one capable of action heroics in extremity. When the rest of the commando-raid party are wiped out in a gun battle, Goodspeed's reaction is to go almost to pieces while Mason, a former SAS man, is largely unmoved. Confronted with the twitching limbs of a crushed body, Goodspeed is barely able to continue; to Mason it is all in a day's work. There is a good deal of play with the issue of Goodspeed's competence in this arena, but when it comes to the final conflict he is able to prevail, earning his spurs as a fully-fledged action hero. He defeats the last and craziest of the bad guys and injects himself in the heart to negate the effects of a breached nerve gas capsule; he retains sufficient self-presence to send the success signal, falling to his knees and holding the flares aloft in a Christ-like position; he does all this just before a flight of jets bombs the island to obliteration. One bomb is released, just enough to create the obligatory climactic explosion and to send Goodspeed flying heroically into the sea.

We never really doubt that this will happen, of course, as the expectation is structured into the narrative in several ways. The early evidence of Goodspeed's skill in the car chase bodes well for his future capabilities, but the strongest expectations are forged by the familiar conventions of the genre. It would be a big surprise, and a frustration to most viewers, if a star character whose action abilities are constantly under question did not turn out to deliver the goods in the end. The associations brought to the part by a particular performer play an important part in the shaping of these expectations. If the star of an action movie is Sylvester Stallone or Arnold Schwarzenegger there will be little doubt that the character ultimately has what it takes. The associations brought by Nicholas Cage are rather different. *The Rock* established Cage in the noisy action genre, a characterization developed in *Con Air* (1997) and *Face/Off* (1997). Cage as an established star, carrying associations across a body of performances, brings to the genre echoes of more quirky roles in films such as *Birdy* (1984), *Wild at Heart* (1990) and *Leaving Las Vegas* (1995). The existence of different associations at an intertextual level may strengthen the ability of the performer to reconcile or blur differences within any single text.

If Stanley Goodspeed embodies contradictions between dullness/routine and excitement/adventure the same goes even more explicitly for the central character of *The Long Kiss Goodnight.* The plot is organized around the dilemma facing a woman suffering from amnesia. Samantha Caine (Geena Davis) works as a schoolteacher in New Jersey and has memories going back only eight years. She lives with a nice man and has a daughter conceived towards the end of her earlier life. Her past starts coming back to haunt her after she is injured in a car crash. Samantha Caine turns out to be Charlene 'Charly' Baltimore, an assassin who worked on illegal 'black bag' operations for the State Department. At the start of the film Caine occupies a world of cosy domesticity: warm, enveloping and Christmassy. The world of action spectacular gradually invades this domain. From endearingly incompetent chopping of vegetables for supper, Caine suddenly becomes possessed by the spirit of her past. She wields the sharp knife with a skill and dexterity that develops from chef-like slicing of carrots to expertly spearing a thrown tomato against a cupboard door. Before long one of the bad guys from her past breaches the family sanctum, breaking in amid bursts of explosive gunfire. Caine hurls her daughter Caitlin through a blast-hole in the wall to the safety of a treehouse before engaging the assailant in a tough and painful fight, the violence of which is felt more deeply for its location within the domestic scene.

Most telling in *The Long Kiss Goodnight* is Caine/Baltimore's shifting attitude towards Caitlin. In between the two incidents described above Caine takes her daughter ice-skating. Caitlin is nervous and uncertain on the ice. Caine is unsympathetic. Caitlin falls, hurts her arm and cries, saying she wants to go home. Caine's voice turns icy as she snaps at the girl to 'stop being a little baby and get up'. She adds, sternly: 'Life is pain: get used to it.' Her past life is beginning to take over and the possessing demon makes her a bad mother. A contradiction is established between the world of the assassin and that of the home-maker. The two appear to be mutually incompatible and a struggle begins for the woman's soul. Samantha Caine was meant only to be a cover story for one of the assassin's missions. Now consciously choosing the identity of Baltimore, she undergoes a physical change of image, cutting her hair shorter, dyeing it blond and wearing heavy make-up. Challenged by the private detective Mitch Henessey (Samuel L. Jackson) for failing to contact Caitlin at Christmas her angry response is, 'I didn't ask for the kid. Samantha had the kid not me. Nobody asked me.'

The domains of domesticity and assassin are brought closer together when Caine/Baltimore sneaks back into her home in search of a bracelet given to Caitlin which holds the key to a safety deposit box full of money. At first the sequence seems to reconfirm her absence of feeling for the child, whose bedroom she searches roughly before snatching the bracelet from the neck of a favourite bear. She pauses, however, on hearing the sound of carols from the church opposite and uses the telescopic scope of her rifle to watch the scene inside where Caitlin is dressed as an angel, dancing in slow motion. The moment is suspended within the contradiction between her two identities. The tool of cold and pre-meditated killing is used to give access to the world of emotion, love and domesticity. The domain of violent adventure takes over again as enemies turn up and Caine/Baltimore rushes out to rejoin the action. The two dimensions come back together in more sustained fashion when the bad guys kidnap Caitlin and demand that Caine/Baltimore gives herself up in return for her daughter. Caine/Baltimore ends up a prisoner, along with Caitlin, and has to perform a series of unlikely heroics which reaches its climax in the sequence with which this chapter began. Now, however, the action heroics are tightly integrated with the protection of the daughter and the reconstruction of the family unit. Caine/Baltimore is able to combine the two roles at once, offering some reconcilation of the opposition between domesticity and action-adventure.

Henessey suggests, significantly, that both aspects of her personality might always have been present. 'You know, her personality had to come from somewhere,' he says, referring to the Samantha Caine character Baltimore is seeking to banish. Maybe Samantha was not just an act, he suggests later: 'Maybe you forgot to hate yourself for a while.' Caine/Baltimore might *always* have combined elements of both identities. A choice might not be necessary between one extreme or the other. We can have it both ways: the nurturing domestic figure of Samantha Caine *and* the capable action heroics of Charly Baltimore, just as Stanley Goodspeed can combine a dose of all-out action heroics with a relatively normal life. This may be flattering to the audience as it helps to bridge the gap between the world of the cinemagoer and that of the action hero. A huge gulf separates most of us from the all-out action hero, but characters like Caine/Baltimore and Goodspeed offer more easy points of access to and identification with the action universe. 'Having it both ways', as we have seen elsewhere, can be one of the most pleasurable indulgences offered by popular films. Very real contradictions are given imaginary – if superficial – reconcilation in the process. The real limitations of domestic life in the nuclear family are wished away, along with a host of complex social and political issues.

Domesticity plays a relatively small part in *The Rock*, but it is an ingredient carefully added to the mix. Immediately after his first encounter with action thrills and spills, in the laboratory incident, Goodspeed recovers at home and finds out that his girlfriend (now to become fiancée) is pregnant. Goodspeed is rapidly removed from any physical contact with the domestic environment, but the woman and unborn child exist in the background, as another pole in his life and also as potential victims of a nerve gas threat to San Francisco. Mason is caught in a similar dilemma. A reluctant conscript on the mission – he is offered freedom from prison in return for his expert knowledge of the Alcatraz tunnels – Mason has a grown daughter living in the city. In one respect Mason is very much the all-out action hero, capable of extreme feats even at an advanced age. But his character is also qualified by an intellectual capacity that appears to have been shaped by decades of study in prison. Action heroics again meet 'civilization', and it is in terms of a shared knowledge of Greek that Mason and Goodspeed first achieve a measure of personal contact.

Women characters in action movies typically exist on the margins, as in *The Rock*. This is clearly not the case in *The Long Kiss Goodnight*, whose action hero is a woman. The film can be seen in the context of other texts of the 1980s and 1990s in which women performed the action heroics traditionally ascribed to men. Prominent examples are the *Alien* films (from 1979), *Thelma and Louise* (1991) and the *Terminator* films (1984, 1991). As Yvonne Tasker suggests, the existence of such films complicates any one-dimensional view of the gender politics of Hollywood action cinema. In *The Long Kiss Goodnight* the domesticated male figure, the man with whom Caine/Baltimore has set up household with her daughter, performs a role analogous to that of the woman in the male-dominated action film. He stays at home with Caitlin, promising to stick with Caine/Baltimore whatever she finds out about her past, and remains absent from the bulk of the film. The gender-role reversal clearly has major implications and it would be a mistake simply to assert that *The Long Kiss Goodnight* and *The Rock* can be reduced to the same narrative pattern. They have all sorts of possible readings of their own, some of which might be divergent. But they share one quality in the handling of the broad opposition between the worlds of domesticity and action-heroics: a negotiation of a way between these two spheres, and an imaginary reconciliation. If radical changes of meaning occur when the male action hero is replaced by a woman – and much debate has been had on exactly what is the result[19] – it may be all the more significant that some elements of the narrative dynamic remain so much the same.

Parallels can be established between the protagonists of these films and those of the classic western. Their positions can be charted on a continuum that runs from the unmodified all-out action hero (the frontier 'savage', of whatever culture) and the representative of settled domesticity. The central characters tend to occupy a mediating position between the two extremes. The dimension of action heroics is generally favoured, as in the classic western. But characters who stand purely for the world of action, with no hint of domesticity or 'civilization', tend to be negatively drawn. James Bond lacks a domestic life but exudes 'sophistication' and a sense of perspective, which keep him on the right side of the divide. An example from the other side is Timothy (Craig Bierko), one of the principal villains of *The Long Kiss Goodnight.* His place beyond the pale is indicated by a general viciousness, but the case is proved when he is confronted with the evidence that he might be Caitlin's father. The revelation comes as he is about to lock mother and child into a freezer to die: a hint of discomfort crosses his face but nothing sufficient to halt his plans.

The favoured action-oriented characters are located on terrains that have the characteristics of a modern equivalent of the frontier. Charly Baltimore operated secretly in the margins of the state apparatus. Mason was with the British SAS, an elite commando unit. The team he accompanies into the Alcatraz tunnels is made up of SEAL commandos. General Frank Hummel (Ed Harris), the 'madman' who threatens San Francisco with a nerve gas attack in *The Rock*, is from a Marine reconnaissance unit with a history of illegal operations behind enemy lines. They are all distinguished from mainstream forces or bureaucratic procedures. They require the kind of operation on the terrain of the enemy that characterizes the classic image of the frontiersman in American mythology, committed to direct and stealthy action that involves immediate hands-on skill and remains free from the confines of formal rules of engagement. The significance of this characterization is highlighted by what might seem to be the anomalous placement of Hummel in this scheme. Hummel's character and motivations are carefully delineated to ensure that he is not the real bad guy of the piece. His motivation is presented as honourable, even if his methods seem extreme.

Hummel has taken direct action only after exhausting all possible avenues of complaint, and his case is handled sympathetically. His protest is against the failure of the military or government to provide for colleagues who died in the course of unconventional duties in Iraq and elsewhere, while the ransom he demands is to come from a Pentagon slush fund, the proceeds of illegal arms sales. The real enemy is not Hummel but anonymous state forces that treat its servants badly and countenance activities such as arms sales. It is made clear that Hummel never intended to fire the rockets but hoped to succeed through bluff. Two members of his team who are eager to go ahead with the attack are detached from close association with Hummel, singled out as individuals who have not worked with him in the past and generally characterized as crazed-action-movie-bad-guys. In frontier terms, they are men of action and adventure who have crossed the line into all-out savagery and inhumanity. In terms of contemporary gender politics, their macho posturing is an excessive masculinity, separated off to avoid contaminating versions of 'masculine' action heroics the film wants to celebrate but to reconcile with domestic and more general human responsibility.

Dark forces of the state are also responsible for Mason's fate, imprisoned for 30 years without trial after being caught trying to escape with microfilm records from the files of FBI chief, J. Edgar Hoover. The files contain 'all our most intimate secrets from the last half century', including those paranoid conspiracy favourites the 'alien landing' at Roswell and the truth about the JFK assassination. The heroes are able to unveil these secrets, stolen by Mason and picked up by Goodspeed after Mason reveals where they have been hidden. *The Long Kiss Goodnight* is equally careful in its apportionment of blame. The climax involves a plot to kill 4000 innocent civilians by exploding a chemical bomb in the centre of a town. This is not the work of 'terrorists', however, although designed to look that way. The plot is hatched by the CIA to scare Congress into voting through funds cut since the end of the Cold War.

Baltimore is also an embarrassment to the 'new' CIA, a hangover from the past who must be eliminated. Again, it is the machinations of shady forces located in the state bureaucracy that is the source of evil. Individual heroics are in each case juxtaposed with the corrupt and dissembling powers of vast institutions. A blatant intertextual reference is made in the epilogue, when Caine/Baltimore has been enriched and secured by the case of money and documents recovered from a safety deposit box. She is driving through what appears to be a western landscape in an open-top car which, together with the scarf she is wearing, is an obvious nod to the part played by Davis in the 'women's frontier/road movie' *Thelma and Louise*. Caine/Baltimore ends up in a setting that establishes a classic compromise between the world of the 'savage' frontier and that of 'civilization': a large 'pioneer' style house that appears to be made of logs in a green and hilly open landscape. She has settled down with her man, but removed from a suburban setting to the pastoral: a gorgeous late-afternoon light bathes the scene as the family group frolics in the grass with a dog and several sheep. This is domestic tranquillity in that ideal 'middle landscape', civilized but close enough to nature for any corrupting potential to be avoided. Caine/Baltimore can still throw a handy knife, however, as she demonstrates just before the credits roll. Goodspeed is also glimpsed in an epilogue in which he and his partner are out on the road, this time at a church in Kansas where Mason hid the microfilm containing all those dark federal secrets. Freedom and openness; the rural landscape and the airing of conspiracy: again, the associations are strongly drawn.

The Long Kiss Goodnight and *The Rock* are not exceptional in their engagement with these issues. Similar oppositions between the realms of domesticity and action-adventure and similar juxtapositions between 'frontier' heroes and corrupt or incompetent institutions are commonplace in the contemporary action genre. One of the most explicit versions is found in *True Lies* (1994), in which Arnold Schwarzenegger plays a secret agent who adopts the cover disguise of a dull computer salesman: even to his wife. He resembles a Charly Baltimore who has not forgotten that Samantha Caine is only a façade. His wife, bored with the all-too-convincing front of domestic routine, takes up with a used car salesman who poses as an agent in order to pick up women. The Schwarzenegger character finds out and sends his wife on to a fake mission to give her the dose of excitement she craves. Things go awry and the fake mission becomes confused with reality. The wife becomes involved in real danger and excitement. A large-scale semi-parodic spectacular finale is followed by an epilogue in which the husband and wife have become a secret-agent double-act, neatly overcoming the contradiction between the demands of married stability and glossy excitement. Similar narrative themes are also to be found in the *Lethal Weapon* series (from 1987) and on the margins of the *Die Hard* films (from 1988): two big-grossing cycles that are among the most high-profile of Hollywood action spectaculars. In all of these cases the action heroes are individuals with at least some characteristics that can be linked to those of the mythical 'frontier' tradition, carefully positioned outside the mainstream of bureaucratic institutions but also distinguished from contemporary versions of the 'savage' existing beyond the pale.

If the high-budget action spectacle of these films has to be understood in terms of the particular strategies adopted by Hollywood in the 1980s and 1990s, the narrative themes can certainly be read up to a point in terms of the gender politics of the time. The male action hero was given a new lease of life from the 1980s onwards, a decade that saw the rise to mega-stardom of hyper-muscled performers like Stallone and Schwarzenegger.[20] The popularity of such figures has often been seen as part of a backlash against the demands of feminism, reasserting a particular brand of macho heroics. Some have argued that these performances can be read differently, their hysterical excesses manifesting a version of masculinity in crisis and overproduced in an act of desperation that lays bare its artificiality.

As Yvonne Tasker suggests, such opposed readings are better replaced by a 'both/and' approach that allows for the possibility of a multiplicity of available meanings.[21] It is not easy to draw a line between representations that reflect or express confident realities and those which might compensate for absence or doubt. The way discourses of gender are manifested in these films certainly appears far from solidly fixed. To some extent they attempt to square the circle, to wallow in orgies of action and destruction conventionally characterized as 'masculine' but ameliorated or perhaps excused by a measure of 'feminine' domesticity and emotion. This is partly a matter of narrative thematics, partly of trying to include some cross-gender audience appeal.

Racial stereotypes can also enter the equation. In the *Lethal Weapon* series the gap between action heroics and domesticity is mediated by the figure of the more mature and nurturing black detective (Danny Glover), who to some extent fulfills the role of the stereotypical black 'mammy'.[22] Similar roles are performed by Mitch Henessey in *The Long Kiss Goodnight* and the black patrolman (Reginald VelJohnson) who serves as ally to John McClane (Bruce Willis) in *Die Hard* (1988).

In the *Lethal Weapon* films the all-out action hero Riggs (Mel Gibson) is portrayed initially as unstable, his connection to the 'normality' signified by the domestic scene having been severed by the death (which later turns out to have been the murder) of his wife. By the end of *Lethal Weapon IV* (1998) Riggs appears to have been brought back into the fold, after a series of movements towards and away from the edge; he fathers a child and is on the verge of marriage. Like his partner, he has to face up to the facts of increased age and responsibility; not that this prevents the pair from continuing to engage in a series of unlikely comic-action set-pieces. Many 'real' issues that do not admit of neat solutions are conveniently bypassed by the mythic or ideological sleights of hand that seem to be performed in these films across heavily loaded terrains of race and gender, a process that does not necessarily 'fool' viewers but offers an enjoyable fantasy located again in the utopian possibility of 'having it all ways'.

There is plenty of significant narrative 'work' going on in these films, whether it is grounded in broader social dynamics or industrial-commercial strategies, which brings us back to Barker and Brooks' comments on the limited importance of narrative in the contemporary action cinema. For Barker and Brooks the role of narrative is strictly secondary:

> For those wishing to be 'done to', narrative is like a carrier-wave, similar to the role that rails play on a big dipper – necessary to carry you along, but in themselves not the point of the exercise. Only if badly designed, if they don't get you safely and unobtrusively to the heights and depths, are they even worth mentioning. For those seeking spectacle, narrative is the means by which decisive moments of technology and effects can be reached appropriately. They frame those moments, and help them intensify our experiences properly – but again, are only worth noticing in themselves when they intrude awkwardly.[23]

This concept of narrative as a carrier-wave is useful up to a point but tends to underestimate the importance of narrative to the overall experience of the films. In its own terms, taking narrative at the level of linear plotting, it still suggests that narrative organization matters a great deal. If the carrier-wave is faulty the thrill ride will not work. But this makes narrative organization sound like an essentially separate and secondary process. A distinction has to be made between elements explicitly noticed and discussed by viewers and those that remain taken for granted. It is precisely the nature of Hollywood narrative strategy to appear more or less 'invisible' to the viewer except where it goes amiss. This does not in any way reduce its significance, including its importance to those whose priority is an effective delivery of action-spectacle. Even in terms of merely 'framing' the action sequences Hollywood narratives are carefully constructed devices.

Films such as *The Long Kiss Goodnight* and *The Rock* are more than just a series of action spectacles loosely strung together on a haphazard plot. *The Long Kiss Goodnight* has a finely-tuned narrative structure. Information about Caine/Baltimore's background is supplied to us (and to her) in precisely measured details throughout the film. The narrative is based around a central enigma (Samantha Caine's mysterious background). The viewer is given numerous partial answers to the question, but also led astray by 'snares' such as the discovery that she was engaged to be married just before losing her memory (it turns out that the 'engagement' referred to being locked-on to a target for assassination).[24]

Viewers are offered the sensual pleasures of high-impact action but are also invited to take part in a measured and enjoyable game of knowing and not knowing, concealment and revelation. Many small matters of detail in the early part of the film turn up with added significance as the plot develops, a quality typical of Hollywood narrative. The action sequences do not occur randomly but within a structured pattern. They play an important part in the narrative juxtaposition of domestic and action-spectacular realms, particularly during the climax in which the two realms are brought decisively together. This is another case in which spectacular impact is used to reinforce rather than to undermine narrative dynamics. There is also an internal structure to the relations between different moments of spectacle. The finale is the third in a series of sequences involving explosive fireballs, each building to a grander scale than its predecessor.

The narrative structure of *The Long Kiss Goodnight* is perhaps more carefully delineated than that of some other examples of the genre but this remains a matter of degree. It might be contrasted to *The Rock* in some respects, which contains a larger proportion of sequences devoted primarily to action. Lengthy action sequences are spread throughout the film, while the only extended sequence in *The Long Kiss Goodnight* occurs at the end. The big car chase is prolonged for some four and a half minutes quite early in the film and seems to have only minimal relevance to the main plot action on Alcatraz. It might be seen as a spectacular distraction from the business of the narrative, but it also plays a part in the establishment of narrative patterns, particularly in establishing the credentials of Stanley Goodspeed.

The action sequences in these films are centred around the main characters, the principal bearers of the narrative dynamic. *The Rock* has its own structures of enigma, partial answers and eventual resolutions. Background information about Mason is supplied in carefully measured doses across the length of the film. *The Rock* is a more 'down the line' action movie than *The Long Kiss Goodnight*, and as such forces in quite large chunks of exposition in the early stages. There is a sense that much of this is being got out of the way to enable the viewer to sit back and enjoy the action spectacle. But the various issues with which the film engages remain in play throughout. A strong linear narrative thread remains important throughout, most obviously in the countdown/deadline structure around which this and so many action narratives are organized.

What about 'underlying' narrative themes such as the negotiation of the relationship between domestic and action realms that is close to the surface in the films considered here? A political analysis might try to reverse the proposition of Barker and Brooks, to argue that the appeal of action sequences might be the 'carrier-wave' for the ideological implications of the narrative themes. Action and spectacle could be the sugar on the ideological pill. This would be a polemical claim, however, of no more help than a disregard for the importance of narrative. What is needed instead is a recognition of the importance of both dimensions. The importance of action spectacular is easier to measure, although this has not been done very often, because it is the kind of thing most viewers of these films appear to talk about if asked. Attributing significance to thematic structures, to which viewers allow little if any importance, is inevitably a problematic business. There is no hard empirical evidence, although the extent to which similar structures are found repeatedly in successful products does provide grounds for the construction of at least a plausible case. There is always a danger of analytical flights of fancy that have little demonstrable root in the real experiences of filmgoers. But there is an equal danger in dismissing aspects of popular cultural products on the grounds that they are not explicitly addressed by audiences.

Barker and Brooks found what they describe as 'a virtual disinterest in the plot of films. These could be digested, and spat out, in a single phrase: "just the usual. Goody wins, baddy dies." '[25] Narrative content could effectively be discounted, an attitude that seems to confirm the conception of narrative as just a 'carrier-wave' for action-spectacle. From the perspective of an ideological analysis, however, that which is discounted or almost invisible on the grounds of its routine familiarity is precisely the material that needs to be interrogated. This is often the stuff of dominant ideological formulations, familiar 'common sense' understandings that construct very particular interpretations of the world (with particular social and political implications) but that have become sedimented into the level of 'taken for granted' everyday assumptions, the conceptual air we breathe. Nothing, perhaps, is more deserving of investigation than that taken to be merely 'obvious'.

To take one further example, *Indiana Jones and the Temple of Doom* (1984) is an 'action-adventure' film that at one point literalizes Barker and Brooks' image of narrative performing a role like that of the rails on a fairground ride. A lengthy chase sequence takes place on the underground rail wagon system of a mining complex (a similar incident occurs, much more briefly, in *The Rock*), the tracks carrying the protagonists through a rollercoaster series of thrills and spills. The whole film is a good example of the action cinema in which a relentless series of big set-pieces appears to move mechanically from one high point to another, overriding any serious narrative interest. The film is bristling with fairly explicit themes, however, generally of a decidedly racist and sexist tenor. When the primary concern is to shape narratives as 'carrier waves', to move viewers effortlessly from one action spectacular to another, it is the most conventional and familiar cultural frameworks that are usually pressed into service, precisely because their currency renders them relatively invisible.

A set of narrative themes organized to provide a challenge to racism or sexism would more likely be perceived as trying to impose a 'message' on the audience. The imposition of such 'messages' is anathema to the respondents of Barker and Brooks. They express this not in relation to any challenge that might be made to their own assumptions about the world, but purely in terms of the harm the imposition of a 'message' might do to the seemingly otherwise undiluted experience of the spectacle. That which is a familiar part of the institutionalized and taken-for-granted cultural reality we inhabit is far less likely to be experienced as a 'message', and therefore serves better as a 'carrier-wave' for the action. This, rather than any more active participation in a 'backlash' against the limited gains of anti-racism and anti-sexism, might be one of the main reasons for the generally reactionary nature of the narrative stuff of so many contemporary Hollywood action features.

Much of the concern of Barker and Brooks is directed at a reading of such 'implications' of Hollywood films because of what this is assumed to mean in terms of the 'effects' of popular cultural products, an agenda often pursued in the interests of censorship and on the grounds of non-existent evidence. I am not suggesting that the ideological assumptions that appear to be built into so many of the films discussed in this book have 'effects' as such. They can have 'implications' without actually bringing about any discernible or measurable change in attitudes or behaviour. This is because they tend to re-confirm or negotiate already dominant cultural assumptions, a process that itself seems likely to be pleasurable for the viewer. The films do not need to have a conscious 'meaning' which audiences 'take away' from the experience. The fact that familiar taken-for-granted meanings exist within the film enables members of the audience to pay them little attention; they constitute a comfortable ground from which to enjoy the action. Discourses based on dominant ideologies tend to render the world in reassuring and recognizable form. As Jean-Louis Comolli and Jean Narboni put it, in a now classic editorial from the French journal *Cahiers du Cinema*: 'when we set out to make a film, from the very first shot, we are encumbered by the necessity of reproducing things not as they really are but as they appear when refracted through the ideology.'[26]

This is not the result of some devious political manipulation but an appeal to the already-familiar that is explicable in commercial terms. It seems more plausible to make a case for the role of products such as Hollywood films in a broader cultural process of re-confirming or negotiating existing meanings than to make claims about the specific 'effects' of individual texts or genres; effects that, if they exist, are impossible to isolate from other factors. What kind of balance might be struck between a passive 'reflection' and a more active 'reinforcement' or 'negotiation' of dominant norms is a big question not easily answered. Cultural meanings are always in process to a significant extent. Meanings are fixed quite rigidly by particular discourses in particular times and places but they remain ultimately provisional, open to question or in need of ongoing reinforcement.

5

Seriously Spectacular: 'Authenticity' and 'Art' in the War Epic

> The practical effects gave us all – the crew, the actors, and myself – a feeling of actually being under combat conditions, and the actors couldn't help but react to it. Often we would walk away from a setup with our hands shaking, and it informed everyone's performance. It certainly reinformed me, from shot to shot, how I needed to tell the story.
>
> Steven Spielberg[1]

> I am violently, viscerally affected by *this* image and *this* sound, without being able to have recourse to any frame of reference, any form of transcendental reflection, or any Symbolic order. No longer does a signifying structure anticipate every possible perception; instead, the continual metamorphoses of sensation preempt, slip and slide beneath, and threaten to dislodge all the comforts and stabilities of meaning.
>
> Steven Shaviro[2]

The door of a landing craft opens, exposing the troops inside to a hail of machine-gun bullets. An extremely unsteady hand-held camera puts us in the thick of the mayhem on board, blood spots flecking the lens. Soldiers eventually scramble ashore under unremitting gunfire, cowering behind anti-tank obstacles in a surf that soon runs red with blood. The camera stays close and highly mobile, to dizzying effect, following the troops up the beach, most of them falling on the way. A cacophony of bullet impacts and explosions pounds oppressively in the ears. Gore and agonized suffering fills the screen on all sides. We are made to endure this painful spectacle, shot tightly in close and mid shots, for a solid 20 minutes, with only the briefest moments of respite, before moving into a quieter interlude in which one infantryman sobs. The opening D-Day landing sequence of *Saving Private Ryan* (1998) is an assault on the viewer almost as much as on the beaches of Normandy.

Another war epic, *Apocalypse Now* (1979), starts with a rather different kind of spectacle. A long shot of a line of jungle trees is held for a full minute. Helicopters drift lazily past the camera in the foreground, the beat of their rotors slowed to create a dream-like mood. Wisps of smoke start to rise from the foreground. Music builds slowly, The Doors reaching a climactic 'This is the end' as the tree-line erupts into giant plumes of flame. The camera pans to the right to reveal more burning jungle before the image dissolves into the face of Captain Willard (Martin Sheen) lying in a sweaty hotel bed. A series of double-exposures place the image of Willard over a background of flaming jungle as we are only gradually relocated from the world of Vietnam combat to that of his tortured consciousness.

What do these sequences have in common, as Hollywood spectacles, and what distinguishes them within that category? War, like space or 'action' defined more generally, is an arena that lends itself to the spectacular impact sought by many contemporary Hollywood films. But the spectacle of war can be presented in a variety of ways. *Saving Private Ryan* and *Apocalypse Now* might be defined as, respectively, spectacles of 'authenticity' and of the 'artistic imagination'. Warfare also offers another opportunity for a return to versions of the American 'frontier' experience. Such an observation is hardly unique in relation to films of the Vietnam war, almost all of which have been injected with heavy doses of frontier mythology. This is worth another look if only because of the force with which the mythic/ideological recuperation has been asserted in this instance. It might also be related more directly to the transformation of the 'reality' of the Vietnam war, and others, into cinematic spectacle. The imposition of so familiar a framework might leave the viewer free to enjoy the sensual pleasures of the spectacle without being greatly challenged by less comfortable implications.

Hollywood action movies are relatively free to indulge in all sorts of death and destruction, often amounting to miniature wars of their own, without any great concern about issues of historical veracity or responsibility. Spectacular films based on real conflicts face a rather different, critical, and often self-imposed, agenda. Particular demands have to be met if Hollywood products are to be treated as 'respectable' representations of war rather than more 'lowly' works of action-exploitation. Films such as *Rambo* (1985) and the *Missing in Action* series (from 1984) are placed on one side of this divide. *Saving Private Ryan* and *Apocalypse Now* are among war films that locate themselves on the 'higher' ground opposite, in keeping with an epic tradition including works such as *The Bridge on the River Kwai* (1957) and *The Longest Day* (1962). One way they do this is through the brand of spectacle offered. Another involves the structure and underlying patterns of narrative.

There are obvious differences between the action cinema examined in the previous chapter and more 'serious' or 'respectable' war films, but they have some things in common. *Saving Private Ryan* and *Apocalypse Now* offer similar pleasures in important respects, but packaged to appeal to viewers who might shun the allegedly more 'gratuitous' impact of the action cinema. 'Serious' war films offer spectacular impact that satisfies the more general requirements of contemporary Hollywood production while allowing both audiences and filmmakers to distinguish themselves from more 'disreputable' aspects of popular culture. A similar effort was made by James Cameron to associate *Titanic* with the romantic epic tradition of *Doctor Zhivago* (1965) rather than less prestigious displays of special effects or melodrama.

Saving Private Ryan: the spectacle of 'authenticity' vs. Hollywood's 'same old story'

The Normandy landing sequence from *Saving Private Ryan* makes its bid for respectability in the name, above all, of 'authenticity'. We are not meant to wallow in the glorious sensual experience of Hollywood-created warfare but to be stunned by a sense of what the 'real event' must have been like. A decision was taken to 'risk not entertaining anyone or not having anyone attend any of the performances',[3] proclaimed the director Steven Spielberg. Such is the carnage that the film allegedly ran the additional risk of earning an NC-17 rating in the United States, a category usually viewed as commercial suicide. Spielberg has the industrial power to take such 'risks', given his general clout and the fact that the film was made jointly by his own company DreamWorks and Paramount. The same is true to a lesser extent of Francis Ford Coppola's position as architect of *Apocalypse Now*, a production for which he retained financial responsibility. The industrial dimension is a key determinant of the availability of one aesthetic strategy or another, in this case the ability of the filmmaker to depart from some of the most immediate concerns about the potential response of a large audience.

The impression of authenticity constructed by *Saving Private Ryan* is offered on at least two levels. Spielberg's comments suggest an attempt to create a degree of authenticity in the pro-filmic event, the action staged in front of the camera. The sequence includes digitally-composed special effects added in post-production, but many of the effects are 'physical', created in the staging, and having an impact on performers and crew. Working in the midst of thousands of physical special-effects explosions and 'bullet impacts' provides, according to this account, an experience something like that of the original combat situation. Unusually, for Spielberg, he did not draw up storyboards in advance and shot the Omaha Beach sequence 'in religious continuity'[4] to maintain the illusion of a series of events unfolding according to their own logic rather than choreographed in advance.

If *Saving Private Ryan* seeks to create an impression of reality for those involved in the production, the aim, of course, is to increase the 'authenticity' of their performances and of the overall experience for the viewer. The formal devices used by Spielberg are designed to force us to share certain aspects of the experience of going into combat. Some of these devices are similar to those used in the cinema of action spectacle. Rapid and unsteady camerawork serve much the same purpose in both cases. The main difference in the landing sequence from *Saving Private Ryan* is that such techniques are used in a deliberate effort to make the viewer

The spectacle of 'authenticity': troops under fire in the opening sequence of Saving Private Ryan, *© DreamWorks L.L.C. and Paramount Pictures and Amblin Entertainment. Ronald Grant archive*

uncomfortable. The experience is claustrophobic, with few long or establishing shots. The viewer has to wait some 15 minutes before being given a relatively long shot in which the action on the beach can be seen in the context of the sea and a few ships framed behind. It is not until 36 minutes into the film – by which time the beach landing sequence has given way to the development of the 'saving Private Ryan' plot back in the United States – that we are given a grand vista of the entire beach, the sea, barrage balloons overhead and dozens of ships. This contrasts with the usual regime of the action movie, in which assaults on the viewer by aggressive bursts of 'in your face' spectacle are tempered by regular cuts to more 'objective' seeming perspectives and often undercut by comic quips. During the landing the viewer's perspective is tightly integrated with that of the troops. One of the first images is what appears to be a point-of-view shot, looking unsteadily from one landing craft to another alongside. The hand-held camera creates the same effect throughout the sequence. It bobs up and down, above and below the surface of the water, along with disembarking troops dragged under by the weight of their equipment. It maintains a very low angle and jerky motion throughout most of the movement up the beach. Blood again spatters the lens as medics attempt to stanch the flow.

With the exception of a couple of shots from the position of German machine guns, our perspective remains that of the troops on the ground. When the troops are pinned down behind a low ridge of sand near the top of the beach, so is the camera, its viewpoint not privileged above that of the protagonists. A 'documentary' type of effect is created, in other words, as if the camera were carried by one of the troops engaged in the assault.

One of the sharpest contrasts between the Normandy landing in *Saving Private Ryan* and the action-movie sequences examined in the previous chapter is the relative absence of editing. Impact effects based on cutting are generally eschewed in favour of camera movement, thus maintaining a greater sense of the substance of the pro-filmic event. Rapidity of movement combines with other photographic techniques to create a kinetic impact and disorientation effect as powerful as action-montage. Increased shutter speeds remove the element of blurring inherent in conventional camerawork, creating a strobing effect, noticeable especially in some of the rapid camera movements (an effect directly opposite to that achieved in Spielberg's *Jurassic Park*, in which an illusion of authenticity is created by the deliberate addition of motion-blur).[5] The impression given is that the cinematic technology is unable to keep up with the pace and violence of the events.

Some of the techniques employed involve a deliberate 'handicapping' of the means of representation, a denial of the full scope of the cinematic apparatus. A technology such as the Steadicam, which permits highly fluid mobile camera movements, is replaced here by a reversion to the precise opposite: a patenting, almost, of the radically 'unsteadicam.'[6] The 'documentary' effect is heightened by processing techniques used to desaturate colour from the images, which have a brownish tone vaguely reminiscent of historical footage. Such techniques are carefully contrived, of course, and the overall effect depends on digital augmentation of both image and sound, the latter playing an important part in the impact the sequence has on the viewer. 'Authenticity' remains itself a special effect and, like all special effects, can be viewed both as an absorbing recreation of reality and as impressive special effect in its own right. The strategic intention in *Saving Private Ryan* appears to be to emphasize the former and downplay the latter, again in the name of cultural respectability. Too much enjoyment of the spectacle might damage the film's claim to be something more than 'gratuitous' entertainment. How this really plays is open to question. Should Spielberg's comments about being willing to lose viewers be taken at face value or be seen as part of a strategic effort to position the film in the marketplace, to claim attention and distinguish it from the more 'disreputable' style of action-adventure? Does the unrelenting nature of the spectacle make it genuinely uncomfortable, or just allow the viewer to enjoy the dizzying hyperreal spectacle freed from any feelings of guilt? It is not easy to answer such questions with any certainty, although the issues might be clarified by examining the location of the beach landing spectacle within the broader narrative structure of the film.

The beach landing is presented as something like a solid 'slab' of recreated reality, seeking to immerse the viewer in the appalling chaos of the events. But this is still a Hollywood production, so there is a limit to how far this can be taken. The beach landing is the experience of a mass of men. The film respects this up to a point, highlighting moments of the nightmare endured by a fairly large number of soldiers. The principal mediation remains that provided by the star system, however, and the convention of focusing on a small group of individuals.

From landing craft to secured beachhead, the sequence is organized centrally around the perspective of Captain John Miller (Tom Hanks) and a few immediate colleagues. Miller is the first figure to be picked out as an important individual, in an early shot of the trembling hand that will become a signifier of human fragility. His perspective is especially privileged in two early slow-motion sequences in which the oppressive noise of battle is drowned out by the distant roar of his interior consciousness. The emphasis on what might be taken to be a representative sample is institutionalized by the narrative frame when we are introduced to the particular (fictional) story isolated from the broader scale of (historical) events. Miller and a small team are to locate Private James Ryan (Matt Damon), one individual paratrooper among hundreds mistakenly scattered around the French countryside. His three brothers have been killed in action, earning him a ticket home in the interests of family and compassion. The bruising spectacle of the beach landing is followed by the establishment of the 'Ryan' narrative. An overhead pan across the dozens of bodies comes to rest on the bag carried on one soldier's back and imprinted with the name of one of the dead Ryan brothers. Harsh realistic spectacle is replaced by more familiar Hollywood fare as gently melodramatic music plays over the sequence in which the coincidence of the three Ryan deaths comes to light, the mother is informed and the Chief of Staff General Marshall quotes from Abraham Lincoln to justify his order for the mission to 'save' the surviving brother.

The move from general scenes of warfare to a story based on a few particular individuals is the stuff of familiar Hollywood narrative. *Saving Private Ryan* ends up playing very much by the book. The way it does this, however, is worth closer examination. The issue of the relationship between the bigger picture and that on which the film focuses is explicitly taken up within the narrative. The initial and sustained reaction of Miller and his crew is that the mission to 'save' Private Ryan is an absurdity, a sentimental gesture made by the brass that risks the lives of eight men in the hope of saving one. Two of them die before Ryan is located. Their criticisms of the mission could apply equally to the narrative focus selected by the film: the business of winning the war is more or less ignored in favour of a small detail of no direct relevance to the bigger picture. The painful impact of the beach landing sequence is replaced by the working through of more familiar combat movie conventions focusing on the relationships between a small group of men. A questioning of the sentimentality of heartstring-tugging devices focused on individuals seems also to be implied in the scene where one member of the patrol dies after ignoring Miller's order not to take a child handed down by anxious parents from the ruins of one of the towns through which they pass. The soldier takes a risk in order to do what he defines as 'the decent thing', to help get a child to safety for the sake of its parents: in some respects an echo of the plot of *Saving Private Ryan*.

There is a contradiction, then, within the film that can be read to some extent as questioning its own narrative structure, its own complicity in a deeply sentimental project. Sentimental concerns, based on an excessive focus on a few individuals, are opposed to the business of larger life-and-death statistics not so easily grasped at a personal-emotional level, and thus less easily accommodated by the usual Hollywood frame. This is an issue central to the positioning not just of this film but of Spielberg himself, a populist filmmaker who has sought greater 'respectability' and gravitas in the pursuit of avowedly 'serious' projects such as *Ryan*, *Schindler's List* (1993) and *Amistad* (1997).

Miller describes how he has to 'rationalize' the death of men under his command: 94 deaths mean saving the lives of 10 or 20 times as many. That is how he weighs up the balance between the mission and the men. In this case, he is reminded – as the tagline for the film has already informed us – the mission *is* a man, a glib phrase that seems to sidestep the issue. The film contrives a way to reconcile the opposition. The unease expressed about the narrative from within seems to be in the name of remaining loyal to the aesthetic of authenticity so prominently displayed in the recreation of the beach landing. Maybe this is what Spielberg means when he talks about the impact of the filming having 'reinformed' him in how he needed to tell the story. The movement of both narrative and spectacular dimensions of *Saving Private Ryan* is towards a reconciliation of the two. The film ends with an even longer sequence of spectacular warfare, a climactic battle that lasts a good 30 minutes. Rather than standing opposed to the conventions of Hollywood melodrama, however, this sequence manages to combine elements of conventional narrative and the spectacular-authentic.

Private Ryan is eventually found among a band of troops protecting a bridge that has become a key strategic point in the Allied campaign. He declines to leave his post, declaring that his comrades there are the only brothers he has left. Miller declares that they have crossed a strange boundary: 'The world has taken a turn for the surreal.' If anything, the opposite is the case: the world of the film takes a turn for the conventional. Miller is left with little choice but to add his men to the complement defending the bridge, turning the remainder of the narrative into a familiar 'last stand' affair in which the outnumbered rag-tag band holds out against an assault by a much larger enemy equipped with tanks. Improvised 'sticky bombs' are used to disable one of the German tanks, blocking the main street and delaying the advance sufficiently to enable the 'cavalry' of US aircraft and troop reinforcements to save the day, although not before Miller is killed.

The battle is shot in much the same style as the earlier beach landing sequence. It is a bruising encounter, again, for both fictional characters and filmgoers, but the aesthetic of 'authenticity' plays rather differently when the event has been framed in terms so conventional that the last holdout is labelled 'the Alamo'. It does not seem to be a question of the formal devices simply validating the more familiarly conventional action, or the cliché detracting from the power of the spectacle. Instead, the two seem to coexist, sitting together rather awkwardly or offering some measure of reconciliation of two dynamics that appear to be in competition during much of the film. It would be wrong to suggest that the more disturbing and visceral aspects of the film, especially on the beach, are entirely or simply 'contained' by the narrative frame. The experience of film viewing does not lend itself to such neat formulations. Audio-visual spectacle can have resonances not so easily pinned down or balanced by other dimensions of the text. It is not a question of mathematical calculations or equations, but of certain tendencies towards a reconciliatory dynamic that combines the aesthetic of authenticity with a more familiar narrative context.

If reconciliation is offered in *Saving Private Ryan*, its tenor is influenced by a prologue/epilogue framework constructed around the principal action. The film opens with the present-day Ryan visiting the war graves with his family. It concludes with a return to the family group and Ryan's expression of emotion at the cross marking Miller's grave. Miller's dying words to Ryan are 'earn this', to make the sacrifice on his behalf worth while. That Ryan has succeeded in doing so is implied in the epilogue by the presence of the family group in the background. Ryan is anxious for reassurance that he has led 'a good life' and is 'a good man'. His wife replies: 'You are', and the framing of Ryan with what appears to be an ideal family group, together with his humility, encourages us to believe her. The values of 'family life', the enshrining of which underpinned the 'illogical' mission to save Private Ryan, return, in other words, to validate the entire project. That this should be seen as a move to recuperate any doubts established earlier in the film is supported by the extent to which the effort to 'make sense' of the mission is overdetermined. One justification is the future trajectory of Ryan's life, and it seems significant that this includes bringing into the world descendants who are part of the generation of moviegoers today.

This way of structuring into the text an appeal to target audiences is an important aspect of Hollywood production. *Saving Private Ryan* has an inbuilt appeal to an older audience, despite the criticism it received from some of those involved in the historical events, but it is also structured to appeal to younger viewers.

The way these appeals are negotiated is rather similar in *Saving Private Ryan* and *Armageddon*, a film more clearly targeted at a primarily youthful audience. In *Armageddon* the characters of AJ and Grace are probably closest in age and attitude to the primary target audience. A tension results from the way they are initially set up in opposition to the older figure played by Bruce Willis, who is clearly the star and an important element of the film's box-office appeal; a tension that the film is careful to work out and resolve. *Armageddon* ends with the death of the father figure – but one still young, vigorous and sexy enough to appeal to a youth audience – and the delirious union of the young couple.

Saving Private Ryan also ends with the sacrificial death of a star who stands in the text as a father figure – a schoolteacher and mentor to the younger of his charges – but also retains an appeal for the younger viewer. Figures like Willis and Hanks are 'mature' enough to play paternalistic roles while maintaining a sufficiently glamorous movie-star aura to appeal to younger generations to whose more immediate representatives in the films they might seem opposed.

Stars, as Richard Dyer suggests, can themselves effect the kind of 'magical' reconciliation of apparently irreconcilable terms that appears to be offered so often in the narrative dimension of Hollywood films.[7] This is important in industrial terms, especially to the efforts of Hollywood to keep up with changing audience demographics.[8] Centre stage in the epilogue to *Saving Private Ryan* is given to the elderly Ryan and his wife, but it is the younger generations of Ryans in the background – and, by implication, some of their contemporaries in the audience – who are offered implicitly as what made the mission of saving Ryan himself worthwhile. As we have seen, however, the film has already given the mission more than adequate justification. If Miller and his crew had not gone in search of Ryan, the bridge might not have been saved from German control. It is Miller who designs the strategy used to hold out against the overwhelming odds, to make their limited resource count. However inadvertently, the Ryan mission ends up playing an important part in securing a key military objective, precisely the kind of factor in the 'bigger picture' from which it seemed a distraction. The narrative of *Saving Private Ryan* ends up conforming to a familiar Hollywood D-Day invasion movie device: a focus on the 'vital bridge' that serves as a microcosm of the broader conflict.

Apocalypse Now: hallucinatory spectacle and the 'art' of darkness

If *Saving Private Ryan* makes its claim to 'serious' respectability through an appeal to the authenticity of its spectacle, however much qualified by the demands of Hollywood-style narrative, *Apocalypse Now* might be viewed in terms of 'art', a creative interpretation of reality brought about by an act of visionary 'genius'. The quotation marks put around terms like 'art' and 'genius' will suffice for the moment to indicate their problematic nature. The issue is less a matter of whether such labels are justified or appropriate than how these films appear to have tried to position themselves.

Apocalypse Now has been criticized for failing to provide anything like an 'authentic' portrayal of aspects of the Vietnam war, a dimension in which most representations of the conflict have been found wanting. Unlike *Saving Private Ryan*, *Apocalypse Now* gives little indication of ever having been intended to do such a thing. Vietnam appears to be little more than a backcloth for an exploration of supposedly more 'universal' questions about 'good' and 'evil', the problem of distinguishing between the two, and the 'nature' of 'man'. The film is based partly on Joseph Conrad's novel *Heart of Darkness* (1902), from which it gains the resonances of a literary-artistic work.

The spectacular dimension of *Apocalypse Now* also appears to be structured to establish associations with the world of visionary 'art' rather than a texture of 'surface' authenticity. The opening sequence makes use of the startling imagery of fireballs so important to the genre of action-spectacular, but uses it rather differently. For one thing, the location of these images is far from certain, especially on first viewing. In retrospect, they appear to be a flash-forward to the air-strikes that will be called down on the Cambodian village ruled by the renegade Colonel Kurtz (Marlon Brando) after his assassination by Captain Willard. The song line 'This is the end' might help to confirm such a reading, but none of this is very clear at the time of watching. Steven Shaviro's characterization of the cinematic experience as one in which perceptions can shift and slip beneath stabilities of meaning seems to have some purchase here, although the case can be overstated. It is by playing up such protean qualities that a work distinguishes itself from the commercial mainstream, a lesson learned by filmmakers such as Coppola from post-war European 'art' cinema.

Rather than as a clearly locatable example of action-destruction, or part of more concrete representation of the horrors of war, the opening of *Apocalypse Now* is presented in terms of Willard's uncertain subjective state: very much the stuff of the cinema of 'art' rather than that of popular escapism. The film itself can be located as a product of the 'Hollywood Renaissance' period, from the late 1960s until the mid-to-late 1970s, in which a combination of particular social and industrial factors created a measure of space for the deployment of such strategies by a group of 'auteur' filmmakers of which Coppola was a leading member.[9] The overlapping images and the increasingly strange, disorienting noises on the soundtrack designed by Walter Murch create a nightmarish impression sustained throughout much of the film. In one of the most celebrated sequences – or one of the most notorious, depending on the viewer's perspective – Willard hitches a ride with an 'Air Cavalry' helicopter-based unit that attacks an enemy village to the accompaniment of Wagner's 'Ride of the Valkyries'. This is grand big-screen spectacle, a spine-tingling sequence that uses its 'high art' point of reference to create in the viewer something like the thrill the attack offers to some of the American participants.

The spectacle offered by *Apocalypse Now* is often one of incongruity: Wagner and aerial attack; a Colonel Kilgore (Robert Duvall) who insists on a demonstration of the attractions of a good surfing beach while still under fire; a religious service conducted in the foreground while a mobile flamethrower spews out flames and the conflict continues behind; the spectacle of a USO performance by Playboy centrefolds on a stage erected in the middle of nowhere; the weird sounds and images of the Do Long bridge, a chaotic realm and apparently the farthest American outpost, beyond which Willard must continue his odyssey.

With the exception of a couple of sequences rendered into a nightmarish slow motion, the viewer of *Saving Private Ryan* is battered over the head during the spectacular battle sequences, sometimes barely able to keep up with the disorienting motion of the image. *Apocalypse Now* offers a more contemplative and allusively textured spectacle. The pace and rhythm is at times closer to the pole represented by *2001: A Space Odyssey* than any of the other examples considered so far. In both cases the viewer is invited to enjoy the sensuous pleasures of unhurried spectacle. In *Apocalypse Now* this often takes the form of elaborate tracking or crane shots in which the nightmarish panorama unfolds before our eyes. Both films also draw the viewer into what are styled as 'profound' disquisitions on the nature of humanity.

This is also a feature of *The Thin Red Line* (1998), a close contemporary of *Saving Private Ryan* and another striking example of the 'artistic' war epic. *The Thin Red Line* offers a bruising spectacle of warfare, sold partly in terms of the 'realism' of its battle sequences. Warfare is rendered harsh and brutal, but the movement of troops up a deadly hillside under the eyes of machine guns is also given seductive qualities in sweeping passes of the crane-mounted camera through long, wind-blown grass. Above all, the film sets out to establish 'artistic' credentials, through a complex, multi-character structure of focus and a series of allusive voice-overs and flashbacks giving access to interior states manifested often in highly 'literary' form. The specific events of the Guadalcanal campaign of 1942 are largely subordinated to the supposedly 'universal' question of the origin of evil, signified by the intrusion of war into a seemingly timeless Pacific island paradise.

If *Apocalypse Now* shares some characteristics with *2001: A Space Odyssey*, its narrative structure remains a good deal more explicit. Much of the narration is done overtly. An early briefing scene sets out Willard's mission to 'terminate' the irregular operations of Colonel Kurtz. Throughout the film we are given Willard's voice-over commentary, both his own observations of events and the contents of briefing materials on Kurtz. The movement of the film could be seen as an alternation between moments of narration, in this form, and moments of lavish spectacle. The forward-moving narrative dynamic of the mission is interrupted by a series of elaborate set-pieces. The two dimensions are rather more integrated than that might suggest, however. Willard's narration continues through some of the more spectacular set-pieces, and its tone often seems to contribute to the atmosphere of hallucinatory spectacle, especially in the later stages of the journey up-river. Narrative and spectacle seem to interpenetrate to a considerable extent, as befits one of the major themes of the film: the merging of exterior and interior journeys, Willard's mission into the jungle and the exploration of his own self on the way.

Apocalypse Now is without doubt a powerful example of cinematic spectacle, and as such very much a product of the Hollywood landscape of the late 1970s. The release included a 70 mm version and was among the first generation to take full advantage of the extra dimension offered by the latest advances in stereo sound. But the film is also heavily overdetermined by a range of narrative frames. It has the structure of a quest, a narrative form with a long tradition. The same is true to a lesser extent of *Saving Private Ryan*. Both films take the viewer on a journey across a wartime landscape of suffering and chaos in search of an object of uncertain value. In each case we are introduced along the way to examples of absurdity: the surfing incident in *Apocalypse Now*, for example, and in *Saving Private Ryan* a troop-carrying glider that crashed because it had been weighted down with steel plates bolted to the underside to protect the seat of a general.

The exploration of such diversions give the narrative something of a picaresque quality, a format well suited to the inclusion of spectacular set-pieces. In *Apocalypse Now*, the quest is pursued towards darker extremes, while *Saving Private Ryan* finds a more recuperative escape. The familiar trope of the 'bridge mission' central to the more conventional dynamic of *Saving Private Ryan* is undercut in *Apocalypse Now*. The Do Long bridge is a signifier not of important strategic objective, but of the absurdities of which the American effort in Vietnam was often accused: destroyed every night by the enemy and rebuilt each day just to enable the brass to say the road is open. Blowing up a bridge is the kind of 'heroic' behind-the-lines-mission on which Willard is assumed to be engaged by a member of the boat crew assigned to take him up river, not the morally ambiguous task of assassinating an American officer.

Apocalypse Now has been widely criticized for an apparent narrative 'weakness' in its later stages at the jungle temple compound where Kurtz mutters darkly and quotes from Eliot's *The Hollow Men*. The film's literary–artistic aspirations are rather openly on display here, including what Gilbert Adair describes as the 'rather too artfully composed still-life shot' in which Kurtz's bedside reading is exhibited: Jessie Weston's *From Ritual to Romance*, an influence on the work of Eliot, and James Frazer's early anthropological classic, *The Golden Bough*.[10] What some take for a 'failure' of narrative might further strengthen the modernist or 'artistic' credentials of the film as a complex text that refuses to deliver the satisfaction of an immediate climactic pay-off. The narrative is crowded with mythical and literary illusion, including references to the Bible and to Dante's *Inferno*. The co-writer John Milius cites a list in which Willard is cast variously as Adam, Faust, Dante, Aeneas, Huckleberry Finn, Jesus Christ, the Ancient Mariner, Captain Ahab, Odysseus and Oedipus.[11] Willard's laconic voice-over adds to the mix the 'lower' cultural narrative forms of detective fiction and *film noir*.

The existence within *Apocalypse Now* of such a diversity of narrative frameworks and potential allusions has left the film open to a variety of readings. Michael Ryan and Douglas Kellner convict the film of expressing a 'quasi-fascist' version of conservative ideology.[12] The narrative focus, they suggest,

> is on Willard's progressive identification with Kurtz's power and ruthlessness and on his concomitant transformation into an effective warrior. The point is made, through Willard's increasing disgust with the ineptitude of the leaderless army and his admiration for Kurtz, that the latter's brand of authoritarian warrior leader is needed as a solution to the disarray of the war.[13]

Ryan and Kellner conclude that the confusion and doubt that characterize much of the film are eventually resolved into certainty and authority, through Willard's identification with Kurtz and his eventual acquisition of Kurtz's power. The 'meaning' of the film seems rather less stable than this suggests, however. Willard does grow increasingly to respect and to be intrigued by Kurtz. He finds it hard to see any clear distinction between warfare as practiced by 'madmen' such as Kurtz or the officially sanctioned Colonel Kilgore. A recognition of the moral ambiguity of all such judgements seems to characterize Willard's response more than any clear-cut process of identification with Kurtz. The landscape through which he travels offers images of chaos and of authoritarian leadership, neither of which appear to be endorsed unambiguously.

Apocalypse Now has it both ways, as Frank Tomasulo suggests, especially in terms of its political resonances. Ambiguity may be a quality often associated with complex works of art, but it can also be a feature of more popular cultural products that seek to appeal to large audiences by leaving themselves open to more than one reading. Such a requirement may have been particularly acute for a project such as *Apocalypse Now*, one of the first in a wave of films to deal directly with the contentious subject of the Vietnam war. Thus, for Tomasulo, the film 'is filled with double binds and mixed messages in its attempt to have it both ways'.[14] Many scenes 'depict the absurdity and outright lunacy of America's Vietnam policies, as well as the machinations of high-level military commanders'.[15] Other aspects of the content and style have the opposite effect. Tomasulo is not the only critic to have questioned the film on the grounds of the 'aestheticization of violence' in spectacular sequences such as Kilgore's helicopter attack, the structure of which he describes as implicating the audience cinematically 'in the exhilarating superiority of the American attack'.[16]

The sequence remains more ambiguous in some details, as both Tomasulo and Adair suggest. The village attacked is declared to 'belong' to the Viet Cong, yet it is shown immediately before the raid to be a peaceful place filled with schoolchildren. Kilgore's principal motivation for the assault is to put on a display of surfing, yet the village is shown after all to be armed and its population includes a woman who hides a grenade in her hat to destroy a helicopter picking up the American wounded. The sequence does indeed 'have it both ways', a pattern repeated through much of *Apocalypse Now*.

If the film is to be enjoyed primarily on the level of its spectacular attractions, it may be that one side of this equation will be favoured over the other. The thrill of the spectacle seems to override the impact of passing details such as the procession of schoolchildren glimpsed in the village square. This appears to be a more grand and upmarket version of the action spectacle, the 'higher' cultural tone of which – together with its location in a more 'serious' narrative framework – might make its enjoyment more acceptable to some audiences. The spectacle of combat might be inherently ambiguous. Combat sequences offer an exhilarating adrenalin rush, the implications of which cannot be determined by the nature of the spectacle alone, Claudia Springer suggests:

> they elicit both intellectual and heightened emotional responses, and spectators have to sort out their own responses based on their predispositions to the events represented. This would explain why it is possible for an antiwar viewer to praise a combat sequence for powerfully depicting the horrors of war, while another viewer might respond to the same film as if it were a wartime adventure filled with exciting action.[17]

The filmmaker who wants to present an antiwar statement has to do so clearly in the narrative dimension, 'for it has to compensate for the more ambiguous signifying system of spectacle'. The provision of large-scale spectacle is one way Hollywood films can avoid nailing their colours too clearly to any particular mast, since the visceral thrills offered can be open to multiple readings. The destruction of landmarks such as the White House or a famous Manhattan skyscraper might be a source of horror or of undisguised glee. Either response is available. If this ambiguity is a more general characteristic of cinematic spectacle, it is of particular relevance in such potentially controversial territory as representations of the war in Vietnam.

Overall, Tomasulo's conclusion on *Apocalypse Now* seems convincing: 'By subordinating content to style and foregrounding aesthetic ambiguity and richness, the director secondarized the ideological implications of a deeply political question – the Vietnam War.'[18]

Tomasulo criticizes Coppola on this ground, calling for a more 'forceful' and politically unambiguous statement about the war. This is all very well from a political point of view. *Apocalypse Now* is 'guilty' of substituting dehistoricized mythical resonances for any analysis of the more concrete realities of the Vietnam war. The reasons for this need to be understood, however. A rather muddy and ambiguous blend of narrative components and hallucinatory spectacle served two purposes rather well. It gave the film the aura of serious 'artistic' respectability while courting audiences by avoiding a commitment to any one political perspective on the war. Another source of this ambiguity may have been Coppola's own reported confusion during the production about where the film was headed, although the terms in which this has been expressed tend to underline the status of the film as the work of a tortured and visionary artist.[19]

'Way down in the mud': war, Vietnam and frontier mythology

A notable characteristic of the Hollywood action cinema discussed in the previous chapter was the tendency to cast the heroes as maverick figures who perform beyond the borders of large institutions and bureaucracies. This is equally true of the central characters of many films set during the Vietnam war. Operating on missions that officially do not exist and making illegal incursions into Cambodia, Kurtz and Willard in *Apocalypse Now* might have been among the former colleagues mourned by Frank Hummel in *The Rock*. Kurtz, Willard and Kilgore stand in contrast to the representatives of military bureaucracy, especially the two army officers and the CIA man who give Willard his briefing. The bureaucrats sit down to meals of cold roast beef and utter bland platitudes as they send Willard on his mission. Powerful mavericks like Kurtz and Kilgore create their own rules as they go, like latter-day Nietzschean supermen. Willard is also alienated from the military hierarchy.

Each of these characters is framed in ways that resonate with the mythology of the frontier. In Kilgore's case this is flagged rather obviously. His 'Air Cavalry' regiment takes to the air to the sound of a bugle, while the colonel himself struts in a stetson, spurs and the yellow neckerchief of a more traditional cavalry officer. Kurtz is the 'white man' who has crossed the boundary too far into 'Indian' country. His career background is that of the perfect military frontiersman, a prodigy who forsook an obvious route towards the top of the bureaucratic hierarchy, choosing instead to undergo Green Beret marine training at the age of 38, a decision that guaranteed that he could not rise above the rank of colonel. Deep in the jungle, however, Kurtz appears to have 'gone native'. He rules over a small group of renegade Americans and what the film presents as an undifferentiated mass of Montagnard tribespeople. His compound is filled with the conventional signs of 'native savagery': severed heads and what appear to be skinned bodies strewn around the ruins of a 'heathen' temple.

If the military bureaucracy stands at one extreme and Kurtz at the other, Willard occupies the obligatory position somewhere in between. Willard's loyalty to his mission and, by implication, to his superiors, is in considerable doubt. He says he took the mission but did not know what he would do when he found Kurtz. He may come to admire some aspects of Kurtz but this seems to stop well short of total identification. The severed head remains a clear signifier of the gulf between them. Kurtz drops the head of one of Willard's crew into his lap, a gesture with which it is hard to imagine Willard identifying. Kurtz expresses admiration for what he describes as the 'primordial instincts' of the Vietnamese enemy, their ability to kill without feeling, passion or judgement. This quality is demonstrated in the story Kurtz tells about a group of Vietnamese cadres who had the strength of purpose to cut the arms from children who had been inoculated by American special forces: in other words, and in Hollywood terms, the ultimate test of the will to overcome sentimentality in the interests of savage/cunning calculation.

This, again, is not something that we can easily imagine Willard embracing, even if he can kill quite coldly when circumstances demand. Willard remains somewhere in the middle, as he is during most of the film, suspended on the river like Huckleberry Finn on his raft, somewhere between 'savagery' and 'civilization'. In this respect Willard offers a classic updating of the frontier hero The darkness and confusion in which the film ends suggests, however, that a neat mythic reconciliation cannot easily be asserted.

The association of the landscape of Vietnam with that of the original American frontier is no accident, and far from limited to the narrative structure of *Apocalypse Now*. Elements of frontier mythology are evoked in many Vietnam films. They were also common currency in the discourses surrounding the war itself. It was not only fictional characters like Kilgore who brought the insignia of the American West with them to Vietnam. Kennedy's rhetoric of the 'New Frontier' included an attempt by the President to identify himself with the figure of the Green Beret, the special forces agent equipped for unconventional guerrilla warfare in the wilderness. Numerous military units and operations were given names taken from frontier tradition. Ground held by the enemy was habitually known as 'Indian country', and so on. This was more than just a matter of playing with words. Imposing such frameworks helped to make sense of American operations in Vietnam, to secure a meaning that was palatable and flattering to the American position. Rather than a dubious neo-colonialist engagement, the war could be characterized in terms of a 'mission' that was both beneficial to its recipients and healthy for an America otherwise threatened in the 1950s and 1960s by an overly comfortable and decadent complacency.[20]

Such mythological framings did not always prove easy to maintain during the war itself. If it was presented in terms of a frontier mission, it risked damaging frontier mythology through negative association, particularly in the wake of the Tet offensive of 1968 and the revelation of the Mai Lai massacre. The currency of frontier mythology in general appears to have been devalued by the war and its immediate aftermath. As John Hellman puts it: 'Most Americans were not willing to give up their mythic heritage and oppose America as the true Force of Darkness; nevertheless, after Tet, they were left without a convincing story of the conflict in Vietnam with which to oppose that passionate vision.'[21]

The late 1960s and early 1970s was the era of the 'anti-western', a cycle of films that presented the American experience in the west as one of rape and massacre. It is hard to tell to what extent connections can be made between the appearance of such films and more general attitudes within American culture. A declaration of affinity with the Native American victims of the heritage of frontier expansionism was certainly one of the various ingredients of the 'counterculture' of the 1960s and early 1970s. A rejection of the mainstream 'American Way' led quite naturally, for many, towards an identification with its traditional 'Other'. It is doubtful that this extended very far into the entire population of the United States, but it might have been given disproportionate coverage at the time. The financial difficulties faced by the Hollywood studios in the late 1960s, and the search for new audiences, helped to secure for the counterculture a position of some prominence in the cinema, even if films such as *The Graduate* (1967), *Bonnie and Clyde* (1967), *Easy Rider* (1969) and *M*A*S*H* (1970) remained exceptions rather than the rule.

The picture is further complicated by the fact that many of these films retain an attachment to the mythology of the frontier, if from a slightly more radical perspective. One of the virtues of such myths/ideologies is precisely the way they can bend with the times. If the more traditional aggressive white frontiersman was in danger of becoming the villain of the piece, it only required a different inflection of the myth for it to embrace a version of the 'outlaw' more consonant with the culture of hippiedom.

A conscious attempt to revive the more central tradition of frontier mythology is detected by John Hellman in the Hollywood of the late 1970s, as we have seen in his reading of the *Star Wars* trilogy. If *Return of the Jedi* can be read as a move forward from the negative associations of Vietnam to a more positive reassertion of frontier mythology, the same might be said of some of the films about Vietnam that followed *Apocalypse Now*. It would be wrong to suggest that all difficulties were immediately shuffled off, but a renewed appeal to the mythic heritage of the frontier seems to have created a framework within which the conflict could be represented in terms more comfortable to American audiences. Frontier rhetoric translated into familiar terms what might otherwise appear to be some outrageous reversals, the most notorious example being the character of John Rambo in *Rambo*, a thorough-going 'frontiersman' blending into the jungle to take on hordes of Russians and Vietnamese in a mission to rescue prisoners kept in captivity after the end of the war. Rambo fights a one-man war, action-movie style, from the ground, while the Russians have the helicopters. As has often been pointed out, this is an almost total inversion of the situation of the war, in which a clumsy American force mistakenly assumed that its technological superiority would guarantee eventual victory over a guerrilla enemy. Clothing this with the garb of the frontier makes it seem closer to the real 'American way', as if it was the 'reality' of Vietnam that was the aberration. This is not to suggest that a film like *Rambo* offers a one-dimensional ideological recuperation. The film is imbued with confusions of its own which, as Yvonne Tasker suggests, tell us something about the complexities of address often at work in products of popular culture.[22]

The extent to which the mythology of the frontier pervades Hollywood representations of the Vietnam war can be demonstrated by turning from the poles represented by *Apocalypse Now* and *Rambo* to *Platoon* (1986), a film that was widely celebrated on release as the most 'realistic' treatment of the conflict. Its 'authenticity' was trumpeted in a manner not dissimilar to that of *Saving Private Ryan*. Unlike *Apocalypse Now* or *Rambo*, *Platoon* focuses on a group of supposedly 'ordinary' soldiers, not elite individuals from special forces units. In this respect it is closer to the traditional Hollywood Second World War 'combat movie'. The traditional combat film is, as Thomas Schatz suggests, a celebration of the virtues of group integration.[23] A diverse bunch of recruits are, typically, welded together, overcoming their differences in the face of common enemy and hardship. The clear-cut moral framework of the Second World War makes this act of integration relatively easy to achieve. *Platoon*, in the more divisive context of Vietnam, is largely about the disintegration of the group, the contradictions that lead to American troops fighting among themselves.

Platoon was greeted by most critics as a breath of fresh air after the spectacular excesses, of different kinds, that dominated films such as *Apocalypse Now* and *Rambo*. Not only did it focus on 'ordinary' grunts from the infantry, but it appeared to give a powerfully 'realistic' portrait of jungle warfare. The impression created by the film's reception was that the war could, at last, be represented more directly, without the need for the insulation provided by metaphysics, grand spectacle or comic-book heroics. The emphasis in *Platoon* is on life 'on the ground' for the American forces in Vietnam, an experience also 'grounded' in reality. This discursive framework is created in the text but was shaped at the time of release by the efforts of the publicity department. Production notes supplied to journalists emphasized the authenticity of the film, especially the fact that the performers had undergone 13 days of 'real' training, including exhausting jungle patrols, immediately before the start of filming. This line was followed by many reviewers and commentators. The 'authenticity' of the film was further established in the press by the testament of authoritative commentators on Indochina, including David Halberstam and William Shawcross.[24]

The jungle and battle sequences of *Platoon* are shot undemonstratively. The film restricts itself mostly to relatively close shots of combat or jungle patrol, emphasizing the claustrophobic nature of the experience. As Adair puts it: 'When darkness falls, we are prevented from seeing any more than the soldiers themselves do; our own perception of the action is never privileged in relation to theirs.'[25] This, for Adair, 'is the primary, ground-level stratum of *Platoon*'s realism: the spectator's increasingly intense conviction that he is in some sense *there*, vicariously sharing the average grunt's own experience'.[26] The extent to which the creation of such an illusion of presence is a relative phenomenon, dependent on its juxtaposition to other conventions, can be demonstrated by comparing what Adair finds in *Platoon* with the aesthetics of the battle sequences in *Saving Private Ryan*. The impact described by Adair is less apparent to the viewer coming to the film after seeing *Saving Private Ryan*. This does not necessarily undermine *Platoon*'s realist credentials. Its depiction of conflict seems in some ways the more 'naturalistic' of the two. The viewer is less aware of a frenetic effort to construct an impression of authenticity than is the case in *Saving Private Ryan*. The latter, in its very commitment to authenticity, is all the more likely to be experienced as spectacle: the hyperrealistic spectacle-of-authenticity rather than authenticity itself. Such are the knots into which assertions of 'realism' become tied.

Platoon was received largely in terms of its claims to realism. The relative nature of such constructs does not detract from the impression they create in any particular context, and it was the degree of apparent authenticity that marked *Platoon* out most clearly from its predecessors. The realist aesthetic accounts for only one aspect of the film, however. A strongly allegorical framework dominates the narrative structure, including self-consciously 'literary' or 'artistic' features and some familiar elements of frontier mythology. The central character Chris Taylor (Charlie Sheen) is not, after all, just an ordinary grunt, but an educated member of the middle classes for whom Vietnam offers an escape from the world of dull respectability. What he finds in Vietnam is not to his liking but, in characteristic terms of the American brand of frontier-related existentialism, he declares: 'Maybe I finally found it way down here in the mud. Maybe from down here I can start up again, be something I can be proud of without having to fake it, be a fake human being.' A sense of 'authenticity' is sought by both film and protagonist, a feature of a number of the films examined in this book. This is a good example of the overlap that often occurs between narrative concerns expressed in the text and claims made about the status of the cinematic spectacle itself. The same could be said of *Titanic*, for example, with its emphasis on Jack's 'authentic' lifestyle and Cameron's reported insistence on reconstructing elements of the ship in the finest authentic detail.

Platoon is presented largely through Taylor's point of view, including a voice-over narration in the form of rather literary observations made in letters to his grandmother. His narrative is framed by two alternative takes on the war, the models provided by Staff Sergeant Barnes (Tom Berenger) and Sergeant Elias (Willem Dafoe). Both are presented as extremely capable, almost superhuman frontiersmen. Barnes is tough, macho, a Southerner who has little respect for rules that forbid the killing of civilian women and children. Elias is also tough, but lithe and supple compared with the solidity of Barnes. There is more than a hint of homoeroticism in the relations between Elias and some of his followers. A brilliant practitioner of individualist manoeuvres in the jungle, Elias remains within the pale of 'civilized' behaviour, condemned to death by Barnes for reporting him for the murder of a Vietnamese woman.

Barnes, whose followers drink beer and bourbon and listen to country music, is the frontiersman in a rough and traditional white Southern incarnation. Elias is the frontiersman who has crossed a step further into the wilderness territory; not as far as Kurtz but to the point at which new openings become possible. He moves fleet-footed through the forest like a deer or one of the 'natives'; his followers listen to Motown and experience other dimensions through the use of marijuana.

The viewer, and Taylor, are thus offered two different inflections of the frontier hero in *Platoon*. The version manifested by Elias has much in common with the reconfiguration available from a 'countercultural' position that has become hostile to the war. Elias says he believed in what he was fighting for in 1965, the year ground troops were first deployed *en masse*, but no longer. The film opens in September 1967 and Elias speaks of his doubts soon after the following New Year, close to the time of the Tet Offensive. His loss of faith is situated in the period when the war began to be questioned on a wider basis in America, a move that makes him representative of broader trends. The dice are weighed rather heavily in favour of Elias, with whom Taylor soon establishes a bond. Barnes is an unsympathetic figure. The film suggests that Taylor has to negotiate a path between the two alternative visions of the frontiersman, however, rather than simply following the path of Elias. He describes himself as 'like a child born of those two fathers', and eventually kills Barnes himself. 'The only thing that can kill Barnes is Barnes,' we were told earlier: the implication being that Taylor has embraced something of Barnes as well as Elias. Quite what this combination is supposed to comprise need not be particularly clear for some kind of reconciliation to be implied. Taylor takes into himself the duality around which much of the film is structured, suggesting rather glibly that America as a whole can embrace its divisive elements.

'The last stand'

Platoon and *Saving Private Ryan* share one feature important to the way they function on the levels of both narrative and spectacle. Each ends with a 'last stand', in which the heroes are heavily outnumbered by the enemy. This guarantees a spectacular set-piece battle, a climactic pay-off that is found in most examples of contemporary Hollywood spectacle, although denied to many viewers of *Apocalypse Now* as part of its more 'artistic' credentials (the film has been seen in versions with several different endings, only one of which ends explicitly with the fiery destruction of Kurtz's compound). Whatever narrative themes these films pursue they are more or less obliged to provide this kind of pay-off if they are to seek a position in the commercial mainstream. The importance of such imperatives in shaping this kind of cultural product should not be underestimated. In *Saving Private Ryan* the final battle is even more protracted than the earlier landing sequence. *Platoon* offers its own display of fireworks as an American compound is overrun by hordes of Vietnamese. Such is the desperation of the situation that the commander orders an air attack inside his own perimeter and, just as Barnes appears about to kill Taylor, napalm drops and a huge fireball spectacularly whites-out the screen.

The 'last stand' supplies the necessary spectacular climax in both cases, but is also a narrative device rich in associations with the American frontier experience. In its original shape, taken from the events at the Alamo in Texas in 1836 and Custer's fall at the Battle of Little Big Horn in 1876, the 'last stand' was a signifier of 'heroic failure'. As such it seems readily transferable to the mythic recuperation of American involvement in the Vietnam war. 'Heroic failure' is certainly a flattering way of conceptualizing American defeat in Vietnam. The climax of *Platoon* moves partially into this register, but without total conviction. Some of the central characters acquit themselves well enough, but a charge into the enemy by Taylor has the flavour of craziness and loss of control more than heroics. One of the principals survives only by hiding under the body of a colleague while another knocks himself out while attempting to flee. According to Taylor's closing speech, and one of his earlier comments, they fought the enemy less than they fought among themselves.

This lapse into solipsism is rather typical of the myopic perspective that appeared to play a part in the American defeat in Vietnam. The myth of the 'last stand' might be able to contribute towards the film's assertion that internal divisions can to some extent be overcome. That, in Richard Slotkin's reading, was one reason why Custer's 'Last Stand' gained such metaphorical power, becoming one of the most frequently depicted moments in American history. The 'Last Stand', Slotkin suggests, was open to different interpretations: 'The Conservative/Democratic tendency saw Custer as a martyr to Indian savagery empowered by soft-headed philanthropic liberalism; the radical/Republican tendency saw Custer as the "real savage" in his representation of the values of racial bigots and aficionados of violence.'[27] The 'last stand' provided a narrative framework within which different readings of the frontier experience could be unified, in a manner not dissimilar to the rather superficial reconciliation effected within the person of Chris Taylor in *Platoon*. It is also important to note that the defeats at both the Alamo and Little Big Horn proved to be only temporary reverses against enemies that were soon defeated.

Metaphorical reworkings of the 'last stand' or the 'Alamo' complex are not new to Hollywood films set during the Second World War, but more usually associated with the early stages of war in the Pacific theatre, where American troops were forced to make strategic withdrawals in the face of a rapid Japanese advance. Classic examples include *Bataan* (1943) and *They Were Expendable* (1945). Why should the same image be found in *Saving Private Ryan*, a film set against the background of triumphant Allied advance into France? The initial forces landed on the beaches at Normandy are shown to take terrible losses, but this is no Dunkirk or Dieppe. The film depicts no real defeat, so why have recourse to mythic events whose value appears to be largely compensatory? *Saving Private*

Ryan's version of the 'last stand'/Alamo is important to the narrative development of the film, yoking the Ryan mission back into the bigger picture of the post D-Day historic events. But why a motif as specific and loaded as this? Maybe because it is the ultimate signifier of wartime heroics: the brave resistance of a small band against a superior force. In reality the Allied advance was not without its setbacks and serious difficulties, the dramatic stuff of more than one epic reconstruction in the cinema. The 'last stand' framework brings to this context an economical and clear-cut means of resolving the tensions among the characters. It also plays on broader aspects of frontier mythology, of course, pitting a resourceful band of individuals against an enemy equipped with tanks and other heavy weapons. The familiar framework, however contrived in this instance, makes an immediate sense in its own mythic/ideological terms. While Miller appears to be just an ordinary solider, one of many caught up in the conflict, we should note that he is a Texas Ranger, and so ideally qualified to meet a heroic death at the Alamo.

Like the action cinema discussed in the previous chapter, these war films also establish narrative and spectacular dynamics around the opposition between the frontier-like world of 'last stands' and heightened experience and the sphere of the home and domesticity. Full-scale war offers on a much wider canvas the moments of extremity and dazzling spectacle around which the action film is constructed. In *Apocalypse Now* the tension between war and home is one that cannot be resolved. The young men on the boat crew want to find a way home, Willard observes: 'Trouble is, I've been back there and know it doesn't exist any more.' In Willard's case, to take on the role of the frontiersman is to be transformed, to lose all possibility of a comfortable return to, or relationship with, 'ordinary' life. In this respect he seems close to Kurtz, who pens a scrawled letter to his wife saying: 'Sell the house. Sell the car. Sell the kids. Find someone else. Forget it. I'm never coming back.'

This is another issue where *Saving Private Ryan* seems to offer a more positive reconciliation. Miller has repressed his domestic past when we join him and the others on their mission. This is emphasized through references to the pot of money that has accumulated into a betting pool to be scooped by the man who can uncover his background. His refusal to allow his men to be side-tracked into rescuing the French child appears to be part of a resolve to maintain a separation between the worlds of family/domesticity and warfare. Cracks in Miller's armour appear when he cries after one encounter with the enemy and in his shaking hand symptom. It is at the moment of maximum fragmentation among his men that Miller lets out the secret of his other self in the ordinary world. A confrontation at gunpoint arises during an argument about the fate of a German prisoner threatened with summary execution. Miller breaks it up by announcing, abruptly, that he is a teacher of English composition in a small town in Pennsylvania. A speech ensues in which he declares that he has been changed by his experience of war: 'Every man I kill, the farther away from home I feel.' The result of this, bringing the context of normal domesticity and home to bear on the situation, is an immediate resolution of the tension between the men. They combine, romantically backlit in silhouette, to bury a dead comrade.

The film foregrounds the hazardous and sometimes absurd heightened domain of warfare. At the same time, the absent domestic scene remains important, as in the action cinema, as an alternative pole, a point of orientation against which can be measured anything that might stray too far from the permissible limits of 'civilized' behaviour. The film presents numerous images of 'savage' killing, at a distance or close quarters. These are not explicitly condemned, but the implication is that they threaten the possibility of a return to the normality figured by domesticity. To suggest that some forms of violent killing between enemies might be more acceptable than others seems to gloss over a contradiction at the heart of any notion of 'civilized warfare'. The location of the domestic hearth at the absent core of a film like *Saving Private Ryan* might also be reassuring to any viewer facing a similar contradiction between the espousal of 'civilized' humanitarian values in everyday life and the enjoyment of spectacles of bloody devastation.

6

Apocalypse, Maybe: Pre-millennial Disaster Movies

> The social structure which precedes the catastrophe is a schematized but supposedly accurate picture of the contemporary Western world. It is a society which has lost sight of 'frontier values', has grown weak through excessive self-indulgence and total reliance on a protective shell of technology, whose moral codes are threatened by liberalism and permissiveness [...].
>
> Nick Roddick[1]

> We've got front row tickets at the end of the earth.
>
> Rockhound in *Armageddon*

The giant lizard star of *Godzilla* (1998) is hatched in the islands of the South Pacific, the spawn of nuclear testing. From here the beast heads east to Panama and Jamaica, tracked by the destruction it leaves in its wake. It turns up next off the eastern seaboard of the United States, sinking fishing boats and ready to mount the destructive assault on New York City that constitutes the main action of the film. The inevitability of this destination is suggested visually even before Godzilla's appearance in the waters of the Atlantic. An aerial tracking shot in which its trail of massive footprints is followed by helicopter along a dirt road in Panama dissolves into a similar shot above one of the concrete canyons it is soon to terrorize in Manhattan. The narrative explanation for this migration is extremely thin. The beast is pregnant and animals do travel long distances to nest, we are told; Manhattan island offers a good place to hide once it has reached the area.

The film raises the issue but fails to deal with it in more than a perfunctory manner. 'It makes perfect sense', we are told, but it does not really. This might be seen as a classic example of the narrative weakness of the contemporary special-effects-led blockbuster. Nobody really cares much about motive or explanation. All that matters is that Godzilla is transplanted from its traditional home, closer to Japan, so it can run spectacularly amok in the streets of New York. A west coast destination such as Los Angeles or San Francisco might have offered a marginally more plausible proximity, but not quite the instantly familiar iconography of the Manhattan skyline and the compression of landmarks ripe for destruction. The city is the perfect arena for the rampage of Godzilla, and that might appear to be explanation enough. The requirements of spectacle are undoubtedly a major factor, heavily outweighing any great concern about narrative plausibility. But this absence of logical motivation does not prevent narrative issues coming into play. That a destructive beast such as Godzilla should head for the primary American metropolis also makes sense in terms of familiar narrative frameworks. Godzilla is just one of many agents of destruction to have made a bee-line for the metropolis. The devastation that results offers much in the way of cinematic spectacle, but it can also be read as a redemptive assault on manifestations of 'decadence'.

The last few years of the twentieth century were marked by a spate of apocalyptic or disaster scenarios. Meteors fall from the sky, flattening cities and threatening the destruction of the earth. Tidal waves assault the coasts and volcanoes erupt through the land, not to mention the deliberate or incidental destruction wrought by aliens and monsters. What are we to make of this revival of the disaster genre, thought by some to have been a product closely tied, as a sustained cycle, to the social context of the 1970s? Should it be seen as an expression of, or appeal to, pre-millennial anxiety? Or is the disaster film just another vehicle to show off the latest spectacular special effects, a quality not restricted to the recent disaster cycle or its immediate forerunner in the 1970s? Each of these dimensions will be explored further in this chapter, which will also consider how some recent examples appear to have been targeted to audiences on the basis of gender.

Apocalypse postponed

An apocalyptic nightmare marks the opening images of *Terminator 2: Judgement Day* (1991). Cars on a freeway, a child on a swing: images of daily life give way to a dark world of blackened bodies, twisted wreckage and future warfare against the machines that seek to obliterate human life. The film returns later to this moment, revisiting the instant of conflagration in the dreams of Sarah Connor (Linda Hamilton), the character given advance knowledge of the fate of humanity. But by the end of the film the apocalypse has been erased. The designer of a new generation computer chip agrees to destroy his work after being convinced of the future threat it represents. Apocalypse haunts the margins of the two *Terminator* films rather than forming the central action, but the way it is approached here makes explicit a tendency found widely in the contemporary disaster movie. There is a recurrent pattern in which the possibility of apocalyptic destruction is confronted and depicted with a potentially horrifying special effects/spectacular 'reality', only to be withdrawn or limited in its extent. Total destruction is rarely shown, other than its consequences in post-apocalyptic fictions in which the act of destruction is usually located some distance in the past. Images or threats of annihilation underpin many contemporary Hollywood films beyond the more obvious conventions of the disaster genre, including a number already considered in this book. Disaster lurks in many science fiction films, an obvious case being *Independence Day*, so much so that Susan Sontag takes science fiction and 'the imagination of disaster' as virtually synonymous.[2] The action films examined in Chapter 4 are also premised often on threats of more localized apocalypse resulting from the activity of terrorists of one kind or another.

In the *Terminator* films the prospect of near-total destruction is replaced by total removal of the threat. More common to the recent cycle of disaster films is a variation in which major devastation occurs but a larger apocalypse is averted. Global annihilation is threatened in both *Deep Impact* and *Armageddon*, competing blockbusters from the summer 1998 season. Comets or asteroids threaten to wipe out all life on Earth. Smaller particles hit the planet, causing enormous destruction, but the Extinction Level Event, as it is termed in *Deep Impact*, is escaped. Godzilla is not killed without serious damage to Manhattan but the protagonists of the film destroy its offspring before they breed further generations that could displace human life from the planet (except, of course, for the single survivor necessary to keep open the possibility of a sequel).

On a more restricted scale, the eruption in *Volcano* (1997) wrecks a swathe of Los Angeles but is prevented from destroying far more of the city. The entire community of *Dante's Peak* (1997) appears to be devastated by its eruption but much of the population escapes, as do the principals; the latter, in the emotional emphasis of Hollywood narrative, being sufficient consolation. Tidal waves, fiery destruction from outer space, nuclear weapons or lava flows often threaten a dissolution of life as we know it, a return to some kind of primal and undifferentiated state.

This might be advocated by the most extreme millennial fundamentalists of various stripes, religious or ecological: a fallen humanity or one that threatens the existence of the planet is purged in fires or floods of biblical proportions. But the cinematic version usually stops short of apocalypse. Disaster is carefully staged. Sufficient destruction is achieved to offer a cleansing or redeeming potential for the survivors, but any threat of annihilation usually recedes.

The recurrence of this narrative structure seems to support the view that representations of disaster can be seen as offering a warning or a way of confronting fears and anxieties within the culture in which they are produced. A threat of disaster in *The Abyss* (1992) is couched explicitly in these terms.[3] An alien power conjures up vast tidal waves to threaten humanity to change its destructive ways. The waves are suspended just before the point of impact, looming above a watching world long enough to ensure that the message hits home. As Patricia Mellencamp and Mary Ann Doane suggest, representations of disaster play on the anxieties of audiences and offer reassurance. Precisely what kind of anxieties might be involved in the historical contexts of the 1970s and 1990s is an issue to which I return below. There are some broad similarities between the narrative thematics underlying the two cycles, however. Whatever their specific historical inflections, both seem to negotiate these at least partly through the articulation of elements extrapolated from or consistent with frontier mythology.

One theme common to most of these films is that of 'natural' or elemental force breaking into the paved, built-up and 'civilized', 'over-civilized' or 'decadent' and 'artificial' worlds created by humans, worlds that threaten a loss of touch with the mythic values associated with the frontier. The principal targets for destruction are symbols of luxury, decadence, arrogance and the smothering of 'nature'. It is no accident that disaster strikes the luxurious cruise liner in *The Poseidon Adventure* (1972) and *Titanic* (1997), or the world's tallest and most advanced building in *The Towering Inferno* (1974); that a prestigious tower block built by a selfish architect is dynamited to stop the lava flow in *Volcano*, or that favourite targets are the metropolises of New York and Los Angeles. Especially asking for it in *Earthquake* (1974) are a giant dam, elevated freeways and houses built on stilts above a hillside, structures that defy the contours of 'nature'. The eruption of disaster destroys the excessive products of humanity and creates a space of heightened engagement, as was seen in *Twister* and *Independence Day*, a space in which 'frontier' heroics can be reasserted and the imagined 'sins' of a post-frontier society can be purged.

It is less common for the target to be rural. This is partly because rural scenes do not offer the same potential for spectacular destruction, but also makes sense in terms of narrative thematics. An interesting exception is *Dante's Peak*, set in a small mountain resort, but Dante's Peak is depicted as a deserving target in its own way. The town might be a candidate for genuine frontier status but this appears to have become degraded in the cheap tourist Pioneer Days Festival celebrated at the time of the eruption. Custer's Last Stand is reduced here to the neon sign of a motel, ripe for destruction. The setting of *Twister* is also rural, of course, but can be read in terms of a negotiation between pastoral and frontier imaginings of the rural landscape.

An opposition between natural force and metropolitan decadence is clearly structured into the opening sequence of *Volcano*. The film quickly establishes a series of juxtapositions between the worlds above and below ground. Above is a world of metropolitan babble and banality, with the occasional implied horror in the background. Below lurk elemental forces. The very first move is a downward pan from the 20th Century Fox logo into blackness accompanied by a seething/crunching sound. The first image is of a skyscraper skyline and a more general overhead view of the city. The images are overlaid with a medley of broadcast voices: the morning temperature and a traffic jam caused by a drive-by shooting on the freeway. We are introduced to the activities of an ordinary day in Los Angeles: sun umbrellas going up on a terrace, towels placed on loungers around the pool, fixtures being polished. A low angle on another building is broken abruptly when the camera plunges down a crack in the concrete surface into blackness, a louder repetition of the subterranean roar and the main title of the film. More vignettes of life 'California style' follow: a sunbather on the beach; a skateboarder towed by a dog; a jogger wearing a walkman; a man on an exercise bike glimpsed through a window; an advertising poster of tanned and muscled bodies. The soundtrack gives us more news reports and part of a Mercedes commercial.

Cut again to the scene underground: the camera prowls slowly through a cavern that glows red and gives off sparks to the sound of an almost animate growl. Back to the surface, and the sellers of maps of the homes of the stars are setting up shop at the roadside. The montage continues with a shot of a doughnut shop sign; the Hard Rock Café; the legs of a woman crossing the road; a line of roller-skaters on a slalom course; the sign of a smog-check centre; a giant Marlboro Man cut-out. Overlapping voices include a religious broadcaster ranting about the devil. Cut to a screen filled with bubbling red-hot magma, flowing towards the screen, towards us and a rude awakening for the world above.

One implication is that the eruption of the magma is some kind of response to the complacence and decadence of this version of Los Angeles. It is as if 'nature' and the elements have been bottled up, submerged or buried under the weight of layers of encrusted social sedimentation, awaiting only the opportunity to burst through.

Manhattan is an equally or more common target for spectacular destruction in the disaster movie but, Mike Davis suggests, a particular delight seems to be reserved for the imaginary annihilation of Los Angeles. A city of dreams, for some, Los Angeles also stands as the ultimate signifier of decadence and 'unreality'.

> No other city seems to excite such dark rapture. The tidal waves, killer bees, H-bombs, and viruses that occasionally annihilate Seattle, Houston, Chicago, or San Francisco produce a different kind of frisson, an enjoyment edged with horror and awe. Indeed, as one goes back further in the history of the urban disaster genre, the ghost of the romantic Sublime – beauty in the arms of terror – reappears. The destruction of London – the metropolis most persecuted in fiction between 1885 and 1940 – was imagined as a horrifying spectacle, equivalent to the death of Western civilization itself. The obliteration of Los Angeles, by contrast, is often depicted as, or at least secretly experienced as, a victory *for* civilization.[4]

Onto Los Angeles can be projected what are perceived to be the most decadent and deplored tendencies of modern American life, in an act of ritual sacrifice and displacement that implies, reassuringly, that much of the rest of the country remains essentially untainted. If the lava that devastates parts of the city can be seen in some respects as a cleansing force, one that burns away elements of corruption and decay, it is also an intervention that brings to power a figure of heroic 'frontier' qualities in the shape of one Mike Rourke (Tommy Lee Jones), the head of the Office of Emergency Management (OEM) responsible for leading the operation to contain the volcanic eruption. An opening title informs us that in an emergency he 'has power to control and command all the resources of the city.'

A key characteristic of the 1970s disaster cycle for Nick Roddick is the emergence of strong leadership figures, invariably white and male, in the face of threatened chaos, a tradition maintained in *Volcano*. Rourke is presented as a figure who stands above the petty self-interest displayed by various institutions initially caught up in the disaster. He is an individualist with his own way of getting things done. This is indicated during a brief interchange with the Chief of Police, mediated through Rourke's deputy Emmit Reese (Don Cheadle). 'Tell him we've got procedures here. Tell him he's not in Kansas any more,' protests the chief. Rourke: 'St Louis. I'm not in St Louis.' Exactly where he is *not* any more does not much matter, except that it is somewhere outside the decadent metropolis, closer to the mythical 'heartland' and its imaginary freedoms. But Rourke's position is a maverick's dream, if something of a contradiction. His role during the disaster gives him absolute power, answerable to no one. The volcano brings the threat not only of physical destruction, but also of social chaos and looting. Rourke is a benign authority figure whose actions and example can bring everyone back together. A very different version of the use of emergency powers lurks in *The X-Files Movie* (1998), where the Federal Emergency Management Agency (FEMA) is implicated in a high-level conspiracy. The key difference here, as far as popular American myth and ideology is concerned, is that FEMA is a federal body and thus an instant target for popular suspicion. Rourke has extraordinary powers, but only at a local level. He is also given characteristics that owe more to the tradition of the 'frontier' than to backroom bureaucracy.

Rourke is one of those typical Hollywood protagonists, like Harry Stamper in *Armageddon*, who has it all ways. He is the man in charge and architect of the rescue plan, but also a figure of direct hands-on action. The heroic leader spends little time at his desk in the control centre, a space occupied by his deputy. Rourke is caught out on the streets when the eruption strikes, handily placed to lead by example in the thick of the action. He gets involved in a series of dramatic rescues and close calls, even grabbing a drill to help create the trench that eventually contains the flow of lava. This is pretty much a basic narrative rule in contemporary Hollywood: the major male hero can be permitted other roles, such as leadership or authority, but he must also display a strong degree of direct hands-on activity. Rourke is a man of action and as such stands in contrast to many other figures within the narrative, particularly the large number of media commentators whose voices maintain an almost constant background chorus. The reporters on the scene watch and talk: they don't *do* anything. Rourke can be in the middle of trying to analyse the situation, debating what to do next, and can still break off to pull a man clear of the lava flow, get trapped himself and be rescued in the nick of time. Others are full of doubt and caution, but Rourke gets on and does something. He can be both boss and engaged in manual labours, implying no unbridgeable gulf between the two.

Disaster is framed as a mode in which we move from what are constructed as petty and inessential inequalities to what is portrayed as a more essential level of American equality. This implication is also folded into a sub-plot involving racial discourse. Tension brews between the representative of a black residential district and an proto-fascist police officer. The black character is arrested after trying to insist that a fire crew be dispatched to his street. Eventually, however, he is freed and joins in the operation to block the lava flow; in return a fire engine is sent to his neighbourhood. The issue of race is broached only to be wished harmoniously away, and this in a neighbourhood that would have been at the heart of the 1992 uprising. Poor and non-white residential areas of the real Los Angeles are given inadequate fire protection, Davis argues, especially when compared with the efforts expended on brush-fires in wealthy beach and mountain developments. A real and specific issue is raised, in other words, but only to be offered imaginary and superficial reconciliation. Racial difference appears to be dissolved at the end of the film, in a heavy-handed gesture in which coverings of ash and dust make all complexions look the same; a fall of rain soon washes this away, suggesting a return to 'normality' but presumably one in which the experience of disaster–extremity is supposed to have taught its liberal lesson.

One way to gauge the thematic implications of disaster films is to examine the targets that come in for maximum destruction. The lava flow of *Volcano* might be expected to be indiscriminate in its aim, beyond the general principle of assaulting the city, but this is not really the case. Most of the damage is done to glossy stores and museums, the heroic endeavours of the cast preventing the lava from making any major assault on residential areas. The main focus of destruction is a stretch of Wilshire Boulevard to the west of MacArthur Park, in which the first signs of volcanic activity appear. This stretch of Wilshire is singled out by Mike Davis as one of the worst areas of economic decline in the city, a high-rise commercial zone that has suffered a severe bout of capital- and jobs-flight. The lava flow might be seen as offering to purge such decline, cauterizing the wounds of the city and holding out the possibility of federally-funded renewal. MacArthur Park is cleared by the police early in the film, a safety measure in the terms of the narrative but also a gesture with broader resonances given the status of the former 'jewel in the crown of the city's park system', reduced today to being 'a free-fire zone where crack dealers and street gangs settle their scores with shotguns and uzis.'[5] It may or may not be coincidence, but the volcanic activity of the film chooses among its prominent targets two of the most conspicuously 'fallen' features of the city.

In other disaster movies of the 1990s the target list is fairly obvious. The first terrestrial destruction seen in *Armageddon* is a meteor shower raining destruction onto the metropolis. Such is the familiarity of these images in the late 1990s that the filmmakers seem to be playing a game of 'which famous landmarks can be destroyed this time?': in *Armageddon*, it is the Chrysler building (which also loses its distinctive top in *Godzilla*) and Grand Central Station that get shredded prominently. Only the destruction of New York is depicted, although we are told that the meteor storm has inflicted damage from Finland to South Carolina.

The next target shown is Shanghai, chosen maybe as a representative of the old and – in terms of the mythology of the frontier – corrupt and cluttered civilizations of the Far East. The final impact given the full special effects treatment is a direct hit on Paris. The Eiffel tower is toppled and the Arc de Triomphe left standing at the edge of a huge crater. It might be significant again that the filmmakers have chosen to highlight the destruction of a quintessential 'Old World' metropolis, the kind of 'decaying' European splendour against which the mythologies of the 'New World' were often defined. (A rival, or complementary, analysis from the industrial perspective might suggest that the major non-American targets were chosen to include reference points for the two economically most important overseas audiences, in Europe and the Far East.)

Deep Impact provides more evidence for this kind of reading. Part of a comet hits the sea off the Atlantic seaboard of the United States, sending a huge tidal wave inland to wipe out all the major cities of the East. Gone are the centres of power, wealth and federal government. The destruction of Manhattan, again, is singled out for spectacular representation, intercut with scenes in Virginia in which people try to escape the path of the wave. The tidal wave forces them to move inland and to the west, in search of higher ground, in a movement that could be seen as a compressed re-enactment of the original frontier dynamic. The hill climbed by the young protagonists Leo Biederman (Elijah Wood) and Sarah Hotchner (Leelee Sobieski) offers an escape from the reach of the flood waters and also, perhaps, a firmer kind of 'moral' ground on which to rebuild the 'American Way'. They carry with them Sarah's baby sister, passed on to them by the doomed Hotchner parents as a symbol of the fresh start they represent: a couple defined largely in terms of freshness and innocence, 'their' child the product of a kind of immaculate conception.

Immaculate conception: the innocent new family unit established on 'higher' ground in Deep Impact, *© DreamWorks L.L.C. and Paramount Pictures and Amblin Entertainment. Ronald Grant archive*

One of the most familiar conventions of the genre is that death tends to come to those who are associated, sometimes more or less innocently, with the forces of 'decadent' civilization. In *Deep Impact* this is the role played to some extent by one of the central characters, Jenny Lerner (Téa Leoni), a television news reporter who makes her career by stumbling across the story of impending doom while attempting to dig up dirt on a former member of the cabinet. Lerner does nothing especially wrong, but might be sufficiently tainted by her work in the media to be marked out as a sacrificial victim. She eventually dies on a beach in the direct path of the tidal wave, redeeming a troubled relationship with her father. Lerner's earlier cooperation with the government earns her a place among those offered survival in an underground complex of tunnels, but she sacrifices herself, giving up her place in favour of her colleague Beth (Laura Innes) who has a baby and thus represents another investment in a new future. A similar pattern of sacrifice is found in *Volcano.* Rourke's efforts are obstructed by an official involved in the construction of an extension to the Red Line metro that has contributed to the destabilization underground. The official appears to be a classic 'blame' figure in the disaster tradition, associated with an arrogant disregard for the forces of nature, but is able to redeem himself by taking a hands-on role in an underground rescue mission, dying redemptively in a pool of lava while saving a train driver.

In *Dante's Peak* the character singled out for this treatment is Paul Dreyfus (Charles Hallahan), the superior of the main protagonist Harry Dalton (Pierce Brosnan), whose sin is to have doubted his colleague's instinctive reading of the situation. None of these characters is personally unpleasant or particularly unsympathetic. What counts is their structural position in the narrative. However much they might be converted or attempt to rectify the situation, they are lined up on the wrong side of the oppositions and their fate is determined accordingly.

Elements of frontier-related discourse are present in the contemporary disaster movie, as they were in the 1970s cycle. But we also need to examine these films in their own specific social and historical context. The 'imagination of disaster', to use Susan Sontag's phrase, is by no means an uncommon cultural phenomenon, and the Hollywood version is not limited only to the cycles of the 1970s or 1990s. As Sontag suggests, the disaster film can be seen as 'one of the new myths about – that is to say one of the ways of accommodating to and negating – the perennial human anxiety about death. (Myths of heaven and hell, and of ghosts, had the same function.)'[6] Human self-consciousness of the inevitability of death goes some way to explain the existence of such myths. But we need to move beyond such generalities, as Sontag suggests, to examine the 'historically specifiable twist' found in any particular context. The same goes for analysis of the mobilization of elements of the myth or ideology of the frontier. These myths have demonstrated great longevity in American culture. The fact that they are reiterated in a range of specific historical circumstances does not mean that their meanings are entirely fixed, however; familiar mythologies can be inflected in particular ways at particular moments. Evidence for mythic continuity across periods of social or historical change is not evidence of stasis. Some active process must be in play if similar mythic structures are to be maintained. That is often precisely the way mythology is worked: to create a sense of timelessness and of eternal verities to which we can look for authority (usually conservative) in the face of change.

The 1970s disaster films have usually been interpreted in terms of their immediate historical context, which is not surprising given the acute nature of some of the social, economic and political events of the late 1960s and early 1970s. For Michael Ryan and Douglas Kellner: 'Natural disaster in the early seventies films is often a metaphor for the "immorality" and "disorders" of the late sixties, or for the "democratic distemper" which conservatives saw at work during the period. In crisis films, a stern paternalist male order is reimposed upon such troubles.'[7] If the Other rejected in frontier-related discourses as essentially alien to American identity is often figured in terms of 'decadence', the upheavals of the 1960s and early 1970s offered plenty of targets. The 'counterculture' and other challenges to the dominance of white capitalist patriarchy might be the real source of a threat translated metaphorically into natural catastrophe. The disaster, for Roddick, 'reflects a widespread contemporary phobia that traditional values are somehow threatened, if indeed they have not already collapsed. The disaster itself [...] can thus be seen as an expiation of the guilt felt about this and a punishment of the implied transgression.'[8]

Representations of disaster were certainly ways of advocating the more traditionally authoritarian order sought by opponents of that for which the 1960s appeared to stand. The authority figures that emerge are presented, as Roddick suggests, as 'natural' rather than official leaders, who demonstrate by example their fitness to exercise control over others. A classic example is Reverend Scott (Gene Hackman) in *The Poseidon Adventure*, a renegade clergyman whose unconventional methods have led to his rejection by the church establishment but whose tough have-a-go individualist approach makes him an ideal hero of the disaster-frontier. Many of these films also include an element of criticism of capitalism, but this is a gesture that for the most part leaves its core values largely intact. A few 'excesses' are singled out, such as the greedy cost-cutting that undermines the integrity of the eponymous star of *The Towering Inferno*, leaving the remainder mostly untouched.

What about the 1990s variant? If a good deal of thematic and mythic continuity can be identified between the 1970s disaster narrative and the contemporary cycle, what more specific social or historical factors might be in play in recent examples? If representations of disaster can be seen as a response to cultural anxieties, the 1990s or early 2000s does not appear to be quite such a fertile terrain as the 1970s, or other post-war decades marked by fears of nuclear holocaust. To this overarching anxiety during the Cold War the 1970s added a now familiar litany: the general fall-out of the 1960s and the Vietnam War, the loss of American dominance of the global economy, the oil crisis and the loss of faith in American government encouraged by Watergate. The current period, we might think, is a rather more confident time. The Cold War is over and there is little overt challenge to the rule of the American political and economic establishment. What, then, is so fearful? One answer appears to be: instability and uncertainty.

The Cold War generated fears of global nuclear war, but it also froze solid a whole range of geopolitical stresses and fractures that have since threatened to break apart. The fear of all-out nuclear war was replaced by anxieties about weapons falling into the 'wrong' hands, which usually meant anyone other than the powers that already possessed them. An assortment of former Soviet republics line up to offer precarious bases for the villains of action films such as *Airforce One* (1997) and *The World is Not Enough* (1999). Godzilla is created by fall-out located safely in the past, but need not be seen as merely a quaint historical or genre throwback when the film was released not long before the mutually hostile India and Pakistan conducted rival nuclear tests. A standard plot contrivance of the contemporary action movie is the 'mad', or simply 'greedy', protagonist who uses stolen nuclear devices for purposes of extortion. At the same time, nuclear weapons have also been treated as possible sources of redemption, a narrative move used earlier in *Meteor* (1979), in which American and Soviet militaries are persuaded to turn their 'defensive' weapons against the threatening object rather than each other. Nuclear devices are used for a similar purpose in both *Deep Impact* and *Armageddon*. The nuclear device uncoupled from its missile housing, usually complete with bleeping countdown timer, has become a familiar icon in contemporary Hollywood, whether used for good or ill.

Other anxieties continue to revolve around the products of science and technology. A current favourite is genetic engineering, which joins global warming as a focus of (western, middle-class?) fears. Nuclear power is only one of a range of potentially apocalyptic threats resulting from human action. As Richard Landes, director of the Centre for Millennial Studies, puts it: 'Thus we come upon a last (although hopefully not final) irony: despite being part of an "elite" culture which rejects God and mocks apocalyptic beliefs, we now have good scientific reasons to fear the End – toxic waste, atomic war, ozone depletion, overpopulation ...

the list is endless.'[9] Representations of disaster can be read as moments when faith in science and technology is challenged. As Mary Ann Doane suggests: 'Catastrophe signals the failure of the escalating technological desire to control nature.'[10]

One variety of disaster is directly caused by the failure or arrogant use of technology: plane crashes, sinking ships, the *Challenger* shuttle explosion, various forms of nuclear or chemical fall-out. Others are not blamed on technology as such, but demonstrate its limits, its inability always to guarantee solutions or to provide sufficient warning. Doane detects a blurring of a distinction previously maintained between catastrophes caused by natural forces such as hurricanes or earthquakes and those that derive from the failings of technology: 'the purview of catastrophe keeps expanding to encompass even phenomena which had previously been situated on the side of nature – earthquakes, floods, hurricanes, tornadoes. Such catastrophes no longer signify only the sudden eruption of natural forces but the inadequacy or failure of technology and its predictive powers as well.'[11] The dictates of 'progress' suggest that we should be able to gain some mastery over even the most capricious of natural threats. A central dynamic of *Twister* is a response to this situation, a demonstration of the failure of technology to provide adequate warnings coupled with a narrative enterprise designed to create a better warning system; but, as we have seen, the technological remedy is made available only through the intervention of a particular brand of human agency.

Warnings are provided in *Deep Impact* and *Armageddon*, but they are not very advanced in the latter. 'We didn't see this thing coming?', queries the President. NASA's Dan Truman replies that the 'object collision budget' is $1 million which enables them to track only about 3 per cent of the sky. Technological shortcomings are mixed up with budgetary issues, which helps to implicate federal parsimony as a bonus factor in the apportioning of blame. In *Dante's Peak* the technological monitoring continues to suggest that there is no problem but is proved inferior to the hunches of Harry Dalton.

The shortcomings of technology are presented as a problem in many of these films, but they also provide the opening through which can be asserted the importance of frontier-style heroics at the individual level: another way in which these films seem both to play on audience anxieties and to offer their own brand of reassurance.

What about an increase in the number of real or potentially imminent disasters? This would offer a more obvious and seemingly 'material' explanation for the prevalence of cinematic disaster narratives. The plot of *Volcano*, revolving around instability created by the work on the new Red Line metro, plays directly on real-world anxieties. The Red Line extension is not a product of the Hollywood imagination, but an ongoing and controversial fact of life in Los Angeles, having swallowed up vast sums of money and the occasional road surface as a result of subsidence (the film includes a passing reference to the undermining of Hollywood Boulevard). Fears of meteor impacts or tidal waves are not limited to screen or other fictions, either, but are the subject of real concerns, especially on the vulnerable western coasts of the Pacific rim. The Los Angeles region underwent an unprecedented succession of disasters in the first half of the 1990s, ranging from earthquake and urban uprising to a succession of hurricanes, floods and fires. 'This virtually biblical conjunction of disaster, which coincided with the worst regional recession in 50 years, is unique in American history,' suggests Mike Davis. 'After a century of population influx, 529,000 residents, mostly middle class, fled the Los Angeles metropolitan region in the years 1993 and 1994 alone.'[12]

Disasters are widely blamed on rampant 'nature', but as Davis suggests this draws attention away from the social and economic factors underlying many apparently 'natural' phenomena.

> For generations, market-driven urbanization has transgressed environmental common sense. Historic wildfire corridors have been turned into view-lot suburbs, wetland liquefaction zones into marinas, and floodplains into industrial districts and housing tracts [...]. As a result, Southern California has reaped flood, fire, and earthquake tragedies that were as avoidable, as unnatural, as the beating of Rodney King and the ensuing explosion in the streets.[13]

Natural and social–ideological dimensions interpenetrate quite closely. The natural geography of the region is a key factor in its vulnerability to disaster. Climate and landforms are unstable and given to sudden nonlinear shifts. But, Davis argues, this has been exacerbated by the production of myths or ideologies in which southern California has been presented as a kind of earthly paradise. A refusal to acknowledge the nature of the terrain has itself contributed to the inappropriate land-use and development that increases the risk of environmental threat on several fronts.

The association of contemporary disaster with the millennium is another way of avoiding the social or political implications of land use or topics such as the emission of greenhouse gases and global warming. Pressing political issues are subsumed to a 'higher' realm of biblical inevitability, a classical ideological manoeuvre. To what extent might the 1990s disaster film be seen as a reflection of millennial or pre-millennial anxieties, though? It is rather simplistic to suggest that these films simply plug into 'the mood of the millennium', even when focusing only on the level of narrative themes, as if this were some clearly identifiable current of popular feeling. A more diffuse connection might be made, however. It would be surprising if Hollywood did not make some attempt to play on the greater currency gained by millennial discourses in the immediately preceding years, more obvious examples including *End of Days* (1999), in which the action-heroics of Arnold Schwarzenegger avert a literal biblical apocalypse.

Millennialist groups, whether religious or secular, often predict an imminent and redemptive apocalypse of the kind anticipated and at least partially realized in disaster films. The presence of some millennial tendencies in the disaster film might be explained by the fact that they can be seen as a heightened variety of more familiar features of American culture, including aspects of frontier mythology. There is not always a clear break between the two. We should not forget that the 'New World' of America was itself seen by some early enthusiasts as marking the potential arrival of the millennial kingdom on Earth. There is continuity in the structure of the mythology that links the original European move to America with the hopes and fears aroused by the approach of the second millennium. In both cases the myth or ideology is rooted in notions of a fresh start, a sloughing off of the old and corrupt in favour of a new and supposedly more authentic beginning. More general anxieties about the dangers of over-reliance on technology were also given a specific millennial twist in discourses playing on fears about the 'millennium bug', the potential impact of the date 2000 on global computer systems. The serious attention this problem was given may help to establish a bridge of some kind between 'real' and more fanciful anticipations of the millennium, especially as it involves attitudes towards technology that are amplified in other aspects of millennialist culture.

Millennialism in contemporary America is in some cases associated with right-wing religious sects and self-styled militia that dissociate themselves from the 'evils' of metropolitan and federal complexes, modelling themselves instead on an armed and self-sufficient lifestyle redolent in some respects of the mythic frontier. These attitudes can be located socially and historically, tending to proliferate among social groups – often white, working and middle class – that have lost ground in recent bouts of economic restructuring.[14] Economic and other factors have combined to create significant growth among such groups in the past 20 years.[15] It would be wrong to lump them all together or to suggest a precise match between their concerns and those associated with the frontier, but certain resonances are hard to resist. Hollywood films do not exactly propagate the ideologies of these groups, some of which – including explicit white supremacism, anti-semitism and anti-feminism – are far too controversial to be embraced by an industry that thrives on blurring issues sufficiently to appeal to broad and heterogeneous audiences.

There are numerous points at which the extreme ideologies and paranoias shade over into more commonly held beliefs on which Hollywood is likely to play, however: a diffuse distrust of 'big government', for example, rather than a concrete belief in active federal conspiracy, the one able to feed into the other; seemingly relatively minor individual concerns opening into awareness of more encompassing theories. It is at a point somewhere in between such extremes that these ideologies have a widespread presence in contemporary Hollywood, including many of the examples analysed in this book. Millennialist sects and the audiences for Hollywood blockbusters share, for example, a certain delirious investment in the destruction of the metropolis, a key image in fundamentalist religious rhetoric, survivalist literature, millennialist groups and the disaster film.

There is a widespread sense of governmental or other conspiracy lurking at the edges of many Hollywood films, as we have seen in the case of *Independence Day* and examples of the action cinema. In *Armageddon* it is made clear that the amateur astrologer who makes the first report on the rogue comet is immediately put under FBI surveillance. Little is made of this, except that it falls into the same broad pattern of assumptions that includes the Kennedy-conspiracy references in the same film and in *The Rock*. The fact that such details form relatively minor elements of the texts suggests that they are available as taken-for-granted reference points for a mass audience.

The various conspiratorial shadows of *The X-Files Movie* include a clear reference to the bombing of the Alfred P. Murrah federal building in Oklahoma City in 1995. A bomb wrecks a federal building early in the film, one side torn away to resemble the wreckage of its counterpart in recent history. Initially assumed to be a terrorist attack, the fictional bombing proves to be the work of conspirators within the federal bureaucracy, seeking to destroy all traces of an alien encounter. Timothy McVeigh, the man convicted of the Oklahoma bombing, is believed to have carried out the attack partly in revenge for the siege by federal forces that led to the destruction of the Branch Davidian compound near Waco, Texas, in 1993: an event that lent itself strongly, for those inclined, to interpretation in terms of a pre-millennial confrontation with the forces of Satan.[16]

The X-Files Movie offers a reversal of the official version of the facts, taking at face value a millennialist conspiracy theory and no doubt helping to reinforce the doubt of sceptics about the truth of what *really* happened in Oklahoma. Some claim that the bombing was the work of federal forces and/or that FEMA is directly implicated in an international conspiracy to take control of the United States. The usual counter to these conspiracies is a strong assertion of individualistic heroics. The action–excitement conclusion of *The X-Files Movie* offers a conventional picture of individual endeavour, climaxing on the frontier terrain of the Antarctic. The conspiracy goes on, suggests the coda, but so do the inquiries of our trusty protagonists.

The same cannot be said of the hero of *Arlington Road* (1999), a film unusual in tackling some of these issues from the opposite direction. Michael Faraday (Jeff Bridges) teaches a course on right-wing extremists, of which his neighbour turns out to be a dangerous example. The film ends with a disastrous bombing of the FBI building in Washington and includes other incidents fictionally extrapolated from real events such as Oklahoma and the siege at Ruby Ridge, Idaho, in which the wife and child of a far-right activist were killed by US marshals. The film is primarily a critique of the extremist, resorting to noisy rhetoric on the soundtrack and the narrative ploy of having the hero's child kidnapped to underline our emotional identifications. Federal agencies do not escape criticism, however, their failings presented as being responsible for unnecessary deaths including that of the hero's FBI agent wife. *Arlington Road* turns towards the usual assertion of individual action-heroics, as Faraday engages single-handedly in an attempt to foil the bombers. The end has the devastatingly bleak character of a 1970s conspiracy thriller such as *The Parallax View* (1974), however, a rarity in contemporary Hollywood, with Faraday not only failing to prevent the bomb attack and dying in the effort but also being made to take the blame. Conspiracy is on the other side, here, although its texture remains familiar, especially in the mistaken finding that Faraday was a 'lone bomber'. *Arlington Road* goes against the grain in several respects, but still ends up offering a mixture of resonances.

A range of contemporary resonances can be identified in the disaster films of the 1990s. Some caution is required, however, in any sweeping assertion that such films capture the mood of the times. Any transmission of social currents into Hollywood films is complex and multiply-determined. To broader qualifications it is also worth adding some background on the processes that led to the appearance of some of the films considered in this chapter. Hollywood films do not spring entirely formed out of the *Zeitgeist.* They come about as the result of often tortured processes of development, planning and negotiation. If a clutch of disaster films appeared in a brief period at the end of the decade they did not necessarily come from the same place; not industrially, at least, even if they invite readings as part of the same cultural moment.

Deep Impact had been around for 20 years, conceived by co-producer David Brown as an updated remake of *When Worlds Collide* (1951).[17] Early scripts by Anthony Burgess and Sterling Silliphant were rejected and the project languished until revived when Steven Spielberg took an interest in

1993. It went through several more stages before Mimi Leder was brought on board to direct and it was given the eventual shape that will be examined later in this chapter. *Armageddon* came by a very different route, initially based on screenwriter Jonathan Hensleigh's interest in the oil-fire fighter Red Adair.[18]

Why films based on such similar narrative events should eventually appear almost simultaneously in the cinema is unclear. Peter Bart, editor of the industry bible *Variety*, reports that he was unable to pinpoint any common point of origin for the two projects. At one stage, in fact, two other asteroid pictures were also in the pipeline, one to be developed by Peter Hyams and another planned by the producer–director team Dean Devlin and Roland Emmerich, who went on to make *Godzilla* after learning of the competition.[19] Hollywood is an incestuous place and it is not surprising or unusual for similar ideas to hover somewhere in the atmosphere at different studios at the same time. Two volcano movies appeared one year, *Dante's Peak* and *Volcano* in 1997; two asteroid films the next. The fact that these and other films offered disaster scenarios close to the end of the 1990s might still be related to the broader cultural or pre-millennial context in which they might be expected profitably to play. That similar films traceable to different processes of development should appear at the same time might be further grounds on which to support a claim that they can be explained in social–cultural terms. It is useful to consider some of the messier and more proximate industrial detail, however, before leaping to any such conclusions.

The spectacle of destruction

Manhattan's streets are laid waste in *Godzilla*, gaping holes are torn out of its skyscrapers by meteorites in *Armageddon* and the entire profile of the skyline is submerged on a grand scale in *Deep Impact*. These are not just elements in a narrative but powerfully realized cinematic displays of large-scale destruction. What is their most immediate appeal? Are audiences interested in thematic patterns and oppositions, or are they just along for the spectacular thrills offered by the latest generation of special-effects technologies? Such questions are not easy to answer, as we have seen before. The argument of this book is that the underlying narrative patterns are a significant dimension of these films, but we can hardly doubt the importance of sheer spectacular attraction to the film industry. If we were forced to make a choice, to suggest which factors were dominant in the industrial decision-making process, it would be hard to resist opting for the domain of spectacle rather than narrative thematics. There is a close fit between the spectacle delivered by these films and the perceived needs of the industry in the late twentieth century.

A volcano, for example, is the perfect vehicle for the delivery of an excess of the kind of flame and fireball effects so beloved of the contemporary action format. It is no accident, from an industrial as well as a thematic point of view, that the disaster genre was established in a sustained and concentrated sense during the early 1970s. The first entry, *Airport* (1970), played a significant part in re-establishing the viability of a blockbuster strategy in the period when the Hollywood studios were at a low financial ebb. *Airport* and the other successes that followed form something of a bridge between the spectacular epics of the 1950s and 1960s and the new breed of blockbuster that came to the fore by the mid-1970s. More sporadically, disaster films have also offered spectacular attractions dating back to D.W. Griffith's *Intolerance* (1916) and beyond.[20]

We might not need to make such clear-cut choices, however. Hollywood cinema is causally overdetermined. More than one plausible explanation can be found, something perhaps in the nature of cultural products structured to try to reach a mass audience by offering multiple grounds of appeal. It might be hard to imagine the disaster genre being revisited with such prominence in the 1990s if it were not for the presence of computer-generated special effects. It exists up to a point precisely for the purpose of spectacular display. Yet it might be equally unlikely for these films to be made without the familiar narrative framework. That this framework persists, even when spectacle might be the most immediate industrial determinant, says a great deal about its significance. The fact that many of these films are driven primarily by the desire to produce extravagant spectacle does not mean that they become evacuated of narrative dimensions. Even if the spectacle comes first, in the economic and aesthetic calculation, that does not mean narrative is forgotten, contrary to the impression given by some commentators. The subtleties of narrative might not always get as much attention as we, or some critics, might desire, but that is hardly unique to the disaster movie or other contemporary blockbusters. Even at their most blundering and heavy-handedly spectacular these films retain significant investments in narrative structure, in terms of both story construction and underlying dynamics.

Close links can be identified between the dimensions of narrative and spectacle in the disaster movie. If the narrative thematics depend partly on redemptive destruction within the metropolis, then the spectacular manner in which this is realized is not a minor detail. The narrative dynamic itself calls, where possible, not just for a quick brushing away but a more extended sensual enjoyment of the process of destruction. A thematic concern with the purging of the metropolis is likely to be better served by the detailed and sweeping high-definition images produced by *Armageddon* and *Deep Impact* than the shaky sets and assemblage of stock footage that comprise the hit on New York City in *Meteor*. This is not to suggest that the impact of the latter is entirely diminished, or to assert a simple model of progressively improving special effects. Stock footage, models and matte-paintings are combined to considerable effect in *When Worlds Collide*, for example, while rapid impressionistic editing creates a strong impact in the earthquake scenes of *San Francisco* (1936).

As far as 'quality' is concerned, the consumption of special effects has to be seen in historical context. The point is that the pleasure offered by the spectacle is not unconnected with narrative thematics, a fact that complicates the construction of any simple hierarchy. Part of this pleasure may be rooted in a general delight sometimes taken in the imaginary destruction of familiar landmarks or cultural edifices. There is a certain carnivalesque[21] appeal in this licensed enjoyment of destruction. Pleasures of this kind need to be located culturally or historically, however, rather than being ascribed to any 'universal' human traits. Various arguments might be made to ground socially the appeal of the kind of destruction found in the disaster film, not least of which in the American case would be the enactment of the elements of frontier-related discourse considered above. The pleasures of spectacle do not exist in isolation. They gain their resonance from a location within cultural formations and discourses that often take narrative form. The pleasure we are offered in the spectacular destruction of Manhattan or Los Angeles is a very specific one, rooted in particular social contexts.

The spectacle of destruction is often foregrounded in the disaster film, as in some of the other examples examined in this book. The inhabitants of the disaster film do not always have much time to stop and stare, but there are significant moments in which the spectacular experience of the events is replayed within the fictional universe. This can be seen as a way of highlighting the basis of these films in spectacular attraction, as suggested in Chapter 2. But it can also have the opposite effect, as a rhetorical strategy used to make a claim for the authenticity of the events presented on screen.

Examples of this effect can be found in *Godzilla* and *Volcano*. The central characters who pursue Godzilla devote some of their energies to the act of producing images of the monster. One of the second-tier of main characters, Victor 'Animal' Palotti (Hank Azaria), is a television cameraman who risks his life on several occasions for the sake of getting good shots of Godzilla and its offspring. The central character Nick Tatopoulos (Matthew Broderick) stops to take snaps of the monster. How should we interpret this? In one sense it reminds us that we, too, are seeing spectacular images that have been captured photographically, that Godzilla owes its existence to an act of representation. But the insertion of the act of representation within the narrative space can also function as an implicit form of disavowal. It naturalizes the production of spectacle, decreasing the distance between the spectator-as-consumer-of-spectacle and those depicted on screen. The spectacle of Victor standing before the giant lizard with a video camera that is struggling to work in the rain draws our attention away from the fact that he, the camera and Godzilla occupy different levels of fictional construction: the actor and camera are substantially real and present, Godzilla is not. The presence of the camera, in a world in which so many events are mediated through television, acts paradoxically as a signifier of the reality at which it is pointed. We watch the view through a camera pointed at an elaborately staged spectacle, but we watch another camera pointed at part of the same spectacle taken by that cameraman to be reality. The implication is that we are thus taken further into the fictional space, as if our vision were closer to that of Victor and thus located within a world in which the spectacle is real.

A slightly different effect is created in *Volcano*, in which a substantial proportion of narrative information is conveyed through the mediation of broadcast voices. Elements of the spectacle are also mediated in this way. Reese and his team watch some of the action unfold on a large television screen in the OEM control room. In one sequence we are given an image of the screen displaying a big aerial shot of the lava flow, the camera-within-the-frame wheeling around slightly to the right and moving in closer to the lava. Three or more heads and shoulders are visible between us and the screen, figures watching like members of a cinema audience. A reverse-angle shows one of these to be Reese, who comments: 'You guys seeing this shit?' We then cut to an unmediated view of the same fiery spectacle: that is to say, the film itself becomes witness without the intervention of the television broadcast. A helicopter flies into the scene from the bottom left of the frame, exiting from the top. The camera then performs almost exactly the same movement seen in the mediated shot, turning slightly towards the right as it closes in on the spectacle below. The impression given is that we have moved from a mediated to a direct experience of the event. The broadcast images must have been taken from a helicopter, presumably the one seen flying into and out of the cinematic frame. The perspective offered by the film is one that both contains the mediated vision – we see the helicopter – and goes beyond it, continuing after the helicopter has passed.

The first part of this sequence may have the effect of emphasizing the spectacular nature of the film itself, watched in much the same way as the television screen is watched in the control room and underlining the distinction between those who remain as spectators in the office and those more directly engaged on the streets outside. But the subsequent shots seem to have the opposite effect. A mediated vision is presented in order that it can be transcended by what is an apparently more direct or 'authentic' view of the action. A similar effect occurs later in a sequence in which Rourke and the geologist Amy Barnes (Anne Heche) lower a video camera into a tunnel to check for volcanic activity. One shot includes in frame the perspective through the monitor, in black and white, as a fireball heads rapidly towards the camera. A reverse-angle of Rourke's face is followed by an unmediated shot from underground, in which the bright orange fireball rushes directly towards both the video camera, in the foreground, and our perspective through the film camera. The impact of the fireball is signified by a cut back, full-screen this time, to the now-blank vision of the video monitor. The same kind of shift is found, between what appear to be positions within and outside the diegetic space of the film. Shifting registers in this way might be expected to undermine any claim to realism. It risks, at some level, drawing the viewer's attention to the fact that the film is a constructed artefact. But this is no Brechtian 'alienation effect', not the least because the transitions are made very rapidly and slickly. The effect may be subliminal, but it seems to underline the claim of the film to allegiance with the more 'authentic' kind of reality established by the moment of direct engagement rather than the surrounding clutter of mass-mediation.

'An altogether different economy of pleasure'

What about the structure of these films? How are they organized in terms of the (rival or integrated) claims of narrative and spectacle? A useful comparison can be made between *Armageddon* and *Deep Impact*, which have similar disaster scenarios. Each concerns the threat of collision with an inert object from outer space and each includes an eventually successful mission to destroy the asteroid or comet. Yet there are instructive differences in the structure and likely appeal of the two films. *Armageddon* is the epitome of the contemporary noisy non-stop action adventure picture. *Deep Impact* focuses far more on the personal emotional dilemmas generated by the threatened apocalypse. The deployment of narrative and spectacular elements is distinctly different and might partly be explained by the way they have been structured to appeal to audiences on the basis of gender.

Deep Impact displays aspects of what might loosely be called a 'classical' narrative structure, a form contrasted by Fred Pfeil to that of the *Armageddon* brand of action spectacular. The classical narrative structure (which Pfeil describes rather vaguely as 'an older kind of story') has 'an accumulation of unspent dramatic or suspenseful elements throughout the narrative's so-called "rising action" into a force that is discharged most completely at the story's climax".[22]

Deep Impact opens with the gradual unveiling of the threat. A new object is sighted in the night sky and one of the finders dies when his jeep collides with a truck. We shift to a different narrative strand as Jenny Lerner comes across the story. The narrative establishes several distinct threads revolving around the schoolboy who makes the first sighting, his family and friends; Lerner, her career and relationship with mother and re-married father; and the astronauts who take part in the mission to destroy the comet. The term 'classical' may not be altogether appropriate for this multiple-stranded narrative structure. It is usually associated with more lean and linear structures based on no more than two principal threads, although numerous Hollywood films depart from that model. The term does, however, in its conventional usage, capture the sense of a type of narrative that builds gradually in the manner suggested by Pfeil. A number of characters and relationships are carefully established before we are treated to much in the way of action or spectacle. The only moment of noisy spectacle in the first part of the film is the explosive accident in which the astronomer Marcus Wolf (Charles Martin Smith) dies. A space action sequence comes some half way through the film when the astronauts land on the comet. The content of this – the hazardous mission, difficulties, death and injury, and the last minute escape – is not dissimilar to its equivalent in *Armageddon*, but the brand of spectacle is a good deal less pounding and insistent.

The second half of the film continues to develop its various character strands and eventually climaxes with the disastrous and highly spectacular special-effects tidal wave that hits Manhattan. A basic tension is built into the narrative by delaying the key spectacle until the very end. Viewers are likely to have been cued to anticipate some kind of spectacular impact, their expectations governed by publicity material such as trailers, posters and reviews, or by word of mouth and generic convention. The comet looms, menacingly, over the film, sustaining a line of tension that ties together the various threads of the story. The narrative is, in this sense, highly 'disciplined', indulging in prolonged foreplay and making the viewer wait for the final spectacular release. An earlier and more extreme example of this kind of 'classical' discipline is found in *San Francisco*, in which the action is focused entirely on interpersonal dramas until the climactic earthquake spectacle which accounts for a very small proportion of the running time.

The spectacle-hungry viewer of *Armageddon* does not have to be so patient. The film opens with a prologue depicting from space an earlier apocalypse that wiped out the dinosaurs. The narrative-proper starts with the destruction of a space shuttle and moves rapidly to a warning of 'incoming bogies' and the spectacular meteorite bombardment of Manhattan; all of this within an extremely slick and fast-paced opening ten minutes in which many of the transitions are made across wheeling camera movements that create a constant impression of kinetic energy.

There are only two more sequences of destruction caused by fragments of the asteroid. This might appear to be symptomatic of a relatively restrained approach were it not for the fact that the film continues to pile on a seemingly endless series of noisy spectacles in between. The first half of the film has relatively less of this than the second, but *Armageddon* can hardly be described as obeying anything like a 'classical' structure when almost non-stop spectacle marks the opening and is the rule for the entire last 75 minutes. Potentially headache-inducing high-octane sequences include: the launch of the space shuttles; a crisis ending in characteristic fireball explosion when the shuttles refuel at a Russian space station; a juddering 'slingshot' around the Moon; landing and crash-landing noisily on to the asteroid; antics in one of the vehicles crashing and flying around on the surface; the 'blowing' of one of the drilling rigs; a hazardous 'rock storm'; and the final destruction of the asteroid itself.

Spectacle is piled upon spectacle in a manner reminiscent of the 'stacking' of extravagant numbers found towards the end of some of the musicals of Busby Berkeley. In films such as *42nd Street* (1933), Martin Rubin suggests, the effect is 'to inhibit the interpenetration of narrative and spectacle. The big musical numbers, stacked together at the end of the film, coalesce into a semi-autonomous bloc that overbalances the narrative and separates out from it to a significant extent.'[23] This is not quite the case in *Armageddon*. A good deal of spectacular balance is provided earlier in the film and the later cumulation of explosive action sequences continues both to drive forward narrative events and to underline key thematic issues. Pfeil's example is another Bruce Willis vehicle, the third in the *Die Hard* series, *Die Hard with a Vengeance* (1995), but his argument applies equally well to *Armageddon* or other examples of action cinema such as *The Rock*. The film, he suggests, 'offers an altogether different economy of pleasure, in which the giddying blur of the high-speed chase and/or the gratifying spectacular release of aggressive impulse occurs at regularly recurring intervals throughout the film.'[24] This is precisely the structure of *Armageddon* and the basis on which this kind of Hollywood cinema has met with widespread criticism, presumably on the grounds that it offers too 'cheap' and easy a spectacular gratification, without the viewer having to exercise any discipline or restraint.

A politics of taste–judgement is involved in the implicitly (or explicitly) critical tone often adopted here. There is nothing neutral or sacrosanct about the 'rising action' form of narrative/spectacle development and nothing intrinsically virtuous about 'restraint'. The valorization of such cultural forms, just as much as the thematic aspects of the texts, can be located in specific social contexts. An appreciation of 'restraint', delayed gratification or the development of more complex, modulated narrative structures is the product of particular circumstances. It is built into the pleasures taken by those whose social, class or educational backgrounds provide a cultural capital that can be expended enjoyably in the celebration of such qualities. Taste, as Pierre Bourdieu argues, is socially constructed, performing an ideological function by naturalizing real differences, 'converting differences in the mode of acquisition of culture into differences of nature [...].'[25] Popular entertainments such as the Hollywood action film 'offer more direct, more immediate satisfactions'.[26]

There are good material reasons why these are likely to appeal to audiences from less privileged backgrounds. They may seek instant satisfaction because they do not have the time or luxury to gain their enjoyment from the deferral of gratification or to admire narrative or formal complexity for its own sake; and because the general characteristics of their lives might suggest that the sacrifice of short-term pleasure is unlikely to be met by future reward.

The assertion of a 'higher' or more 'noble' taste is achieved not through the intrinsic qualities of the works admired, but though the rejection of those enjoyed by the social groups from which an act of distinction is made. Judgements of taste, when they have to be justified rather than taken as merely natural, 'are asserted purely negatively, by the refusal of other tastes.'[27] To condemn the easy gratifications offered by an *Armageddon* or a *Die Hard with a Vengeance* is, by implication, to locate oneself on a higher cultural plane that is naturalized by being defined only through its negative opposite. A very similar dynamic of class-based taste formations underlay a move towards 'respectable' bourgeois narrative forms at a much earlier stage in cinema history, towards the end of the first decade of the twentieth century.

Before 1908–09, Tom Gunning suggests, the primary sources for films seem to have been vaudeville and burlesque sketches, fairy-tales, comic strips and popular songs. These forms, targeted at a predominantly working-class audience, 'stressed spectacular effects or physical action, rather than psychological motivation.'[28] A growth in the number of films based on famous plays, novels and poems was rooted not in some inherent 'improvement' of the medium but in deliberate efforts to capture a more middle-class audience. The aim was to take the business further up-market. Higher prices could be charged and the industry could gain greater respectability, an important factor in avoiding the threat of censorship and potential closure posed by those who campaigned against movies for being harmful to public morals. Differing valuations of narrative- and spectacle-led forms are never neutral matters of aesthetics, in other words, but part of socially grounded and political configurations of taste. Popular entertainment also tends to involve collective participation rather than contemplative distance, a distinction that helps to explain, with regard to target audiences, the difference noted in earlier chapters between the kind of spectacle/narrative operations found in the action cinema and films such as *2001: A Space Odyssey* or *Apocalypse Now*.

The character of the spectacle provided by *Armageddon* is precisely that of the 'impact aesthetic' examined in Chapter 4, with its promise of immediate sensual stimulation/gratification for the viewer. The viewer is assaulted by a succession of high volume 'in your face' sequences in which a constant stream of objects and debris fly towards the camera. Even the main title flames and explodes outwards. Rapid editing and extremely unsteady camerawork are frequently used to jar and disorient the viewer, to give an impression of participation in the action on screen. Many of the action images are heavily back-lit. Shafts of bright white light project out at the viewer, the pace of editing sometimes creating a strobing effect. These qualities, combined with a heavy emphasis on close and mid-shots, make *Armageddon* a good example of the kind of cinematic spectacle that appears to have been constructed with a view to how it will work within the confines of the small screen.

This style can be attributed in part to the background of the director Michael Bay, an award-winning director of commercials and music videos, a factor also relevant to the design of the action sequences in *The Rock*, also directed by Bay. The impression of subjective participation is often intercut with the comfort and stability of more 'objective' perspectives, as we have seen elsewhere. The top of the Chrysler building

Impact aesthetic: a low-angle 'subjective' shot of the Chrysler building, its distinctive top plummeting towards the camera in Armageddon, *© Touchstone Pictures, 1998. Ronald Grant archive*

plummets directly towards the camera at once instant, only to be seen from the relative safety of a side-on longer shot the next. The crash of the shuttle *Independence* is rendered in a lengthy sequence comprised primarily of three elements: dizzying shots from inside the craft, shots from outside the shuttle as it hurtles towards and past the camera and reaction shots from Mission Control. The first series creates a highly subjective impression; the second is seemingly more objective in being taken from outside, yet still assaults the viewer by sending the space shuttle towards the screen; the third relocates our perspective with that of the physically distanced but still emotionally involved observers.

Pfeil makes an ambitious attempt to situate the shift from one 'economy of pleasure' to another within the very broad ranging context of a movement from a 'Fordist' to a 'post-Fordist' economic formation and a concomitant impact on formations of gender and subjectivity. Traditional narrative structure is associated with 'the preferred rhythms of saving and spending, of repression and release, inscribed into the operations of Oedipal masculinity'.[29] That is to say a stable fixing of (male) gendered identity through Freud's Oedipal triangulation. Pfeil's 'different economy of pleasure' is associated with a pre-Oedipal absence of anchored gender fixity. A post-Fordist landscape, in this account, is one in which the grounding of male identity in older industrial forms of employment has been lost. Fordism, generally, is associated with mass production and consumption; post-Fordism with a shift to a more flexible system based on variety, niche-marketing and the export of heavier industrial concerns to geographical zones of cheap labour. In this respect Pfeil's analysis is in keeping with other accounts that have seen the mobilization of hyper-masculine heroics in the action cinema as a frantic overcompensation for some of the lost certainties of a version of capitalist patriarchy challenged by tendencies towards deindustrialization in parts of the 'developed' world.[30]

Can a connection really be made between broad shifts in the economy of capitalism, the operations of psychic processes and the relative balance of narrative and spectacle in Hollywood cinema? A number of big leaps have to be made to bring each of these dimensions together and oversimplification is hard to avoid, as Pfeil himself concedes. Exactly what kind of mechanism could be shown to make connections from one level to another is extremely difficult to specify. This kind of enterprise is problematic not the least because of the issues that remain to be debated within each of these levels, especially any sweeping claims within Freudian or economic theory. The usefulness of the concept of post-Fordism has been heavily debated, for instance, and the same might be said of the validity of an Oedipal mapping of the development of gendered subjectivity. At best, these would need to be considered as tendencies that have to be located in specific historical, social, economic, geographical and other contexts. Any suggestion of a broad-ranging epochal shift is particularly prone to difficulties.

How, for example, would any such argument account for the co-existence of the differing narrative structures of *Deep Impact* and *Armageddon*? There are tempting resonances, however. The structure of *Armageddon* has a frenetic character that suggests an over-compensatory assertion of its values more than any confident reflection. It could be seen as exhibiting a desperate rearguard action in attempting to batter its audience into accepting a particular form of macho heroics. The need to maintain this level of adrenaline/testosterone, constantly to prove something – and to have it all ways – seems to speak to anxiety rather than assurance. It is not hard to relate this loosely to contemporary gender insecurities, which are never surprising given the ultimately flimsy basis of the cultural terms into which sexual differences are constructed. And the particular gender insecurity of the 1990s might well be connected in some way to shifts in the level of the economy, even if these are not as clear-cut as the Fordism/post-Fordism couplet suggests. It is possible to speculate about such connections, then, and this can be a way of opening up fruitful lines of enquiry. The complexity of the issues should not dissuade us from the attempt, as long as we remain aware of the hazardous nature of the business and the dangers of oversimplification. There is no 'proof' for any of these kinds of arguments, merely varying degrees of rigour and plausibility.

The overblown spectacle typified by *Armageddon* is also the product of uncertainty at the industrial level, adopted perhaps as part of a desperate strategy to throw in a multitude of instant appeals in an effort to build in assurances of financial success. It is at this rather more pragmatic level also that the structures of *Deep Impact* and *Armageddon* merit examination in terms of gender issues. We have already seen that the contemporary action spectacular often has a strong investment in issues to do with family relationships, attempting to square its foregrounding of action–adventure with ideologically potent domestic concerns. This is equally true of many disaster-related films. Thus, the large-scale disaster theme of *Volcano* is played off against the context of Rourke's relationship with his teenage daughter Kelly.

Rourke, like many Hollywood heroes, is presented as a figure partly alienated from and seeking to re-establish connection with the domestic scene. He is separated from his wife and looking after Kelly when the volcano erupts. Rourke is torn between the rival demands of work and family responsibility. He is supposed to have taken a week's holiday during Kelly's visit. Devoting his attentions to the disaster means abandoning his daughter to the care of others. The film negotiates a way through these conflicting imperatives. Rourke gets Kelly into trouble, rescues her and is then obliged to abandon her. The broader narrative of disaster and the domestic father-daughter strand are brought back together – and the contradiction between Rourke's proper role in each is apparently resolved – when it emerges that the lava flow is heading for the hospital to which Rourke has directed both his daughter and all the others injured by the eruption.

In the climactic spectacle Rourke manages to rescue Kelly and a younger boy in a gloriously implausible split-second intervention just before the detonated Beverly Heights building falls on their heads. The film ends with Rourke heading off for his vacation and leaving others to clear up the mess, implicitly united with Amy Barnes as a new female partner. *Dante's Park* offers another implicit reconstitution of the nuclear family relationship. The hero loses his partner in a Colombian volcanic eruption in the prologue but eventually gains a new surrogate family after leading the town's mayor and her children to safety through a series of adventures.

From one perspective, the prevalence of this widespread concern with negotiations around issues of family and domesticity can be read in ideological terms: the thematics of many of the films examined in this book seem to display a strong investment in the reconstitution of, or negotiation of tensions around, the nuclear family. This can also be read from an industrial–commercial perspective, however, and is another example of the overdetermination characteristic of Hollywood cinema. The insertion of narrative elements based on families, relationships and children might be an attempt to broaden the potential audience for films that otherwise appear to be targeted mostly at male viewers, to reconcile some of the demands attributed to male and female audiences.

Young males have been Hollywood's prime target audience since the early 1970s, a strategy that has often failed to capitalize on an untapped female audience.[31] Big-budget spectacle has become a particularly male-centred form since the demise of the female-centred spectacular musical in the 1960s. The major exception to this rule is *Titanic*, which appealed strongly to a young female audience while also offering the requisite dose of action and spectacular effects. It might be tempting to suggest that the romance narrative appealed to women and the spectacle to male viewers, but this would be an oversimplification: spectacle, as we have seen, plays an important part in underlining the emotional impact of the romance. *Deep Impact* appears also to be designed to appeal to women, a factor that goes a long way to explain the difference between its structure in terms of narrative and spectacle and that of *Armageddon*. *Deep Impact* delays its moments of maximum spectacle because one of its major concerns is to build more sustained relationships between its protagonists. Its major source of 'impact' is not really contained in the spectacle of disaster, not even in the spectacular climactic destruction of Manhattan.

A huge wall of water sweeps up the island, toppling skyscrapers in its wake and leaving visible just the tips of the World Trade Centre. It is a fairly clinical affair, however, displayed quite coolly, especially when compared with the noisy rhetoric of *Armageddon*. There are three shots in which the city wavefront rushes towards the camera, thrusting before it the usual debris of cars and buses, but most of the spectacle is conveyed in more lofty and panoramic shots which lack *Armageddon*'s blustering approach. This sequence might constitute the release of the narrative/ spectacular tension built up by the film, but a strong emphasis is also placed on the emotional state of the protagonists.

In the major disaster-effects sequence of *Armageddon*, the initial bombardment of the same city, a few minor character sketches are included to give us some point of human reference, but this is a relatively minor gesture, far outweighed by the display of the spectacle itself. The background extras of *Deep Impact* run and scream, but for some of the principals the focus is on their own relationships. Jenny Lerner and her father stand on a beach in the face of the tidal wave, a location that has been made resonant to the background story of their troubled relationship. Their attention is turned inward, on one another, rather than on the spectacular doom that is imminent. The same goes for Sarah's parents, who stand face to face, blocking out the bigger picture in a last moment of mutual tenderness.

The inattention of these characters to the spectacle seems to speak to a large extent for the film itself, in which spectacle is a relatively minor ingredient. The biggest 'impact' is of a different kind, associated more with the 'women's film' or 'weepie' than macho-action postures. The real climax of the film, or at least a strong rival to the metropolitan apocalypse, is built up through a series of emotion-laden sacrifices focused around the most guaranteed of tear-jerking devices: the baby, two examples of which we have already seen.

If the passing on of the Hotchner baby is one element in the rising action of the baby/sacrifice narrative, another is Lerner's donation of her survival space to Beth and her child. The climax is a positive orgy of emotion in the moments before the astronaut crew sacrifice themselves by flying their craft heroically into the comet. The families of some of the crew members are brought out at Mission Control to say their tearful goodbyes, including the husband and young daughter of Andrea Baker (Mary McCormack) and, at the last second, the wife and new baby of Oren Monash (Ron Eldard). The two sons of the older astronaut Spurgeon 'Fish' Tanner (Robert Duvall) are away on 'active duty' and so cannot be assembled, but Tanner says his own piece to his late wife, joining the wave of domestic emotion via an old photograph of his wife and the two boys as children. All of this – intercut with the escape of Leo,

Sarah and their newly acquired infant – is played for maximum sentimental impact.

An element of this is also present in the climax of *Armageddon*, especially the final exchange between Stamper and Grace. The difference in *Deep Impact* is the greater centrality of this kind of material and the lesser emphasis on the larger scale of spectacle generated by special effects. The differences between the two films can be read, from this perspective, as a classic example of the way Hollywood has always worked to mix and match its ingredients, to offer different takes on similar material, to play around with elements of genres or cycles in the pursuit of one audience segment or another.[32] *Deep Impact* has the texture of a film oriented significantly towards a female audience but it includes elements of action-adventure and spectacular effects. *Armageddon* is a thumping male-oriented action movie that takes care to work in a degree of romance and tearful emotion. Both hold the potential to achieve the useful economic status of a 'date movie', offering something at least to meet dominant expectations associated with male and female viewers. Exactly how such films are pitched to audiences is further complicated and compromised by promotional discourses, especially trailers. One trailer for *Armageddon* opens with the spectacular assault on Manhattan, very much in keeping with the dominant tone of the film. Another, however, puts the initial emphasis on the glowing embrace between Grace and AJ, creating the impression of a relationship-based drama more like *Deep Impact.* The latter, just to complete any confusion, has one trailer that adopts a thumping and flashy *Armageddon*-like aesthetic that sends out further mixed messages. Trailers, just like the films, are not so much 'incoherent' as careful attempts to have it all ways in the search for maximum audience appeal.

7

Conclusion: Into the Spectacle?

> LIVE THE SAGA. Take part in the epic events from the *Star Wars*: Episode I story – and beyond …
>
> Packaging blurb for the PC game *Star Wars – Episode One: The Phantom Menace*

> Historically, spectacle tends to move toward participatory narrative in order to retain our attention, to lengthen the immersive experience.
>
> Janet Murray[1]

A liquid-metallic extrusion comes out from the screen at the viewer. The extremity assumes the visage of the police officer used by the shape-shifting T-1000 terminator in *Terminator 2: Judgement Day*, probing out among startled members of the audience. A real flesh-and-blood actor wearing the same uniform jumps out from the bottom of the screen to fight performers already in the auditorium playing the roles of the film's heroes, John and Sarah Connor. The figure of the original terminator (without quite the build of Arnold Schwarzenegger) comes roaring out of the screen on his motorcycle to join the action, shortly before he and the John Connor figure burst back to the other side of the looking-glass as we are treated to a futuristic on-screen action spectacular including many more 3D effects.

A 'multi-dimensional adventure so real you can't tell what is film and what is live action,' is how the official guide describes *Terminator 2: 3D*, an attraction that opened at Universal Studios, Hollywood, in May 1999. It offers the illusion of an interpenetration of the worlds on and off screen.

Real performers penetrate to 'our' side of the screen, while 3D imagery and other effects project us into the fictional universe. At times we might doubt which exactly is which, raising our 3D glasses to check whether a particular figure is really present in the theatre or just the spectre of a 3D illusion.

Theme-park attractions such as this claim to take us into the physical and experiential space of the movies. Computer games based on films, meanwhile, promise an interactive engagement with something like the world on screen. The latest in giant IMAX or Omnimax cinemas engulf us in vast encompassing images. Virtual reality technologies are celebrated as offering the future potential of truly immersive entertainment environments, the implications of which are explored in a growing subgenre of science fiction. Each of these new dimensions, often seen as exacerbating existing trends in contemporary Hollywood cinema, has been greeted as a threat to the existence of narrative.

What happens when we are projected, one way or another, into the spectacle? What place is there for narrative amid the thrills of the latest attraction at Disneyland or Universal Studios, the computer game, the IMAX screen, or in the simulated worlds of VR? More importantly, perhaps, what is the impact of these spin-offs on Hollywood films themselves? Have rides become more like films, or films more like rides? Which, exactly, is the driving force? To what extent, in the world of a corporate Hollywood that has one eye on potential for exploitation in other media, are some films designed around their ability to be translated easily into the ride or computer game? The debate surrounding films that have become 'inhabitable' in these ways is perhaps the ultimate test of the relationship between spectacle and narrative that has been the focus of this book. Is this the point at which narrative finally succumbs to the demands of spectacle? Or, if narrative persists, how might it function in the space between films and their more emphatically spectacular or interactive progeny? This concluding chapter will consider these issues in relation to the extra-cinematic dimension, especially the Hollywood-based theme-park attraction and the computer game, and also in films that create fictional equivalents of such habitable spaces of illusion.

Riding the movies

Theme park attractions such as *Terminator 2: 3D* offer a more literal version of the 'in your face' spectacle examined in earlier chapters. They project a series of items out into the space of the viewer, in typical 3D style. *T2: 3D* follows the probing T-1000 with a range of weapons and exploding fragments, with miniature armed flying machines and the hyperbolic multi-limbed T-1000,000. There is already a recognizable currency in this kind of attraction.

'In your face': the hyperbolic T-1000,000 appears to penetrate startlingly into the space of the audience in the Terminator 2: 3D *attraction. Publicity still © Universal Studios Inc.*

Similar effects are offered by Disney's *Honey, I Shrunk the Audience*, although with a smaller role for 'real' on-stage performance. A miniaturized flying machine zooms out into the audience space in 3D, like the armed variety seen in *T2: 3D*, and sends out its own debris as it crashes into a neon sign suspended over the front of the audience; the face of a cat extends from the screen, transforming into a roaring lion, and so on. This is nothing new in the history of 3D movies, which have always tended to spend much of their time thrusting objects out at the audience. These attractions go further, however, in offering an assault on the viewer. Both resort to one way of physically touching the audience without any threat of injury: by spraying liquid in their faces. In *Honey, I Shrunk the Audience* the result is a climactic gross-out effect as a giant dog sneezes into the auditorium; in *T2: 3D* the T-1000,000 is frozen solid and then shattered outwards into a shower of liquid metal fragments. These attractions also move their audiences physically, if not always emotionally. The seats in *T2: 3D* push upwards at the start of the last sequence, in which the screen widens to almost 180° and the audience is given the illusion of joining the fictional protagonists in a descending lift. In the final conflagration, as 3D flames explode out from the screen and smoke effects engulf the theatre, the seats drop back abruptly to jolt with the impact of destruction.

More sustained motion effects are used in *Honey, I Shrunk the Audience.* Once the audience has been 'shrunk' the images on screen are blown up to giant proportions and the booming sounds of the movements of gigantic fictional performers are translated into the shaking of the entire ground of the theatre, an effect repeated as the mischievous younger child of the inventor Wayne Szalinski (Rick Moranis) 'picks up' the auditorium, which seems to sway beneath the audience as it is carried and nearly dropped.

If audiences for action films enjoy 'being done to', as was suggested in Chapter 4, then this is 'being done to' quite literally. Stronger motion effects are found in a different kind of theme-park attraction, the movie-based motion simulator ride. Pioneered by Disneyland's *Star Tours* and updated by Universal's *Back to the Future: The Ride*, these are based on technologies developed by the US military for pilot training simulation. Relatively small numbers of viewers/experiencers sit on a motion platform that bucks and yaws alarmingly to synchronize with the apparent movements suggested on screen. In the *Star Wars* spin-off, *Star Tours*, the images are projected on to a relatively small screen that stands in for the window of a spacecraft on a runaway flight through various scenes of the film. *Back to the Future: The Ride* offers more encompassing imagery projected on to an Omnimax dome, a chase through time and space that includes plunging into a volcano and down the throat of a T-rex. Other Hollywood-based attractions, including *Jurassic Park: The Ride* at Universal and Disneyland's *The Indiana Jones Adventure*, take the form of more conventional theme-park rides, moving around tracks that purport to take us through the landscape of the relevant films, and offering thrills such as the 84-foot drop and splashdown that ends the ride based on *Jurassic Park.*

As theme-park 'attractions', these forms remind us of Tom Gunning's 'cinema of attractions', the brand of early cinema that addressed an audience directly rather than establishing an internally focused narrative. Film-based rides and attractions establish a similar kind of relationship with the audience. As participants, we are directly addressed and interpellated in many cases. In *Back to the Future: The Ride* we are addressed on video by the figure of Doc Brown (Christopher Lloyd) as volunteers in his time travel experiments. Both *T2: 3D* and *Honey, I Shrunk the Audience* present viewers as members of an audience at, respectively, a demonstration of high-tech weapons and a scientific awards ceremony. This is a way of attempting to naturalize some of the process and surroundings of the attractions, including in both of the latter cases the wearing of 3D glasses styled as 'safety glasses' needed in the 'unlikely' event of anything going wrong. The modern movie-based theme-park attraction recalls the first film showings, which often took place as novelties at fairs and amusements parks. There is also a striking resemblance to some of the early attempts to create motion simulation illusions coupled with cinematic images, including the Hale's Tours feature of the 1900s, which synchronized moving platforms disguised as railway carriages with projected images designed to create the illusion of the passing landscape.

The *Back to the Future* ride could be seen as the belated fulfilment of a design by H.G. Wells and the inventor and early filmmaker Robert Paul in 1895 for an attraction based on the novelist's *The Time Machine*, a theatre in which the audience would view films and slides from seats on a motion platform, the impression of movement to be increased by blowing air at the viewer.[2] More recent rounds of novelty attraction within the cinema also come to mind, including the 1950s experiments with larger screens, 3D (briefly revived in the 1980s) and other gimmicks including William Castle's production of *The Tingler* (1959), shown in some theatres with seats wired to produce mild electric shocks in the audience.

It is no accident that a rollercoaster ride featured centrally in the first Cinerama feature, *This is Cinerama* (1952), nor that one of the films to follow *Earthquake* in the use of the Sensurround process was *Rollercoaster* (1977). Both use first-person perspectives to give the viewer a sense of being carried on the ride itself. The ride-film, or film-based ride, is taken by some commentators as an index of the state of contemporary Hollywood. The identification of parallels with aspects of early cinema and subsequent novelty attractions has tended to encourage the association of the 'ride film' with the dominance today of a variety of spectacle that is said to be largely unadulterated by narrative. In some cases comparisons are extended to suggest similarities between what are perceived as moments of the 'birth' and 'death' of cinema, at least in its classical form. The 'cinema of attractions' pre-dates the establishment and consolidation of a cinema centred on narrative. Like Hale's Tours, it marks a stage in which what we now recognize as the institution of 'cinema' was still finding its shape. The novelty attractions of the 1950s or today are often described in terms of a crisis of cinema or its threatened end-point. In the 1950s novelty experiments were a response to serious economic difficulties. Today the industry is healthier, but seen as facing challenges from the technological developments of the digital age, including its potential future replacement by more immersive or interactive forms of entertainment.[3]

Spectacular and visceral thrills are the principal and most immediate stuff of contemporary attractions, and for some they confirm the worst tendencies identified within the Hollywood blockbuster: the epitome of apparently vacuous rollercoaster experiences. It has become commonplace to describe many Hollywood products in these terms, as 'thrill-rides' rather than sustained narratives of any kind. This is a term often used approvingly in Hollywood publicity and by some reviewers in the popular press, presumably because a thrill ride is what many viewers want from this kind of cinema. But it has become the basis of a familiar complaint from more 'serious' critics and among some academic commentators. For Scott Bukatman, Hollywood has developed 'what might be termed the "theme park movie" – a set of overdesigned, hermetically sealed, totalizing environments masquerading as movies. *Dick Tracy* (1990), *Batman* (1989), and *Jurassic Park* (1993) all could be considered examples of this phenomenon.'[4] Film-based rides are important, Bukatman argues:

> in the 1980s and 1990s, films became rides, which is to say that they became less narrative than they used to be and more spectacular, with their spectacles more compressed one atop another but also more extended, hammering across an entire two-hour-plus film with scarcely any let-up. Meanwhile, theme park rides and attractions became more narrative than, say, roller coasters had been. They also were extended. Waiting on line for Star Tours was part of the ride, as elaborate sets and amusing droids entertained but also grounded the spectacle.[5]

Bukatman's account is familiar from arguments we have already encountered, including the analysis of *Armageddon* in the previous chapter, and full of sweeping claims. The suggestion that any of the examples he cites merely 'masquerade' as movies is purely hyperbolic, whatever their merits or shortcomings. His latter point is a significant one, however, opening up the possibility of a more fruitful analysis of the relationship between attraction-rides and films.

The films Bukatman and others have in mind do not surrender all investment in narrative, in terms of either story-plotting or underlying thematic structures, in the pursuit of ever grander spectacles. Neither, actually, do the theme-park attractions or rides. Attenuated though they may be, the rides themselves rarely lasting more than about ten minutes, they have their own narrative components. Elements of narrative are, indeed, structured into the process of waiting on line involved in the experience of such popular attractions. *Star Tours*, as Bukatman suggests, provides a theatrical backdrop to entertain the waiting queue, and this has become a standard feature. Video monitors, posters and other media are used as 'warm up' devices, to keep audiences amused during the wait and to prepare them to get the most from the spectacle that follows.

The lengthy preamble/queue for *The Indiana Jones Adventure* at Disneyland, for example, takes the visitor through a series of mock temple chambers and passageways that set the mood for the ride itself. An element of interactivity is introduced, including notices and warnings to read and certain marked paved stones on which we are told to avoid standing. Attractions such as *T2: 3D* and *Honey, I Shrunk the Audience*, displayed in full-sized theatrical auditoria, bring waiting visitors into a vestibule area before the main event, in which they are entertained and prepared through a combination of video-monitor presentations and live hosts. The physical organization of the queue itself has become something of an art form. The lines for *Star Tours*, *The Indiana Jones Adventure* and *Back to the Future: The Ride* are cunningly designed to snake through different chambers to remove the appearance of a single long queue. Something akin to a kind of narrative manipulation of expectation is constructed as the audience moves closer to the end of one section, a miniature crisis of expectation, fulfilment and often disappointment created as we wait to find out if we are 'really' at the end of the line, at last, as we pass from one chamber to the next. It is possible to see the overall experience of the ride-film as in one sense similar to that of the 'classical' narrative pattern discussed in the previous chapter: a lengthy and gradual build-up leading to a relatively brief and spectacular climax.

If this seems to be stretching the point a little, it is worth noting that the ride-film or attraction usually has a more obvious story-narrative of its own. We are not plunged into a direct and unmediated experience of three-dimensional spectacle. So, in *Back to the Future: The Ride* we are briefed on a specific mission based on a plot thread from the films: our task, as time travel volunteers in Doc Brown's Institute of Future Technology, is to chase and bring back to the present the rogue Biff Tannen (Thomas F. Wilson), who has escaped with one of the scientist's time-travelling DeLoreans. *T2: 3D* presents, in microcosm, another *Terminator* sequel, a tale in which the threat to humanity forestalled in *Terminator 2* has been renewed and has heroically to be tackled once again. *Honey, I Shrunk the Audience* is structured in much the same way, as a truncated sequel in which another permutation is worked in the game of comic crisis engendered by shrinking and/or enlargement. These attractions can also be understood in terms of the underlying narrative issues found in their feature-length parents. Many include discourses about the relationship between technology and humanity that have been elaborated throughout this book.

T2: 3D sets up precisely the opposition between utopian and dystopian visions of advanced technology found so widely in Hollywood cinema. Information supplied during the queuing process plays heavily on the utopian side of the equation. Promotional material from the Cyberdyne corporation promises: 'Making you a better person through technology.' A range of wonderful new technologies is unveiled, including virtual doctors and operating theatres and the original T-1 metallic material that can be shaped into anything we desire. Familiarity with the franchise and a general underlying sinister tone lead us to distrust blandishments such as the sight of a mother able virtually to tuck up her child at night, when away from home, through the interface of a pair of robot arms.

The official PR video signal is interrupted as the drama begins, while we are still in the vestibule, when the Connors break in with their rebel message about the threat posed to humanity by the corporation's new generation of computer technologies. Many of these attractions are organized around the theme of the promises, threats and unpredictable hazards offered by new technologies. *Honey, I Shrunk the Audience* is a catalogue of errors and eccentricity, just like the films from which it was spawned. It shares their implication in an ideological presentation of technology: technology associated with innocent eccentricity and family values, rather than a product of giant corporations like Cyberdyne. The imaginary technology of *Back to the Future: The Ride* is a mixed blessing, as in the films, often going wrong or threatened with misuse. It, too, is presented as the product of loveable eccentricity rather than the might of corporate or military R&D.

Star Tours and *Jurassic Park: The Ride* offer the spectacle of technology gone, literally, off the rails. In *Star Tours* our gentle trip to the moon of Endor turns into a hectic ride when the inexperienced robot pilot misses a turning before launch, crashes around inside a space station and sets off on a haphazard journey through a series of zones from which it should have been forbidden. In *Jurassic Park: The Ride* we start off with a relatively bland boat trip through the dinosaur park, having been given repeated assurances on video while waiting in line that Jurassic Park is safe, well guarded and protected by technology. The ride then stages an illusion of 'going the wrong way', as we appear to miss the prescribed route and enter a forbidden 'backstage' area rife with dangers from escaped velociraptors, a T-rex that looms down from above, poisoned atmosphere and the climactic plunge. It is in the act of going 'off the rails', the wrong way, or witnessing the interruption of what are initially presented as routine procedures, that the thrilling aspects of these attractions are usually comprised.

This again suggests continuity with the structure of contemporary Hollywood. What we are given to inhabit in many of these attractions is akin to the position of the Hollywood hero, experiencing the thrills that are found on the wild or rebellious domain juxtaposed to all that is corporate, controlled or immersed in technology.

There is a strong connection between these theme-park attractions and the films, but it is not best described as an eclipse of narrative concerns at either extreme. The attractions are built around and extend the spectacular potential of the films, but they also play on narrative

'Off the rails': a three-dimensional T-rex menaces riders given the illusion of going the wrong way, into danger, in Jurassic Park: The Ride. *Publicity still © Universal Studios Inc.*

resonances. As Murray Smith suggests in relation to *Jurassic Park* and *The Lost World* (1997):

> The dinosaurs in Spielberg's recent films are not just impressive spectacles, but creatures of terror and wonderment – characters, antagonists, in a tale. It is this emotional dimension which, among

> other things, makes the movies memorable, and thus fosters the 'memorialization' of the experience through further purchases – be it games, videos, clothing or theme parks.[6]

The demands of the blockbuster may have led to an emphasis on certain genres and on more episodic forms of narrative, but this is not the same as narrative being displaced. The movie 'provides a primary narrative baseline which both endows isolated movie icons with meaning and emotional resonance, and provides a backdrop against which to toy with these associations in other media contexts'. This is a useful and subtle account of the relationships between the different manifestations of popular media products. The meanings and resonances carried by film icons are important commercial considerations, helping to ensure that expensive theme-park attractions have a ready-made audience and are able to establish clear and positive associations in the minds of visitors. The more intense experience of aspects of the spectacle offered by the films is a major factor in their appeal, but this can be heightened by carrying over narrative associations and identifications and by including elements of narrative within even the most visceral thrill-based attraction. As Janet Murray suggests: 'the movie-rides are providing evidence that audiences are not satisfied by intense sensation alone. Once people do go "into" the movie, they want more than a rollercoaster ride; they want a story.'[7]

Virtual spaces: from immersion to interactivity and beyond

The recent *Aladdin* ride at Walt Disney World offers an extra dimension to the theme-park experience: the freedom for riders to choose their own way through the imaginary landscape and to affect the way the story unfolds.[8] This is a significant development, a shift from a form of 'immersive' attraction to one that offers a degree of 'interactivity'. Most ride-films seek to act physically on the body of the viewer/rider, but allow little space for their subjects to respond. The main reason for this is financial: significant levels of interactivity require more expensive technology and more time-consuming experiences than can easily be accommodated in theme-park settings. Developments in virtual reality technologies may offer new future possibilities of immersive and interactive entertainments. For now, however, one of the most available forms of film-based interactive experience is provided by the computer game, a form that has become increasingly significant in the commercial calculations of the corporations within which the Hollywood studios are located.[9] Like ride-films, interactive computer games based on films offer much in the way of spectacular thrills; but this, again, does not necessarily involve an absence of narrative.

Computer games based on films come in different shapes and sizes, and with varying degrees of narrative structure. At one extreme is the pure action shoot-up or race variety; at the other, more complex puzzles that entail the investigation and exploration of a digital version of cinematic space. All supply a 'back story' of some kind, a narrative that provides a context for the action. The extent and complexity of these varies. *Independence Day: The Game* provides a brief half-page of text based on the plot of the film. The action of the game is drawn, and extended, from the last movement of the film, beginning at the point where the computer virus has been delivered to the alien mother ship. The task is to 'finish the job', which comprises a series of fast-paced flying-and-shooting engagements devoid of much more in the way of narrative. *Star Wars – Episode I: The Phantom Menace*, in contrast, starts with a similarly brief initial sketch of narrative background but develops the more complex series of characters, goals and puzzles characteristic of a hybrid adventure/puzzle/action game.

Spectacle, and a sense of inhabiting the space of spectacular action, is a major ingredient in the appeal of these games. But what exactly is the role of the narrative, both the back story and, in examples such as *The Phantom Menace*, the ongoing developments of plot? Mary Fuller and Henry Jenkins suggest that the framing stories 'play little role in the actual experience of the games, as plot gives way to a more flexible period of spatial exploration.'[10] *Independence Day: The Game* has precious little narrative beyond the initial exposition, which tends to disappear from view during frenetic combat missions. In the more substantially plotted *The Phantom Menace*, narrative also stops, effectively, during all those moments when we become stuck or engaged in the rapid finger-twitching required to survive attack by a platoon of battle droids.

Computer games promise the illusion of inhabiting the central character, rather than merely watching figures on a screen, but the experience may offer less satisfying identification than that achieved in the cinema. We should not forget, amid all the immersive and interactive frills of rides and games, that the impression of 'immersion' is precisely one of the illusions the Hollywood style of filmmaking seeks to create through its continuity editing patterns and emotional identifications with character. As Ted Friedman puts it: 'whereas classical Hollywood cinema is designed in every way to allow one to "lose oneself" in the fantasy on-screen, the stop-and-go nature of the puzzle-solving paradigm makes it very hard to establish the same level of psychic investment'.[11]

Games vary in the degree of interactivity permitted. *The Phantom Menace* game enables the player to explore aspects of the on-screen world passed over rather rapidly in the film. The player gets to inhabit the atmospheric underwater world of the Gungans, for example, to a much greater extent than the protagonists of the film, who zoom away after a short stop. The player is often free to stop and have a more leisurely look and a virtual wander around. This is a major appeal of the film-based game, the chance to go beyond simply revisiting the imaginary world on video or in the sequel. The player's behaviour can sometimes affect the immediate outcome as well, in properly interactive fashion. We are advised not to kill any Gungans, for example, and they respond more favourably if that injunction is followed. The capacity for interaction is limited, however, in any game that follows the film narrative closely. There is ultimately only one way through the action of *The Phantom Menace*, in a series of moves and developments that correspond broadly with the celluloid version.

Increased potential for interactivity is often presented as a benefit of new media such as computer games, DVD or digital broadcasting, but it is worth questioning how far this is likely to be embraced by audiences. A choice between different routes through a story, or alternate endings, may offer a novel experience, useful especially for the promotion of new technologies. It might also undermine some of the most enjoyable characteristics of uni-directional narrative: the delicate balance of familiarity/uncertainty, suspense, emotional tension and relief built into the Hollywood variety and largely dependent on moment-by-moment choice being taken out of our hands.

Narrative structure is an important aspect of the experience of a game like *The Phantom Menace*, although it is narrative of a particular variety. The narrative is built into the fabric of the game world and has to be unlocked by the player, who has some freedom in how to proceed but relatively little ability to control the outcome. The result is what Fuller and Jenkins term 'an alternative tradition of "spatial stories", a different way of organizing narratives that must be examined and evaluated according to their own cultural logic'.[12] They have their own ideological implications. Games that unfold largely through the mastery and conquest of alien spaces, Fuller and Jenkins suggest, enact a colonialist narrative. Their example, a Mario Brothers game, is broadly comparable to *The Phantom Menace* in this respect: 'it allows people to enact through play an older narrative that can no longer be enacted in reality – a constant struggle for the possession of desirable spaces, the ever shifting and unstable frontier between controlled and uncontrollable space, the need to venture onto unmapped terrain and to confront its privileged inhabitants'. Something close to the mythic frontier narrative, in other words.

Resonances from the cinematic narrative carry over into games in the manner suggested by Murray Smith, a crucial point again in the economic equation. Games based on hit films have an added advantage in the marketplace, initially at least. This is partly a matter of cross-promotion, films released in the cinema tending to gain high-profile media coverage and to carry into other forms the kind of cinematic prestige outlined by Peter Kramer. But it also influences the game-playing experience itself. To play a game based on a film like *The Phantom Menace* is to enjoy the illusion of *being* a part of that world and sharing the aura. Players are inserted into the fictional universe in a more testing manner than watching a film. A sense of strength and mastery can be established, qualities that have potential cultural, sociological or psychological implications, not least for the process of male gender construction. The fact that this goes on within the simulated diegetic universe of a film adds an extra dimension to the experience. A player of *The Phantom Menace* might feel justified in acts of death and destruction given the noble cast given to the central Jedi characters, for example, or might even be led to explore less aggressive alternatives.

The *Independence Day* game also situates its destructive missions within a legitimating context: saving the world as part of an outbreak of global unity. Is this just a weak excuse for a typical exercise of male shoot-up aggression? Is it entirely left behind in the second-by-second business of on-screen combat, or do the glowing ideological resonances of the film continue to hover around the experience? It is very hard to quantify this kind of thing, the amorphous resonance brought to one cultural product by its associations with another, and this account remains rather speculative. A degree of evidence is provided by the sheer number of games based on films, particularly on successful franchises such as *Star Wars* and *Star Trek*.

Does the game-potential of films actually help to shape the films themselves? This is a key question, but hard to answer in any definitive way. The film version of *The Phantom Menace* provides an example in the case of the spectacular pod race sequence that was immediately translated into its own computer game, *Star Wars – Episode I: Racer*. The sequence in the film – the alarming high speed negotiation of a wild course, rendered in a blend of first and third person perspectives – is strikingly reminiscent of a computer or arcade game. It is mostly computer-generated except for the shots of Anakin and other principal characters. The game offers a choice of four different perspectives on the action, ranging from an entirely subjective first-person to viewpoints which include within the frame all or part of the racer. It provides dizzying speed and thrills of a kind not dissimilar to the action scenes of contemporary Hollywood. Which comes first is hard to say. Was the sequence worked into the film primarily with the intention to extract it as a distinct game-based profit-line of its own, or is this a secondary benefit? Attempting to compile precise hierarchical relationships is to miss the most important point: it is precisely the nature of the world of the contemporary entertainment conglomerate to work through a process of mutually informing and multiple determinations among and within product streams.

Even if the pod race sequence were designed with the game version very much in mind from the start this would not support the argument that such multiple-media exploitation necessarily undermines the narrative dimensions of the film. Thomas Schatz argues that 'the blockbuster tends to be intertextual and purposefully incoherent – virtually of necessity, given the current conditions of cultural production and consumption'.[13] The 'vertical integration of classical Hollywood, which ensured a closed industrial system and coherent narrative, has given way to "horizontal integration" of the New Hollywood's tightly diversified media conglomerates, which favours texts strategically "open" to multiple readings and multimedia reiteration'. There is much to agree with in this account except that it persists in overstating the extent to which narrative was 'coherent' in the past or is 'incoherent' today. Films made in the studio era 'had their intertextual qualities', Schatz concedes, but 'these were incidental and rarely undermined the internal coherence of the narrative itself'.

Does this really go far enough, to account for the potent intertextual dimensions of phenomena such as genre and star performance in the heyday of 'classical' Hollywood? I would suggest not. The contemporary blockbuster is open to multiple readings in pursuit of a wide-ranging audience, and it is certainly 'open' to multimedia reiteration. The question is whether these qualities add up to a qualitative difference at the level of narrative. Let us return to the pod race sequence, the kind of example that might be used to support the position of Schatz, a classic instance of the extended spectacular special-effects extravaganza that might overwhelm all narrative concerns. But the sequence has its own narrative motivations. Successful completion of the race is presented as the only way to guarantee the onward movement of the plot, in fact, as a victory for the young Anakin Skywalker is necessary to enable the main protagonists to escape from the desert planet of Tatooine and continue their mission. Dizzying spectacle that it is, and sustained for a lengthy seven minutes, the race also has an internal narrative structure. It constitutes a miniature version of the classical Hollywood parable of outsider beset by difficulties and outright sabotage who starts off behind, works hard to catch up, is the victim of sabotage again, and eventually overcomes all adversity to zip home in triumph. Underlying narrative themes are also pencilled in amid the spectacle, as we have seen elsewhere in contemporary Hollywood. Anakin's victory is secured, we are given to assume, through his access to the mystical powers of the 'Force', a dimension the *Star Wars* films repeatedly present in opposition to over-reliance on technological rationality. The broad arc of the narrative may be bracketed during the most exciting parts of the race, but it is doubtful that such a phenomenon is so new in the entire action-and-spectacle-packed history of Hollywood cinema.

Often driven strongly by the demand to produce immersive and/or interactive spectacle, film-based rides and computer games maintain a significant investment in narrative, as do the films on which they draw. The same is likely to go for any sustained development of virtual reality as a form of entertainment technology, although this is a conclusion resisted by many commentators. The body in virtual reality, for Bukatman, 'transcends the need for a surrogate character to experience the diegesis *for* him or her, or for a narrative to ground the exploration of an unfamiliar space'.[14] There may be no *need* for a surrogate character or narrative in new forms of virtual reality entertainment, but that is far from suggesting that they will not be offered. It might be more plausible to suggest that virtual reality entertainments are likely to stick to some kind of mixture of narrative and directly immersive 'ride' experiences. Direct immersion tends to be uncomfortable and/or demanding if extended beyond a brief period. The classical Hollywood *découpage*, still very much in evidence in today's blockbusters, avoids this problem by offering combinations of perspectives located close to those of 'surrogate' characters and apparently more 'objective' positions, as we have seen. This is exactly how *Rollercoaster* organizes its ride sequences: potentially dizzying first-person images from the front seat of the rides are balanced by 'safer' and more stable third-person perspectives. The same goes for the rail chase in *Indiana Jones and the Temple of Doom*, in which immediate 'rollercoaster' perspectives are offered but account for much less of the sequence than various other viewpoints on the action and the plight of the characters.

So far, virtual reality technologies have not been mobilized for entertainment purposes that go greatly beyond the more sophisticated ride-film or computer game. Existing games remain well short of the fully immersive virtual reality created by wearing a full-body data-suit and head-mounted display helmet, or future projections that might require a less clumsy interface. The stronger sense of virtual reality, a world we might feel that we 'really' inhabit, remains the stuff of science fiction. One of the most cited examples is the 'holodeck' of *Star Trek: The Next Generation*, a system in which the player is situated within entirely convincing three-dimensional simulations of imaginary worlds; potentially spectacular to inhabit, but also narrative driven. Hollywood has come up with a number of representations of 'habitable' computer-generated landscapes in films that offer another perspective on the relationship between spectacle and narrative. To take four prominent examples, *The Matrix* (1999), *Johnny Mnemonic* (1995), *The Lawnmower Man* (1992) and *Strange Days* (1995) all present spectacular visions of virtual realities of one kind or another, the appeal of which seems to be at odds with the underlying concerns expressed by the narrative. Each of these films suggests that the virtual landscape is in some way dangerous. The narrative tends towards a dystopian vision of the new technologies involved. This is at its most extreme in *The Matrix*, in which the 'normal' world is shown to be a giant computer simulation designed to conceal the reality of a post-apocalyptic nightmare in which almost the whole of humanity has been reduced to the status of organic batteries creating the energy needed by a race of machines.

In *Johnny Mnemonic* the life of the title character is endangered by the overloaded data chip implanted in his head and much of humanity is suffering from an apparently terminal illness produced by 'technological civilization'. The virtual reality of *The Lawnmower Man* holds the potential for utopian applications including 'the key to the evolution of the human mind', but ends up creating a virtual megalomaniac who threatens to take over the world. *Strange Days* features a 'SQUID' technology that can record and play back experiences in all their original sensory richness: 'You're there, you're seeing it, you're hearing it, you're *feeling* it.' The device offers an ersatz experience of life in a world in which 'reality' is becoming too dangerous to risk; it is treated more like a dangerously addictive drug than a new world of experience or entertainment.

If their narratives tell us that these technologies offer at best mixed blessings, each of these films sells itself as popular entertainment partly in terms of the spectacular deployment of the new visions on offer. *Johnny Mnemonic* and *The Lawnmower Man* are filled with luminous special-effects graphics that highlight the appeal of both the fictional technologies and the cinematic equivalents that enable them to be displayed. *Johnny Mnemonic* presents us with dazzling 'first-person' perspectives through the space of the data stored in Johnny's mind, visions offered for our spectacular pleasure even when they indicate a painful experience for the protagonist. The film also gives us a vision of a VR-mediated computer interface complete with head-mounted display and data-gloves, an experience of manipulating the world within the computer with seductive ease and facility. The spectacular climax has Johnny's virtual equivalent hacking into the brightly coloured landscape of his own brain to find a vital piece of data and do battle with an animated virus.

The Lawnmower Man offers numerous computer-graphics sequences which glory in the spectacular world of virtual space and the capacities a technologically-enhanced being can bring to the exterior world, including the ability to destroy enemies by pixillating their images and deconstructing them, a weapon that seems to involve the application of digital special-effects techniques to the real world. The narrative of *Strange Days* worries about the loss of contact with reality caused by prolonged exposure to recordings of the experiences of others, but it also provides the viewer with a version of those experiences. Examples include the exhilarating first-person perspective of a robbery supplied by a mobile subjective camera that ends up plunging from the top of a building and, more disturbingly, being forced to occupy the perspective of a rapist-murderer.

And then there is *The Matrix*, in which one of the gloomiest of dystopian scenarios is coupled with a positively intoxicating sense of the possibilities unleashed once the protagonist becomes aware that the 'real world' is merely a computer simulation the rules of which can be bent and broken by the initiate. One character eventually betrays the heroes, his price being a return to unconscious acceptance of the illusion. Who could blame him, given the bleak nature of the naked reality and the fantastic possibilities unleashed in the simulation? The film certainly invites us to take much of our pleasure from the latter, a world in which the gloriously absurd choreography of the martial-arts and action cinemas can be both gently parodied and given literal motivation: yes, it is all impossible nonsense, but who said it was reality, anyway? A character can, suddenly, display the skills to fly a helicopter in a major action sequence because, in this virtual world, all she needs is someone to plug in the right software.

One conclusion to be drawn from these films is that there is a contradiction between the dimensions of narrative and spectacle, between what we are told at one level and invited to enjoy on another. Some effort is made to resolve this contradiction, however. In a manner typical of Hollywood science fiction, the narrative 'rescues' the otherwise indicted realm of technology through the insertion of technologically-skilled characters who are not implicated in its dystopian use; figures who, like William Gibson's 'cyber cowboys', are often presented in the garb of frontier-rebels of one kind or another. *The Matrix* and *Johnny Mnemonic* are characteristic in their establishment of rag-tag bands of rebels who stand against the forces of massive domination, the group led by Morpheus (Laurence Fishburne) in *The Matrix* and the Loteks of *Johnny Mnemonic*. These are essentially hackers–heroes, with all of the positive computer-age-frontier-related characteristics the term suggests. They penetrate the technologies of the oppressors and use them for subversive purposes, in the interests of humanity. Technology is transformed from threat to a source of hyper-active human agency. Our enjoyment of the cinematic techno-spectacle is thus legitimated, helping to square the apparent contradiction between the dimensions of spectacle and narrative.

Relatively crude versions of bodily immersive virtual reality are beginning to be used for entertainment purposes in the real world, and these may well succeed initially on the basis of novelty attraction. The sheer sensation of being able to move around and manipulate objects within a computer-generated world might be thrill enough, even if this remains way behind the capacities given to fictional counterparts such as the heroes of *The Matrix*. But how long is this likely to remain the case? Narrative accompaniments are already included in virtual reality games, as they are in theme-park rides. We are reminded here of the narrative component that always existed in the historical 'cinema of attractions'. It is hard to imagine that any sustained move into virtual reality entertainment will fail to be accompanied by more developed narratives. The vision of a future equivalent of the cinema in which virtual reality enables us to inhabit the diegetic space is one in which narrative is likely to play a major role if it is to offer sustained and compelling illusions: assuming, that is, that the entertainment industry conglomerates see a profitable potential in the development of a VR-cinema: something we should not take for granted.[15] We may enter into interactive narrative scenarios, or simply be given a much stronger illusion of 'presence' as spectators to the virtual events. These narratives may not be as new as the technologies within which they are mobilized, as Cheris Kramarae found in the Legend Quest game, a 'dungeons and dragons' style virtual reality adventure. The aim is to survive a number of challenges and defeat the evil master: 'If this sounds familiar it's because all-too-familiar knowledges, stories, adventures, and stereotypes operate in virtual reality.'[16] The myths and ideologies that dominate existing media are the ones most likely to be translated into the new medium. In American popular culture, at least, this means many more doses of frontier-related discourse.

None of this is to suggest that virtual reality technologies will simply repeat a history of cinema characterized as a move from pure spectacle to narrativization (and, in some versions, back again to the dominance of spectacle). A full-scale and sustained virtual reality entertainment medium is likely to follow the Hollywood model, offering a combination of narrative and spectacle, the 'amazing' vistas we would be able to inhabit and the dynamics of both 'surface' plot and underlying narrative thematics. This is not to say that particular representational technologies *inevitably* lead to the production of one dimension or the other; merely that they have proved popular and profitable in the past and are likely to be deployed again. New technologies bring their own specific qualities, but do not automatically change the kinds of materials presented. Narrative, in its various dimensions, has been around for a very long time and is not likely to disappear in future representations any more than it has vanished from the contemporary Hollywood blockbuster. The default is likely to be in favour of maintaining significant narrative elements, however much a technology or its economic context lends itself also to the production of eye-popping spectacle.

Notes

Introduction

1. 'Ideology, Genre, Auteur', 62, in Barry Keith Grant (ed.), *Film Genre Reader II.*
2. 'Theses on the philosophy of Hollywood history', in Steve Neale and Murray Smith (eds), *Contemporary Hollywood Cinema.*
3. A number of theorists who develop this argument will be encountered throughout this book. Beyond the academic sphere, the assumption that narrative has been eclipsed by Hollywood spectacle appears to have wide currency in the work of mainstream film reviewers and more general popular discourses.
4. For a detailed analysis of the extent to which many contemporary Hollywood films, including action blockbusters, retain a large investment in 'classical' narrative techniques see Kristin Thompson, *Storytelling in the New Hollywood.*
5. 'The Classical Hollywood Style, 1917–60', 'Part One' of David Bordwell, Janet Staiger and Kristen Thompson, *The Classical Hollywood Cinema: Film Style and Mode of Production to 1960.*
6. See Richard Maltby and Ian Craven, *Hollywood Cinema: An Introduction*, and Elizabeth Cowie, 'Storytelling: Classical Hollywood cinema and classical narrative', in Neale and Smith.
7. Barbara Klinger, 'Digressions at the cinema: reception and mass culture, *Cinema Journal*, vol. 28, no. 4, Summer 1989, 4.
8. *The Classical Hollywood Cinema*, 4.
9. See, for example, Timothy Corrigan, *A Cinema Without Walls: Movies and Culture After Vietnam*; Justin Wyatt, *High Concept: Movies and Marketing in Hollywood*; Mark Crispin Miller, 'Advertising: End of Story', in Mark Crispin Miller (ed.), *Seeing Through Movies.* I am not

suggesting that such works do not make useful points, merely that there is a tendency to assume a previous norm in which narrative was fundamentally more coherent.

10. 'The Concept of Cinematic Excess', *Cine-Tracts*, vol. 1, no. 2, Summer 1977.
11. *Spectacular Bodies: Gender, Genre and the Action Cinema*, 9.
12. See Rick Altman, 'Dickens, Griffith, and Film Theory Today', in Jane Gaines (ed.), *Classical Hollywood Narrative: The Paradigm Wars.*
13. *Spectacular Bodies*, 6.
14. This approach derives from the structural reading of myths by Claude Lévi-Strauss – see 'The Structural Study of Myth' in *Structural Anthropology* – and has been applied to Hollywood frontier mythology by writers including Will Wright, *Sixguns and Society*, Richard Slotkin, *Gunfighter Nation* and Robert Ray, *A Certain Tendency of the Hollywood Cinema, 1930–1980.*
15. Though a key aspect of the framework within which most westerns were or are made, frontier mythology does not itself feature centrally in the content of all films in the genre, as Steve Neale points out in *Genre and Hollywood*, 136.
16. See Nicholas Garnham, 'The Economics of the US Motion Picture Industry', in *Capitalism and Communication.*
17. See, for example, Rick Altman, *The American Film Musical*, and Kristine Brunovska Karnick and Henry Jenkins (eds), *Classical Film Comedy.*
18. For numerous historical examples see Janet Staiger, *Interpreting Films: Studies in the Historical Reception of American Cinema.*
19. Richard Maltby, 'Sticks, Hicks and Flaps: Classical Hollywood's generic conception of its audiences', in Melvyn Stokes and Maltby (eds), *Identifying Hollywood's Audiences: Cultural Identity and the Movies.*
20. 'Sticks, Hicks and Flaps', 26.
21. See various contributions to Stokes and Maltby.
22. See, for example, Olen J. Earnest, '*Star Wars*: A Case Study of Motion Picture Marketing', *Current Research in Film*, vol. 1, 1985.
23. Ray, *A Certain Tendency.*
24. Many examples of *film noir*, for example, have the *absence* of the frontier as a reference point no less potent for being implied rather than made explicit.
25. Cognitive approaches suggest that 'top-down' schemas are imposed onto narratives, schemas imbued with cultural assumptions and values; see Edward Branigan, *Narrative Comprehension and Film.*

Chapter 1

1. *Gunfighter Nation: The Myth of the Frontier in Twentieth-Century America*, 14.

2. The positive version of the frontier connection with the wilderness, as a place of potential purity and regeneration, is the dominant tendency in works of popular culture. A darker vision also exists, however, and has since the time of early European settlement. The wilderness, here, is seen as a place of demonic threat, the domain of evil or radical otherness, a heritage played upon in fantasy or horror fictions ranging from *The X-Files* television series to *The Blair Witch Project* (1999).
3. For a fuller account of such different strains within the myth see Slotkin, *Gunfighter Nation.*
4. For the classic account of the role of pastoral in American mythology see Leo Marx, *The Machine in the Garden.*
5. William Cronon, *Nature's Metropolis: Chicago and the Great West.*
6. Mark Crispin Miller, 'Advertising: End of Story', in Miller (ed.), *Seeing Through Movies.*
7. 'The Cinema of Attractions: Early Film, its Spectator and the Avant-Garde', in Thomas Elsaesser (ed.), *Early Cinema: Space, Frame, Narrative.*
8. 'An Aesthetic of Astonishment: Early Film and the (In)Credulous Spectator', in Linda Williams (ed.), *Viewing Positions: Ways of Seeing Film*, 121.
9. See various contributions to Elsaesser, *Early Cinema.*
10. 'Early Cinema, Late Cinema: Transformations of the Public Sphere', in Linda Williams (ed.), *Viewing Positions*, 149.
11. 'Early Cinema, Late Cinema', 149.
12. John Belton, *Widescreen Cinema.*
13. Henry Jenkins, *What Made Pistachio Nuts? Early Sound Comedy and the Vaudeville Aesthetic*, 14.
14. Frank Krutnik, 'The Clown-Prints of Comedy', *Screen*, vol. 25, nos. 4–5, July–October 1984.
15. Rick Altman, *The American Film Musical*; Jane Feuer, *The Hollywood Musical.*
16. *Hard Core*, 134.
17. *Hollywood Cinema: An Introduction.*
18. Belton, *Widescreen Cinema*, chapter 9.
19. 'Advertising: End of Story', 235.
20. 'Blockbuster: The Last Crusade', in Mark Crispin Miller (ed.), *Seeing Through Movies.*
21. *Only Entertainment*, 20.
22. 'Advertising: End of Story', 205.
23. 'The Lure of the Big Picture: Film, Television and Hollywood', in John Hill and Martin McLoone (eds), *Big Picture, Small Screen: The Relations Between Film and Television.*

24. Richard Slotkin, *Gunfighter Nation*; Douglas Pye, 'Criticism and the Western', Introduction to Ian Cameron and Douglas Pye (eds), *The Movie Book of the Western.*
25. Notably Edwin Fussell, *Frontier: American Literature and the American West.*
26. *The American Film Musical.*

Chapter 2

1. Leonard Maltin (ed.), *Leonard Maltin's 1998 Movie & Video Guide*, entry on *Jurassic Park*, 700.
2. *Hollywood Cinema*, 324.
3. Justin Wyatt and Katherine Vlesmas, 'The Drama of Recoupment: On the Mass Media Negotiation of *Titanic*', in Kevin Sandler and Gaylyn Studlar (eds), *Titanic: Anatomy of a Blockbuster.*
4. A convention designed to maintain the spatial relationships between objects on screen by shooting consistently from only one side of an imaginary line drawn through the action.
5. I have encapsulated rather briefly here a very large and on-going debate in film study between theorists who argue for a kind of textual determinism (associated, historically at least, with psychoanalytically-oriented work in the journal *Screen*) or for consideration of the particular experiences of specific audiences.
6. 'CGI effects in Hollywood science-fiction cinema 1989–95: the wonder years', *Screen*, vol. 40, no. 2, Summer 1999, 169.
7. 'CGI effects', 176.
8. 'CGI effects', 169.
9. *Hollywood Cinema*, 339.
10. Kristin Thompson, 'Implications of The Cel Animation Technique', in Stephen Health and Teresa de Laurentis (eds), *The Cinematic Apparatus*, 109. I am grateful to Paul Ward for drawing this essay to my attention.
11. 'Implications', 109.
12. 'Implications', 111.
13. Mark Cotta Vaz and Patricia Rose Duignan, *Industrial Light and Magic: Into the Digital Realm*, 221.
14. *Industrial Light and Magic*, 227.
15. See Albert La Valley, 'Traditions of Trickery: The Role of Special Effects in the Science Fiction Film', in George Slusser and Eric Rabkin (eds), *Shadows of the Magic Lamp.*
16. 'Photography and Modern Vision: The spectacle of "natural magic" ', in Chris Jenks (ed.), *Visual Culture*, 219.
17. 'Photography and Modern Vision', 220.

18. 'Photography', 223.
19. 'Photography', 223.
20. Joseph McBride, *Steven Spielberg: A Biography* (1997).
21. On *Titanic*, Martin Barker, 'How Special Effects Matter: From A(lien) to Zee', 'Science Fictions, 9-9-99', Brunel University, 9 September, 1999.
22. John Mueller, 'Fred Astaire and the Integrated Musical', *Cinema Journal*, vol. 24, no. 1, 1984, 30.
23. 'Fred Astaire and the Integrated Musical', 28.
24. Ron Magid, 'ILM's Digital Dinosaurs Tear Up Effects Jungle', *American Cinematographer*, vol. 74, no. 12, December 1993, 50, 54–5.
25. 'Fred Astaire and the Integrated Musical', 29.
26. 'Making Culture into Nature', in Annette Kuhn (ed.), *Alien Zone Cultural Theory and Contemporary Science Fiction Cinema*, 67.
27. For other examples of this strategy see Brian Winston, *Technologies of Seeing*.
28. Asu Askoy and Kevin Robins, 'Hollywood for the 21st century: global competition for critical mass in image markets', *Cambridge Journal of Economics*, 16, 1992.
29. Benedict Carver, 'Illusions of Grandeur', *Screen International*, 27 September 1996.

Chapter 3

1. *Hollywood Cinema: An Introduction*, 132.
2. Quoted in John Hellman, *American Myth and the Legacy of Vietnam*, 209.
3. *American Myth and the Legacy of Vietnam*, 217.
4. See Walter McDougal, *The Heavens and the Earth: A Political History of the Space Race*, and my *Mapping Reality*, chapter 5.
5. 'Zooming Out: The End of Offscreen Space', in Jon Lewis (ed.), *The New American Cinema*, 259.
6. 'Zooming Out', 261.
7. For examples, see Geoff King and Tanya Krzywinska, *Science Fiction Cinema: From Outerspace to Cyberspace*.
8. *Narrative Comprehension and Film*, 98.

Chapter 4

1. *Knowing Audiences: Judge Dredd, Its Friends, Fans and Foes*, 149–50.
2. 'Americanitis', in Ronald Levaco (ed.), *Kuleshov on Film: Writings of Lev Kuleshov*.
3. James Chapman, *Licence to Thrill: A Cultural History of the James Bond Films*, 58, 126–7, 144; Leon Hunt, personal communication.

4. 'The Virtues and Limitations of Montage', in *What is Cinema?* Volume I, 46.
5. 'The Virtues and Limitations of Montage', 50.
6. 'Aesthetics in Action: Kung Fu, Gunplay, and Cinematic Expressivity', 21st Hong Kong International Film Festival, Hong Kong 1997, programme notes.
7. See Leon Hunt, 'Once Upon a Time in China: Kung Fu from Bruce Lee to Jet Li', *Framework*, 40, April 1999.
8. *Licence to Thrill*, 58.
9. 'The Montage of Film Attractions', 34, in *Selected Works,* Volume I.
10. 'The Montage of Film Attractions', 39.
11. *Knowing Audiences*, 146.
12. *Knowing Audiences*, 146.
13. *Knowing Audiences*, 53.
14. *Old Hollywood/New Hollywood: Ritual, Art and Industry*, 3.
15. See, for example, Thomas Austin, 'Desperate to see it': Straight men watching *Basic Instinct*, in Melvyn Stokes and Richard Maltby (eds), *Identifying Hollywood's Audiences: Cultural Identity and the Movies.*
16. 'Video Replay: families, films and fantasy', in Victor Burgin, James Donald and Cora Kaplan (eds), *Formations of Fantasy*, 172.
17. 'Video Replay', 196.
18. A point made in relation to action movies by Yvonne Tasker in *Spectacular Bodies: Gender, Genre and the Action Cinema.*
19. *Spectacular Bodies*, chapter 7.
20. *Spectacular Bodies.*
21. *Spectacular Bodies*, 109.
22. See Donald Bogle, *Toms, Coons, Mulattoes, Mammies and Bucks: An Interpretative History of Blacks in American Films.*
23. *Knowing Audiences*, 150.
24. For an analysis of such narrative devices see Roland Barthes, *S/Z*, or Robert Stam, Robert Burgoyne and Sandy Flitterman-Lewis, *New Vocabularies of Film Semiotics.*
25. *Knowing Audiences*, 53.
26. 'Cinema/Ideology/Criticism', in Bill Nichols (ed.), *Movies and Methods*, Volume 1, 25.

Chapter 5

1. Ron Magid, 'Blood on the Beach', *American Cinematographer*, vol. 79, no. 12, December 1998, 62.
2. *The Cinematic Body*, 32–3.
3. Magid, 'Blood on the Beach', 56.
4. 'Blood on the Beach', 66.

5. I am grateful to Richard Franklin and Alan Miller for help in explaining the technical basis of this effect.
6. The association of such camerawork with authenticity has been established in home-video based 'reality' television and is exploited to similar effect in *The Blair Witch Project* (1999).
7. Richard Dyer, *Stars*, 30.
8. For an account of recent demographic trends and their impact on the inter-generation appeal of another kind of Hollywood product, see Robert Allen, 'Home Alone Together: Hollywood and the 'family film', in Melvyn Stokes and Richard Maltby (eds), *Identifying Hollywood's Audiences: Cultural Identity and the Movies.*
9. The degree of freedom granted to filmmakers such as Coppola was limited, in both time and extent. For a fuller discussion of these issues in relation to Coppola's career and the limitations of auteurist approaches to Hollywood, see Jon Lewis, *Whom God Wishes to Destroy: Francis Coppola and the New Hollywood.*
10. Gilbert Adair, *Hollywood's Vietnam*, 118.
11. Frank Tomasulo, 'The Politics of Ambivalence: *Apocalypse Now* as Prowar and Antiwar Film', in Linda Dittmar and Gene Michaud (eds), *From Hanoi to Hollywood: The Vietnam War in American Film*, 156.
12. *Camera Politica: The Politics and Ideology of Contemporary Hollywood Film*, 239.
13. *Camera Politica*, 238.
14. 'The Politics of Ambivalence', 153.
15. 'The Politics of Ambivalence', 149.
16. 'The Politics of Ambivalence', 149.
17. 'Antiwar Film as Spectacle: Contradictions of the Combat Sequence', *Genre*, XXI, Winter 1998, 484.
18. 'The Politics of Ambivalence', 154.
19. See Eleanor Coppola's memoir, *Notes on the Making of* Apocalypse Now.
20. See John Hellman, *American Myth and the Legacy of Vietnam*, and my *Mapping Reality: An Exploration of Cultural Cartographies*, chapter 6.
21. *American Myth and the Legacy of Vietnam*, 90.
22. *Spectacular Bodies: Gender, Genre and the Action Cinema*, 104.
23. *Old Hollywood/New Hollywood: Ritual, Art, and Industry*, 82.
24. David Halberstam, 'Two Who Were There View "Platoon": The Correspondent', *New York Times*, 8 March 1987, 21; William Shawcross, 'The unseen enemy', *Times Literary Supplement*, 24 April 1987.
25. *Hollywood's Vietnam*, 148.
26. *Hollywood's Vietnam*, 148.
27. Richard Slotkin, *The Fatal Environment: The Myth of the Frontier in the Age of Industrialization, 1800–1890*, 501.

Chapter 6

1. 'Only the stars survive: disaster movies in the seventies', in D. Bradby, L. James and B. Sharratt (eds), *Politics and Performance in Twentieth Century Drama and Film*, 257–8.
2. 'The imagination of disaster', in *Against Interpretation and Other Essays.*
3. The following is based on the 'director's cut' version.
4. *Ecology of Fear: Los Angeles and the Imagination of Disaster*, 277.
5. *Ecology of Fear*, 378.
6. 'The imagination of disaster', 223.
7. *Camera Politica: The Politics and Ideology of Contemporary Hollywood*, 51.
8. 'Only the stars survive', 257.
9. 'While God Tarried: Disappointed Millennialism and the Making of the Modern West', 13.
10. 'Information, Crisis, Catastrophe', in Patricia Mellencamp, *Logics of Television*, 231.
11. 'Information, Crisis, Catastrophe', 231.
12. *Ecology of Fear*, 8.
13. *Ecology of Fear*, 9.
14. Daniel Junas, 'The Rise of the Militias', 1.
15. Damian Thompson, *The End of Time: Faith and Fear in the Shadow of the Millennium*, 307–17.
16. Thompson, *The End of Time*, 294.
17. This and the following detail is from Peter Bart, *The Gross: The Hits, The Flops – The Summer that Ate Hollywood*, 140–3.
18. *The Gross*, 80.
19. *The Gross*, 40.
20. Maurice Yacowar, 'The Bug in the Rug: Notes on the Disaster Genre', in Barry Keith Grant, (ed.), *Film Genre Reader II.*
21. The concept of carnival is from Mikhail Bakhtin's *Rabelais and His World*, a study of medieval periods of licensed indulgence and overturning of cultural norms.
22. Fred Pfeil, 'From Pillar to Postmodernism: Race, Class, and Gender in the Male Rampage Film', in Jon Lewis (ed.), *The New American Cinema*, 180.
23. *Showstoppers: Busby Berkeley and the Tradition of Spectacle*, 99.
24. 'From Pillar to Postmodernism', 181.
25. *Distinction: A Social Critique of the Judgement of Taste*, 68.
26. *Distinction*, 34. For Bourdieu's own survey evidence for the class markings of cinematic taste, including the favouring of spectacular films by those from the commercial and industrial sectors, see 271–2.
27. *Distinction*, 56.
28. 'Weaving a Narrative: Style and Economic Background in Griffith's Biograph Films', in Thomas Elsaesser, *Early Cinema: Space, Frame, Narrative*, 340.

29. 'From Pillar to Postmodernism', 180.
30. See Steven Cohan and Ina Rae Hark (eds) *Screening the Male: Exploring Masculinities in Hollywood Cinema.*
31. Peter Kramer, 'A Powerful Cinema-going Force? Hollywood and Female Audiences since the 1960s', in Melvyn Stokes and Richard Maltby (eds), *Identifying Hollywood's Audiences: Cultural Identity and the Movies.*
32. Rick Altman, *Film/Genre.*

Chapter 7

1. *Hamlet on the Holodeck: The Future of Narrative in Cyberspace*, 112.
2. Raymond Fielding, 'Hale's Tours: Ultrarealism in the Pre-1910 Motion Picture', in John Fell (ed.), *Film Before Griffith*; Brooks Landon, *The Aesthetics of Ambivalence*, xv.
3. See Landon, *The Aesthetics of Ambivalence.*
4. 'Zooming Out: The End of Offscreen Space', in Jon Lewis (ed.), *The New American Cinema*, 266.
5. 'Zooming Out', 266.
6. 'Theses on the philosophy of Hollywood history', in Steve Neale and Murray Smith (eds), *Contemporary Hollywood Cinema*, 14.
7. *Hamlet on the Holodeck: The Future of Narrative in Cyberspace*, 50.
8. See Murray, *Hamlet on the Holodeck*, 50–51.
9. The gaming industry is expected to outstrip the film industry in global revenues for the first time in 2000, according to Oliver Burkeman, 'Mortal Combat', *The Guardian*, G2, 3 September 1999, 2; Sony, which owns Columbia Pictures, is reported by Jack Schofield to derive about 40 per cent of its operating profits from the games business ('Do you dare to dream?', *The Guardian, Online*, 14 October 1999, 2).
10. 'Nintendo and New World Travel Writing: A Dialogue', in Steven Jones (ed.), *Cybersociety: Computer Mediated Communication and Community*, 62.
11. 'Making Sense of Software: Computer Games and Interactive Textuality', in Jones (ed.), *Cybersociety*, 78.
12. 'Nintendo and New World Travel Writing: A Dialogue', 71.
13. 'The New Hollywood', in Jim Collins, Hilary Radner and Ava Preacher Collins (eds), *Film Theory Goes to the Movies*, 34.
14. *Terminal Identity*, 239–40.
15. See Brian Winston, *Technologies of Seeing.*
16. 'A Backstage Critique of Virtual Reality', in Jones (ed.), *Cybersociety*, 40.

Bibliography

Adair, Gilbert, *Hollywood's Vietnam* (London, 1989).

Allen, Robert, 'Home Alone Together: Hollywood and the 'family film', in Melvyn Stokes and Richard Maltby (eds), *Identifying Hollywood's Audiences: Cultural Identity and the Movies* (London, 1999).

Altman, Rick, *The American Film Musical* (Bloomington, 1987–89).

—— 'Dickens, Griffith, and Film Theory Today', in Jane Gaines (ed.), *Classical Hollywood Narrative: The Paradigm Wars* (Durham, 1992).

—— *Film/Genre* (London, 1999).

Askoy, Asu, and Kevin Robins, 'Hollywood for the 21st century: global competition for critical mass in image markets', *Cambridge Journal of Economics*, 16, 1992.

Austin, Thomas, '"Desperate to see it": Straight men watching *Basic Instinct*', in Melvyn Stokes and Richard Maltby (eds), *Identifying Hollywood's Audiences: Cultural Identity and the Movies* (London, 1999).

Bakhtin, Mikhail, *Rabelais and His World* (Bloomington, 1984).

Barker, Martin, 'How Special Effects Matter: From A(lien) to Zee', 'Science Fictions, 9-9-99', Brunel University, 9 September 1999.

Barker, Martin, and Kate Brooks, *Knowing Audiences: Judge Dredd, Its Friends, Fans and Foes* (Luton, 1998).

Bart, Peter, *The Gross: The Hits, the Flops – The Summer that Ate Hollywood* (New York, 1999).

Bazin, André, 'The Virtues and Limitations of Montage', in *What is Cinema? Volume I* (Berkeley, 1967).

Belton, John, *Widescreen Cinema* (Cambridge, Mass., 1992).

Biskind, Peter, 'Blockbuster: The Last Crusade', in Mark Crispin Miller (ed.), *Seeing Through Movies* (New York, 1990).

Bogle, Donald, *Toms, Coons, Mulattoes, Mammies, and Bucks: An Interpretive History of Blacks in American Films* (New York, 1993).

Bordwell, David, 'Aesthetics in Action: Kung Fu, Gunplay, and Cinematic Expressivity', in programme for 'Hong Kong Retrospective: 50 Years of Electric Shadows', 21st Hong Kong International Film Festival, Hong Kong,1997.

Bordwell, David, Janet Staiger and Kristen Thompson, *The Classical Hollywood Cinema: Film Style and Mode of Production to 1960* (London, 1985).

Branigan, Edward, *Narrative Comprehension and Film* (London, 1992).

Bukatman, Scott, *Terminal Identity: The Virtual Subject in Postmodern Science Fiction* (Durham, 1993).

—— 'Zooming Out: The End of Offscreen Space', in Jon Lewis (ed.), *The New American Cinema* (Durham, 1998).

Burkeman, Oliver, 'Mortal combat', *The Guardian*, G2, 3 September 1999.

Carver, Bendict, 'Illusions of Grandeur', *Screen International*, 27 September 1996.

Chapman, James, *Licence to Thrill: A Cultural History of the James Bond Films* (London, 1999).

Cohan, Steven, and Ina Rae Hark (eds), *Screening the Male: Exploring Masculinities in Hollywood Cinema* (London, 1993).

Comolli, Jean-Louis, and Jean Narboni, 'Cinema/Ideology/Criticism', in Bill Nichols (ed.), *Movies and Methods*, Volume I (Berkeley, 1976).

Coppola, Eleanor, *Notes on the Making of* Apocalypse Now (London, 1995).

Corrigan, Tim, *A Cinema Without Walls: Movies and Culture After Vietnam* (London, 1991).

Cowie, Elizabeth, 'Storytelling: Classical Hollywood cinema and classical narrative', in Steve Neale and Murray Smith (eds), *Contemporary Hollywood Cinema* (London, 1998).

Cronon, William, *Nature's Metropolis: Chicago and the Great West* (New York, 1991).

Davis, Mike, *Ecology of Fear* (London, 1999).

Doane, Mary Ann, 'Information, Crisis, Catastrophe', in Patricia Mellencamp (ed.), *Logics of Television* (London, 1990).

Dyer, Richard, *Only Entertainment* (London, 1992).

Earnest, Olen J., '*Star Wars*: A Case Study of Motion Picture Marketing', *Current Research in Film*, 1, 1985.

Eisenstein, Sergei, 'The Montage of Film Attractions', in R. Taylor (ed.), *Selected Works, Volume I* (London, 1997).

Feuer, Jane, *The Hollywood Musical* (London, 1982).

Fielding, Raymond, 'Hale's Tours: Ultrarealism in the Pre-1910 Motion Picture', in John Fell (ed.), *Film Before Griffith* (Berkeley, 1983).

Friedman, Ted, 'Making Sense of Software: Computer Games and Interactive Textuality', in Steven Jones (ed.), *Cybersociety: Computer-Mediated Communication and Community* (Thousand Oaks, 1995).

Fuller, Mary, and Henry Jenkins, 'Nintendo and New World Travel Writing: A Dialogue', in Steven Jones (ed.), *Cybersociety: Computer-Mediated Communication and Community* (Thousand Oaks, 1995).

Fussell, Edwin, *Frontier: American Literature and the American West* (Princeton, 1965).

Garnham, Nicholas, 'The Economics of the US Motion Picture Industry', in *Capitalism and Communication* (London, 1990).

Gunning, Tom, 'The Cinema of Attractions: Early Film, its Spectator and the Avant-Garde', in Thomas Elsaesser (ed.), *Early Cinema: Space, Frame, Narrative* (London, 1990).

—— 'Weaving a Narrative: Style and Economic Background in Griffith's Biograph Films', in Thomas Elsaesser (ed), *Early Cinema: Space, Frame, Narrative* (London, 1990).

—— 'An Aesthetic of Astonishment: Early Film and the (In)Credulous Spectator', in Linda Williams (ed.), *Viewing Positions* (New Brunswick, 1995).

David Halberstam, 'Two Who Were There View "Platoon": The Correspondent', *New York Times*, 8 March 1987.

Hansen, Miriam, 'Early Cinema, Late Cinema: Transformations of the Public Sphere', in Linda Williams (ed.), *Viewing Positions* (New Brunswick, 1995).

Hellman, John, *American Myth and the Legacy of Vietnam* (New York, 1986).

Hunt, Leon, 'Once Upon a Time in China: Kung Fu from Bruce Lee to Jet Li', *Framework* 40, April 1999.

Jenkins, Henry, *What Made Pistachio Nuts? Early Sound Comedy and the Vaudeville Aesthetic* (New York, 1992).

Junas, Daniel, 'The Rise of the Militias', at http://www.worldmedia.com/caq/militia.htm.

Karnick, Kristine and Henry Jenkins, *Classical Film Comedy* (New York, 1995).

King, Geoff, *Mapping Reality* (Basingstoke, 1996).

King, Geoff and Tanya Krzywinska, *Science Fiction Cinema: From Outerspace to Cyberspace* (London, 2000).

Klinger, Barbara, 'Digressions at the cinema: reception and mass culture', *Cinema Journal*, vol. 28, no. 4, Summer 1989.

Kramarae, Cheris, 'A Backstage Critique of Virtual Reality', in Steven Jones (ed.), *Cybersociety: Computer-Mediated Communication and Community* (Thousand Oaks, 1995).

Kramer, Peter, 'The Lure of the Big Picture: Film, Television and Hollywood', in John Hill and Martin McLoone (eds), *Big Picture, Small Screen: The Relations Between Film and Television* (Luton, 1997).

—— 'A Powerful Cinema-going Force? Hollywood and Female Audiences since the 1960s', in Melvyn Stokes and Richard Maltby (eds), *Identifying Hollywood's Audiences: Cultural Identity and the Movies* (London, 1999).

Kuleshov, Lev, 'Americanitis', in Ronald Leaco (ed.), *Kuleshov on Film: Writings of Lev Kuleshov* (Berkeley, 1974).

Landes, Richard, 'While God Tarried: Disappointed Millennialism and the Making of the Modern World', at http://www.mille.org/wgt-prec.htm.

Landon, Brooks, *The Aesthetics of Ambivalence* (Westport, 1992).

La Valley, Albert, 'Traditions of Trickery: The Role of Special Effects in the Science Fiction Film', in George Slusser and Eric Rabkin (eds), *Shadows of the Magic Lamp* (Carbondale, 1985).

Lévi-Strauss, Claude, 'The Structural Study of Myth', in *Structural Anthropology* (Harmondsworth, 1968).

Lewis, Jon, *Whom God Wishes to Destroy: Francis Coppola and the New Hollywood* (Durham, 1995).

Magid, Ron, 'ILM's Digital Dinosaurs Tear Up Effects Jungle', *American Cinematographer*, vol. 74, no. 12, December 1993.

—— 'Blood on the Beach', *American Cinematographer*, vol. 79, no. 12 December 1998.

Marx, Leo, *The Machine in the Garden* (London, 1964).

Maltby, Richard, 'Sticks, Hicks and Flaps: Classical Hollywood's generic conception of its audiences', in Melvyn Stokes and Richard Maltby (eds), *Identifying Hollywood's Audiences: Cultural Identity and the Movies* (London, 1999).

Maltby, Richard and Ian Craven, *Hollywood Cinema: An Introduction* (Oxford, 1995).

Maltin, Leonard (ed.), *Leonard Maltin's 1998 Movie & Video Guide* (Harmondsworth, 1997).

McBride, Joseph, *Steven Spielberg: A Biography* (London, 1997).

McDougal, Walter, *The Heavens and the Earth: A Political History of the Space Race* (New York, 1984).

Miller, Mark Crispin, 'Advertising: End of Story', in Miller (ed.), *Seeing Through Movies* (New York, 1990).

Mueller, John, 'Fred Astaire and the Integrated Musical', *Cinema Journal*, vol. 24, no. 1, Fall 1984.

Murray, Janet, *Hamlet on the Holodeck* (Cambridge, Mass., 1997).

Neale, Steve, *Genre and Hollywood* (London, 1999).

Pfeil, Fred, 'From Pillar to Postmodernism: Race, Class, and Gender in the Male Rampage Film', in Jon Lewis (ed.), *The New American Cinema* (Durham, 1998).

Pierson, Michele, 'CGI effects in Hollywood science-fiction cinema 1989–95: the wonder years', *Screen*, vol. 40, no. 2, Summer 1999.

Pye, Douglas, 'Criticism and the Western', in Ian Cameron and Pye (eds), *The Movie Book of the Western* (London, 1996).

Ray, Robert, *A Certain Tendency of the Hollywood Cinema, 1930–1980* (Princeton, 1985).

Roddick, Nick, 'Only the stars survive: disaster movies in the seventies', in D. Bradby, L. James and B. Sharratt (eds), *Politics and Performance in Twentieth Century Drama and Film* (Cambridge, 1986).

Rubin, Martin, *Showstoppers: Busby Berkeley and the Tradition of Spectacle* (New York, 1993).

Ryan, Michael and Douglas Kellner, *Camera Politica: The Politics and Ideology of Contemporary Hollywood Film* (Bloomington, 1990).

Schatz, Thomas, *Old Hollywood/New Hollywood: Ritual, Art, Industry* (Ann Arbor, 1982).

—— 'The New Hollywood', in Jim Collins, Hilary Radner and Ava Preacher Collins (eds), *Film Theory Goes to the Movies* (New York, 1993).

Schofield, Jack, 'Do you dare to dream?', *The Guardian*, *Online*, 14 October 1999.

William Shawcross, 'The unseen enemy', *Times Literary Supplement*, 24 April 1987.

Shaviro, Steven, *The Cinematic Body* (Minneapolis, 1993).

Slater, Don, 'Photography and modern vision: The spectacle of "natural magic" ', in Chris Jenks (ed.), *Visual Culture* (London, 1992).

Slotkin, Richard, *The Fatal Environment: The Myth of the Frontier in the Age of Industrialization, 1800–1890* (New York, 1985).

—— *Gunfighter Nation: The Myth of the Frontier in Twentieth-Century America*, (New York, 1992).

Smith, Murray, 'Theses on the philosophy of Hollywood history', in Steve Neale and Murray Smith (eds), *Contemporary Hollywood Cinema* (London, 1998).

Sontag, Susan, 'The Imagination of Disaster', in *Against Interpretation* (New York, 1978).

Springer, Claudia, 'Antiwar Film as Spectacle: Contradictions of the Combat Sequence', *Genre*, XXI, Winter 1998.

Staiger, Janet, *Interpreting Films: Studies in the Historical Reception of American Cinema* (Princeton, 1992).

Stam, Robert, Robert Burgoyne and Sandy Flitterman-Lewis, *New Vocabularies of Film Semiotics* (London, 1992).

Stern, Michael, 'Making Culture into Nature', in Annette Kuhn (ed.), *Alien Zone: Cultural Theory and Contemporary Science Fiction Cinema* (London, 1990).

Tasker, Yvonne, *Spectacular Bodies: Gender, Genre and the Action Cinema* (London, 1993).

Thompson, Kristin, 'The Concept of Cinematic Excess', *Cine-Tracts,* vol. 1, no. 2, Summer 1977.

—— 'Implications of the Cel Animation Technique', in Stephen Heath and Teresa De Laurentis (eds), *The Cinematic Apparatus* (London, 1980).

—— *Storytelling in the New Hollywood: Understanding Classical Hollywood Narrative Technique* (Cambridge, Mass., 1999).

Tomasulu, Frank, 'The Politics of Ambivalence: *Apocalypse Now* as Prowar and Antiwar Film', in Linda Dittmar and Gene Michaud (eds), *From Hanoi to Hollywood: The Vietnam War in American Film* (New Brunswick, 1990).

Vaz, Mark Cotta, and Patricia Rose Duignan, *Industrial Light and Magic: Into the Digital Realm* (London, 1996).

Walkerdine, Valerie, 'Video Replay: families, films and fantasy', in Victor Burgin, James Donald and Cora Kaplan (eds), *Formations of Fantasy* (London, 1989).

Williams, Linda, *Hard Core* (London, 1990).

Winston, Brian, *Technologies of Seeing* (London, 1996).

Wright, Will, *Sixguns and Society: A Structural Study of the Western* (Berkeley, 1975).

Wood, Robin, 'Ideology, Genre, Auteur', in Barry Keith Grant (ed.), *Film Genre Reader II* (Austin, 1995).

Wyatt, Justin, *High Concept: Movies and Marketing in Hollywood* (Austin, 1994).

Wyatt, Justin and Katherine Vlesmas, 'The Drama of Recoupment: On the Mass Media Negotiation of *Titanic*', in Kevin Sandler and Gaylyn Studlar (eds), *Titanic: Anatomy of a Blockbuster* (New Brunswick, 1999).

Yacowar, Maurice, 'The Bug in the Rug: Notes on the Disaster Genre', in Barry Keith Grant (ed.), *Film Genre Reader II* (Austin, 1995).

Index